Connections Between Neuroscience, Rhetoric, and Writing

This book argues that contemporary neuroscience compliments, extends, and challenges recent and influential posthuman and new materialist accounts of the relations between rhetoric, affect, and writing pedagogy. Drawing on cutting-edge neurophilosophy, Comstock rethinks both historical and current relations between writing and power around questions of affect, attention, and plasticity. In considering the uses and limits of exciting new findings from the neurobiology, this volume both theorizes and offers pedagogical strategies for teaching writing in a digital age characterized by the erosion of wonder and pervasive disaffection. Ultimately, in response to recent critiques transcendental reason and subjectivity, and related calls for the increased inclusion of multimodal and digital writing and rhetoric, Comstock argues for an embodied pedagogy that values the substantial relations between writing and pedagogical care.

Edward J. Comstock is Senior Professorial Lecturer of Literature at American University, USA.

Routledge Research in Educational Psychology

The Routledge Research in Educational Psychology series is a forum for scholars across the field of Educational Psychology to present their latest research and contribute to the development of the field.

Books in the series include:

Beyond Bullying
Researching Student Perspectives
Simone Paul

Student Motivation and Quality of Life in Higher Education
Edited by Marcus Henning, Christian Krägeloh and Glenis Wong-Toi

Verbal Protocols in Literacy Research
Nature of Global Reading Development
Susan E. Israel

Challenging the Cult of Self-Esteem in Education
Education, Psychology, and the Subaltern Self
Kenzo Bergeron

Wellbeing in Higher Education
Cultivating a Healthy Lifestyle Among Faculty and Students
Edited by Marcus A. Henning, Christian U. Krägeloh, Rachel Dryer, Fiona Moir, D. Rex Billington and Andrew G. Hill

Connections Between Neuroscience, Rhetoric, and Writing
A Plastic Pedagogy for the Digital Age
Edward J. Comstock

Connections Between Neuroscience, Rhetoric, and Writing

A Plastic Pedagogy for the Digital Age

Edward J. Comstock

Routledge
Taylor & Francis Group
NEW YORK AND LONDON

First published 2018
by Routledge
711 Third Avenue, New York, NY 10017

and by Routledge
2 Park Square, Milton Park, Abingdon, Oxon, OX14 4RN

Routledge is an imprint of the Taylor & Francis Group, an informa business

Library of Congress Cataloging-in-Publication Data
A catalog record for this book has been requested

ISBN: 978-0-415-79177-9 (hbk)
ISBN: 978-1-315-21182-4 (ebk)

Typeset in Sabon
by Apex CoVantage, LLC

Contents

Introduction

In many ways, our field's skepticism towards neuroscience reflects the best in the rhetorical tradition that informs writing studies. Even as neuroscience gains cache in popular culture as a crude explanation of seemingly *everything*, from the behavior of your teenager to your tendency to vote republican, it's understandable if the first reaction of writing studies scholars to "neurorhetoric" involves eye rolling. After all, to the extent that neuroscience is understood as the study of the causality between brain locations and behavioral and experiential phenomenon, it must be understood as *anti-rhetorical*. It also cuts against the grain of our progressivist and Deweyan heritage, particularly John Dewey's instance—adapted from Alfred North Whitehead's process theory—that: "no two conscious experiences exactly duplicate one another. Creativity and novelty are characteristic of nature" (171). Following Whitehead and Dewey (and the influence of scientific theories of evolution and relativity upon them), toppling Lockean faculty psychology and the historical primacy given to presence, symbolic representation, and ideas, writing pedagogy is founded on the idea that knowledge is not discovered in substances or locations, but created through phenomenological introspection into our embodied, affective experience. For Whitehead and Dewey, it is through this introspection, not through once-removed cognitive representations, that we gain *direct* access to things and causes (an idea that, as we'll see, is still playing out in "new materialist" theories today); through experience, yielding habits and dispositions through introspection, learning, growth, and change happen.

In these ways, Whitehead and Dewey have had an obvious influence on our process pedagogies, and, perhaps less obviously, on our theories of rhetorical situatedness and attunement. And within this tradition, we can see too the limits of conventional understandings of neuroscience. To the extent that we follow Whitehead and Dewey in the idea that the ultimate reality of nature and experience is a *property*—i.e., creativity—as opposed to a presence or substance, appeals to mechanized, localized brain functions and intelligence are invalidated. From this perspective, reducing complex human phenomenon to brain locations threatens to return us to something like Lockean faculty psychology, idealism, or worse, phrenology. Taking influence from the modernist tradition, writing studies—even more than other fields of pedagogical study—remains resistant to the kind of naïve "*locationism*" associated with neuroscience, which it quite correctly views as overly reductive, as lacking an understanding of the social and rhetorical situatedness of the types of mental phenomenon involved in composing. In short, we have long recognized the non-reciprocity of rhetorical situations—and the nature of experience—to pre-determined forms and mechanistic modals. Again, the best impulses in rhetorical theory, following Whitehead and Dewey, view all compositions as *becoming* as opposed to as *being*.

It's for this reason too that invention, influenced by rhetorical theory, has again become so important in contemporary pedagogy (e.g., Hawk; Muckelbauer). While a re-discovering of invention was central to the rise of composition as the discipline we know today (Worsham), this renewed interest has taken shape around various "posthuman" ontologies that—to generalize—complicate the received student-centered foundations of our field. This diverse range of rhetorical theories have in common a certain challenge to conventional accounts of the primacy of reason, cognition, the symbolic, and the subject; invention, from this perspective, must be understood beyond acts of conscious deliberation and "critical thinking," beginning instead in forms of attunement and tacit and indirect knowledge (e.g., Rickert; Rice; Shipka). Therefore, beyond learning the codes of institutionalized discursive forms or socially directed critical reasoning—hallmarks of the social epistemic perspective—today invention is being understood first as an embodied habit or disposition, and in relation to the work of a public (as opposed to a scholastic) rhetoric. Much of this thinking suggests that these embodied dispositions and habits—as opposed to a mastery of discursive forms—are what is required in a world (and a "public") increasingly characterized by flexibility and complexity. As we'll see, these theories forefront, one way or another, the rhetoricity of the complex networks and entanglements that both precede and give rise to conscious experience and other compositions—whether those networks be embodied, affective structures, built or material environments, or complex ecologies in which objects greet each other with no regard for human designs.

Beyond "inventing the university," rhetorical ontology today challenges us to invent new posthuman bodies and ways of being. And in doing so, while the trace of progressivist process philosophy and pedagogy remains, posthumanism rethinks the foundations of Dewey's understanding of experience; from the perspective of contemporary rhetorical theory influenced by posthumanism and new materialism, we can still see this trace in our privileging of human cognition, symbolic abstraction, and reason (what Quentin Meillassoux calls "correlationalism"). After all, what exactly is this Deweyan transcendental "introspection" that gains us direct access to things from some Archemedian point? How is it empirically different from "regular" cognition? What is the status of the "meta" position, beyond consciousness, from which we practice phenomenology? One thing posthumanism has demonstrated is that conscious experience is always preceded by ecological complexities that introspection may fail to give us purchase over (much like Michel Foucault's *episteme*, except non-reducible to symbolic discourse formations). While Dewey, in his theorization of habits and dispositions, recognized early on that there is a level of embodied, non-reflective and non-representational "thinking," as we'll see, his privileging of a reflective introspection ultimately privileged the disciplined intentionality of a prefigured, reasoning subject that would become the very definition of "educated."

While recognizing and building on these important ontological advances, in this work I wish to return to Dewey's attempt to imagine an embodied pedagody that links the humanities and sciences. I will embrace much in posthumanism and new materialism along the way, while addressing the limits of simply abandoning the question of transcendental subjectivity—as the most radical accounts, like Object Oriented Ontology (OOO) claim to do. Indeed, what these theories have offered, as I'll demonstrate, is a more compelling and complicated picture of ecological complexity—irreducible to subjectivity—and of the primacy of rhetorical circulation over signification. And it's precisely because science has reduced the complexity of experience to predetermined natural forms, efforts to bridge pedagogy and theories of writing have heretofore failed. For example, writing studies scholars have come to understand the limits of theorizing writing in terms of universal cognitive structures. And earlier attempts by Dewey to link pedagogy to the natural sciences—especially the theory of relativity—reflected the epistemic limits of modernism (as we'll see in Chapter 4). Unable to see beyond the terms of the evolutionary naturalism and functional psychology that informed his theory, Dewey failed to realize the constructedness of embodiment itself. As a result, metaphysics sneaks in through the back door in Dewey's philosophy.

On the other hand, deconstructing the binary between the symbolic and the natural, the conscious and the material, Dewey understood learning in relation to an individual experience that is always already discoverable in nature: "Everything that characterizes human experience is found in the natural world. Conversely, what is found in the natural world is found in human experience. Hence the more we find out about the natural world, the more intellectual agencies we have for analyzing, describing, and understanding human experience" (171). In fore fronting experience and process in terms of affect and desire as opposed to consciousness and reason, Dewey offers an early and vital theorization of the primacy of embodiment that dismantled classical metaphysics. Despite Dewey's limitations, his insistence on bridging the material sciences and the humanities remains prescient and necessary.

But again, why neuroscience? To the extent that contemporary neuroscience rests on a mechanistic account of the brain, a primordial correspondence between its universal structure and human behaviors, it remains at odds with a rhetorical perspective that instead discovers our open potential for difference.

But what if this *locationism* is not the lesson neuroscience teaches after all?

This will be a main contention of this book, one that has not been fully realized in the neurorhetorical discourse to date. Neuroscience today discovers what Dewey was looking for and what even Derrida, perhaps, could not fully see: the process of deconstruction in nature itself. That is, it discovers in embodied subjectivity an ontological openness to difference that remains both decentered and thoroughly material. This moment therefore presents us with something different—a new scheme through which we can reimagine the symbolic in relation to the material. Through its posthuman account of the primacy of material, of *embodied affectivity* over reason's symbolic abstractions, neuroscience today reinvigorates important questions about the embodied nature of rhetoric, composition, and invention that will be explored across this book. As Kia Jane Richmond argues, affect theory has been underused because of an association with personal development and expressivism that influential social epistemic theorists like Joseph Bartholomae and James Berlin had thought inappropriate to the study of writing. Neuroscience allows us to return to these questions without positing an *anti*-rhetorical, *anti*-social subject in the ways that concerned Bartholomae and Berlin, and without privileging the discursive and symbolic (as both author's did) over "nonverbal" forms of knowing.

Carelessness Today

Student embodiment and the materiality of writing disappears as process pedagogies look towards the symbolic, discursive, and ideological work of composing. As Alex Reid argues, "To be sure, we have discussed materiality and material conditions to no end, but almost always in the context of discourse and ideology."[1] And while composition and rhetoric have long considered emotion through the study of *pathos*, and while some following rhetoric's "affective turn" have theorized the significance of *care* to, for example, teacher–student relationships, argument, invention, and empathy, contemporary theory has had surprisingly little to say about our students' embodied, material, and affective relationship *with the embodied experience of writing itself*. This experience, as we'll see, demands that we confront ideology not—as in received rhetorical theory and writing pedagogy—at the level of symbolic critique, but instead by turning the question of ideology back onto writing pedagogy, and pedagogical care, itself.

Although we lack an adequate theory of embodied care—or perhaps because of this lack—there's a lot of hallway talk these days about our student's increasing *carelessness*. To many, this generation seems both less interested and less capable of producing the writing we require of them. This, despite the fact that—in the digital age—students are likely writing more than ever. Some have argued that our students seem less attentive or less emotionally present; some have argued that they lack necessary intellectual and emotional self-awareness. The former is reflected, for example, in the growing literature on AD/HD, and the latter, for example, in former president Obama's claim that there appears to be an "empathy deficit" with today's students. But whatever the cause, for many, the differences in the classroom are tangible if not easily quantifiable.

Of course, one might argue that there's nothing to see here but age-old intergenerational dispute, or another "Why Johnny Can't Write" moment for the digital age. However, moving beyond "the kids are alright/the kids are not alright," I'll argue across this book that there is indeed good reason to think something different, something new, is emerging at this moment. In doing so, I'll follow the great philosopher of plasticity, Catherine Malabou,[2] who describes a metamorphosis having taken shape in our culture, producing widespread carelessness and indifference.[3] This indifference often appears to us in the classroom as a disaffection or lack of attention—a lack of meaningful self-presence. And in addition to creating predictable forms of carelessness and blockages, it may also be possible (seemingly paradoxically) that this disaffection presents in students as a difficulty handling criticism about their writing—that is, as an emotional over-attachment masking an underlying *rigidity*.

Put simply, in this moment of increasing frustration and disaffection, subjectivity recedes and an affectless and careless subject—what Malabou calls the "new wounded"—is emerging. For Malabou, it is neuroscience that best describes the emergence of the potentially "disaffected" subject—a subject deprived of empathy and wonder—that characterizes, as we'll see, both neuropathology and subjectivity in the 21st century. In our own field, Brian Jackson goes so far as to argue that "ultimately our viability as a discipline specializing in argument may depend on how carefully we engage with affective neuroscience on some level" (474–475). What is emerging in this moment, therefore, is not only a pervasive disaffection, but also a new "motor scheme," a new materialism after dialectics and deconstruction, of neuroplasticity.

In a lecture titled "Emotional Life in a Neurobiological Age," Malabou describes the indifference of the "new wounded" in non-philosophical terms that many teachers will easily recognize:

> This indifference, I feel it with my students. I feel it with everyone. It's the end of transferences . . . this lack of focus . . . this absence of interest for things that's so common today. Sometimes I see my students . . . I'm teaching, and [they're] like checking emails, or whatever. It is indifference . . . It is a mode of 'well, I'm not interested'; 'well, I can't focus.' 'I'm bored.' This is a very concrete phenomenon. It's not philosophical. ("Emotional Life")

Malabou counterpoises the blank expression of the student staring at a cell phone screen, a self-presence or attention lost in the competing demands that divide it, with the tradition of deep attention in which most teachers were raised. In that fading tradition, there was a great value placed on disciplined and singular focus, on sitting still in a single room, concentrating on just one thing—in short, staying within oneself in a way that places one closer to meaning and being through care. But after the explosion of technology and new media in the contemporary "attention economy," we are left instead with a regime of divided attention, blank expression, passivity, simulation, a lack of knowledge transfer, and above all, *indifference*. At the same time, many academic disciplines, along with received academic and pedagogical values, are facing a new legitimation crisis in which they are threatened by market concerns, cultural irrelevance, political correctness, and, indeed, social and political indifference.

The question of disaffection has great relevance to writing pedagogy, given our discipline's concern with writerly problems like heuristics, motivation, transfer, and writers block, as well as our theorization of the relations between emotion, expertise, and public rhetoric following the "affective turn." As I'll argue across this book following Malabou and others, contemporary neuroscience challenges us to understand this new situation on the side of the (posthuman, deconstructed) subject, in terms of the brain. Complicating the relationship between affectivity, productivity, and writing, neuropathology shows that the affectivity (specifically, wonder) that precedes invention and reason can in fact be *destroyed*. As a result, students that have become pathologically disaffected simply will not be able to mobilize a more productive identity to surpass their failures and blockages. As Catherine Malabou argues, in the face of indifference, "there is no symbolic cure, there is no symbolic reinvestment of what is lost" ("From Sorrow to Indifference"). No amount of critique can reconstitute the affective engagement of the student, no socially directed rhetoric can produce the care required to engage the world through wonder and reason. Without resorting to rationalism or essentialism, here we discover the limits of both rhetorical theories of emotion, like Daniel Gross', and rhetorical and posthuman pedagogies that emphasize invention and ecological attunement while bracketing the subject. But by building on neuroscientific insights, our own field can account for the role of writing itself—the materiality of the social experience of writing—in both cultivating and destroying care and intelligence.

The Rhetorical and Posthuman Subject Today: Theorizing Writing and Reason After "Funk"

At the same time—following Jane Bennett, Quentin Meillassoux, Bruno Latour, Ian Bogost, Graham Harman, and others—cutting-edge work in our field has already begun to imagine composition pedagogy, in the wake of the deconstruction of transcendental reason, beyond the level of signification and the reasoning subject. As I'll argue, these theories address student disaffection—and the limits of the social epistemic pedagogy, rooted in signification and reason—by *bracketing the question of care* while retaining a concern with metacognitive strategies for invention and public rhetoric. While the received tradition ties rhetoric to signification and situations involving intentional, conscious acts of persuasion, these new theories expand the definition of rhetoric—and concomitantly, writing pedagogy informed by rhetoric—to include, as John Muckelbauer formulates it, "non-linguistic" and other "instances in which persuasion occurs without anyone consciously intending to persuade" (Barnett & Boyle 30). Influenced by posthumanism and new materialism—building on earlier network (e.g. Byron Hawk) and ecological theories (e.g., Marilyn Cooper), as well as a large body of rhetorical scholarship on emotion and affectivity (which I'll address below)—the most radical of these theories (especially OOO) further decenter the subject by examining objects as themselves influencers and *actants*, bracketing the ontological primacy of subjective agency, human value, and meaning. Nathaniel Rivers, for example, builds on the work of Laurie Gries, Sid Dobrin, Byron Hawk, Thomas Rickert, and other rhetoricians in subverting the primacy of reason and epistemology, articulating a pedagogy of wonder and ontological inquiry. Arguing that "Ontology is the single biggest conceptual hurdle in this pedagogy of public rhetorics" ("Tracing the Missing Masses"), this pedagogy looks beyond the meanings and values of things with regard to human correlation and agency, having students focus on (wonder at) objects "in-and-of themselves." As Hawk, Lindgren, and Mara point out, this project of an "object oriented rhetoric"—one specific variant of posthuman and new materialist ontologies that has become especially important in our discipline—is still very much "in the process of being defined and articulated" (192).

Nevertheless, these scholars agree that "things are rhetorical" (Barnett & Boyle 1). For instance, John Muckelbauer theorizes a "heliotropic" rhetorical paradigm in which flowers might be understood to be persuaded by the sun as they turn towards it (Barnett & Boyle 39). Bill Hart-Davidson similarly argues that by conceiving composition as a "collection of objects" (31), we might teach writing not in terms of audience-awareness, but as an awareness of the varied and dynamic roles writing-objects assume within different networks. From this perspective, the features of a writing object emerge not only in relation to human intentionality and meaning—as if that meaningfulness exhausted the essence of the writing-object—but as latent discursive and rhetorical potentialities always only partially articulated as translations made both by humans and other objects in networked relation (this idea will be developed at length in Chapter 2).

Alex Reid calls this "correlationalism" between the world and the subject that comes at the cost of object relations "perhaps the most significant philosophical glitch." This "hermeneutics of suspicion," following Jane Bennett and Bruno Latour, calls into question the "illicit" process in which sovereign, human agency is projected into objects (Rivers "Tracing the Missing Masses"). Instead, the new materialist theories (including, as I'll argue, contemporary neuroscience) argue that we need to understand objects themselves, beyond sovereign subjectivity, as rhetorical actants. Writing pedagogy influenced by new materialism invests students in the work of public rhetoric by contemplating—through wonder—the plights and even the "objections" of objects themselves, questioning the ontological prioritization of humans over their writing technologies (and all objects). It requires that students understand how objects (like writing) "overlap in various constellations at various times in various situations to produce a singular object for those moments," recognizing that "What we write participates in the objects, co-produces their coherence" (Hawk, Lindgren, & Mara 198). Writing is doubly important from the perspective of new materialism, given its role in "producing any material coherence that can be brought to objects from their smallest fragments to their largest networks of assemblages" (195). Furthermore, as Rivers argues, at the limits of epistemic discourse and critique, writing pedagogy "must trace humans and nonhumans alike if it ever hopes to be fully public and intensely rhetorical."

Relatedly, at the intersection of new materialism and affect theory, in *Inessential Solidarity*, Dianne Davis argues in her critique of Kenneth Burke against the received view that presumes a prior divisiveness of the subject guaranteed by the "separation of one central nervous system from another." This "biological estrangement" acts as an "insurance premium" (22) for our discipline's privileging of rational unity and symbolic identification—the universal desire of the subject, forming the libidinal economy through which the young appropriate the language and symbols of the parent culture—over the *ad hoc* singularity of affective relationality. In other words, for Davis, subjective identification is not a symbolic, cultural affiliation following the fact of the subject's biological individuation. Instead, there is an "originary repetition," an "abysmal mimesis . . . from which symbolic structure could provide no real transcendence" (34). That is, instead of a multiplicity of divisive singularities, there is an endless affective repetition or mimesis of the same: a flat ontology in which there is nothing but the circulation of affective connections preceding the intentionality of conscious agency. Finally, we identify with the other as the condition of our own identification with our self.

But it's not just the new materialists and cutting-edge rhetoricians that call into question the primacy of sovereign reason in composition pedagogy. Brian Jackson's neurorhetoric argues explicitly against " 'They Who Believe We Act Rationally,' " seeking to "completely obliterate the traditional rational model" in favor of a rhetoric based on "affective intelligence" (474). Todd DeStigter has argued that in privileging argumentative writing, we overemphasize reason, reinforcing the rationalizations of Western ideology following the Enlightenment, leaving our students ill-equipped to do the "impolite, illegal, or even violent things" that are necessary in "their struggle for justice" (24).

Each in their own way, these theorists have in common a renewed concern with heuristics. And together these critiques of the sovereign primacy of reason suggest that our received pedagogy—rooted in rationalized process and social reasoning—creates as many problems as it solves. In the introduction to *Presence of Mind: Writing and the Domain Beyond the Cognitive* by Alice Brand and Richard Graves, James Moffett reflects on a problem familiar to those of us that teach writing in the wake of composition's social turn:

> The futility of a course in which one is supposed to just write, in a vacuum, can be seen in several telltale symptoms, the most notable of which is the head scratching, paper-staring search for something to write about. The instructor resorts to assigning "provocative" essays or other texts (not only supplying subject matter but the same subject matter for all). Other symptoms of stripping down to focus on the "cognitive" are notoriously poor motivation and chronically disappointing results.
>
> (xi)

In *Non-Discursive Rhetoric: Image and Affect in Multimodal Composition*, Joddy Murray echoes Moffett's concerns with received pedagogy, arguing for a turn to multimodal forms:

> The expository essay that springs from controversial readings; writing exercises intended to just practice writing as if that function is a skill that can simply be turned on or turned off; and, consequently, a student who does not care to write anything at all. . . . writing is taught as if people are in a "vacuum," divorced from their emotional state, coolly and completely. Such an emphasis on student writing outside of this artificial rationality reinforces the need for an expanded view of writing that includes image and emotions through the use of non-discursive text.

Together these authors describe the disturbing possibility that our students increasingly view our writing assignments as artificial hoops they need to jump through, devoid of "real world" significance, producing the very opposite of the productive emotional effect we intended—even as we focus, as Gross and Alexander contend, almost singularly on inculcating "positive" emotions and habits of mind. Or as Lance Langdon, editor of a recent special edition of *Composition Forum* on the "affective turn" in rhetoric contends: "by urging students into a 'happy' relationship with their writing classes, we ignore that those very classes—and here I'm thinking of the measurement and shaming and competitiveness inherent in them—regularly produce emotions opposite those called for in the framework. . . ."

In nearly every case, this critique of sovereign reason is tied to calls for writing pedagogy to multiply its modes and technologies. For example, Adam Banks, in his 2015 CCCC chair's address, argues that it's time to "bring the funk" by expanding the kinds of compositions we value to include new technologies and non-traditional forms. Relatedly, Richard Lanham argued that "We need new spaces between words, and new spaces for words, in order to depict [today's] new and more complex information flow" (115).

The emerging posthuman and new materialist rhetoric similarly frequently argues for the importance of composing with new media (Dobrin, Writing Posthumanism 3), stipulating that by understanding how new writing technologies enable students to not only "do old things differently" but also "do different things altogether," they can better "foreground the rhetorical agency of objects" (Rivers). Alex Reid gives this object-oriented rhetoric a special urgency by intuiting the breakdown of received modes of composing: "I am increasingly certain that we are entering an ever-stranger compositional environment where the rhetorical roles we imagined for ourselves as modern humans will not function." Therefore, his pedagogy calls for embracing technological "glitches" as a way to move beyond the reduction of composition to the usual questions of subjectivity, ideology, and discursivity. Relatedly, offering the example a student composition written on pink ballet slippers, Jody Shipka argues we should vastly expand our concept of argument beyond the text (2). And Sid Dobrin identifies the future of composition in terms of a posthuman understanding of the extent to which we've already become cyborgs, enhancing our biological capacities through the use of technologies. Clearly, deconstructions of reason and subjective agency in our field have been tied to calls for an expansion of writing media, technologies, and modes in the writing classroom. We can see too how this perspective gives increased importance to *invention* as rhetorical awareness, recognizing that students are better equipped to handle the complexity of the digital age than received social epistemic pedagogies, rooted in symbolic critique. In short, around posthuman and postcompositional critiques of social epistemic process, subjectivity, and contemporary complexity, the future of more traditional forms of discursive composition has never seemed less certain.

Neurorhetoric and Discursive Writing: Is Reason a Priority?

I don't completely disagree with these calls to get funky. And again, in drawing on neuroscience and neurophilosohpy, I mean to extend as opposed to undermine posthuman accounts of subjectivity. However, I'm going to argue against relegating the essay to "genre emeritus" (Banks),[4] and I have a somewhat different opinion on what this moment most demands given the serious psychosocial consequences that may accompany such a relegation. Similarly, while new materialism and posthumanism have offered essential challenges to our privileging of the symbolic and subjective agency, and while I don't question that objects too are actants, I'll argue across this book in light of ultra-contemporary neuroscience that in simply bracketing the subject, some new materialist theory fails to address important pedagogical questions about the relation between care, development, and intelligence. As I'll argue, these questions are best understood through contemporary accounts of neuroplasticity (and therefore, on the side of the subject)—neuroscience, that is, discovers in the materiality of subject (i.e., the brain) subjectivity's self-deconstruction.

In short, the new materialist-inflected pedagogies and postcomposition theories remain deficient in their accounts of the relations between form and difference, affect and learning. In fact, while a cyborg paradigm (identified especially with theorists such as Donna Haraway and Katherine Hayles) has characterized our posthuman relationship to technology in terms of biological enhancement, today, following the neurobiological discovery of plasticity and epigenesis, the situation has reversed itself: in theorizing the potential of technologies, and how they can change, adapt, and learn, we turn to biology and nature. Again, as Dewey had speculated, there is nothing that occurs in the changes and transformations that comprise learning that is not already present in nature. Therefore, tracing the work of various actants in a public rhetoric will require that we follow neuroscience's materialist injunction, recognizing the plasticity of form, its open potential for difference, and also therefore the ways that this potential can be forestalled, compromised, and destroyed by automation and reduction—that is, by *disaffecting power*.

On the one hand, following deconstruction it would be senseless to restore reason to its lofty perch at the top of the mountain. We've come too far to return to the classical account of reason as a transcendental metacognition that gives humanity total purchase over the fluidity of rhetorical situations. However, while reason cannot give us this purchase, I submit that from the materialist perspective of neuroscience, *there is nevertheless an important embodied value to practice in producing long chains of reason through discursive writing*. And while reason does not have a transcending value outside of or above situations from the *top-down*, neurological and cognitive science demonstrates it works perfectly well within situations (especially, as we'll see in Appendix 5.5, in groups), from the *bottom-up*. Recognizing this embodied value of reason in light of contemporary neuroscience will return us to questions concerning affect, wonder, and care. In short, where other new materialist theories have emphasized rhetoric, neuroplasticity reprioritizes pedagogical care, simultaneously revealing the entanglements of rhetoric, composition, writing, and the body.

Indeed, at this moment of increasing indifference, in which powerful technologies are purposefully designed to compete for and capture our students' affects and attention, producing *carelessness*, what we require is new ways to think about care. As Kant argued, "To make public use of reason, as a scholar before the literate world . . . is *to write*" (*Taking Care of Youth* 25), and writing has been the technology in Western society through which individuals connect to and dispute transindividuated culture. The point is not to cultivate reason as "critical thinking" with the idea that doing so will offer a transcendence of our situatedness, but instead to realize the importance of the forms of reasoned writing in inculcating the embodied habits and plastic dispositions required for mature contributions to the highly situated and public work of rhetoric.

So before turning away from the essay—and its careful relationship to what Katherine Hayles calls "deep attention"—we should first ask how it is that have we arrived at this place where our writing assignments too often fail to inspire and respond to the new technological dispensation. Among other things, this will force us to confront that, by returning too quickly to the symbolic even where we've emphasized objects and emotions, we've failed to fully address the frequently negative feelings that accompany writing. On the one hand, process pedagogy and the "social turn" in writing meant—at least in part—to correct for the deadening effects of the classical curriculum and the "current-traditional rhetoric," with its dull focus on correctness and mechanistic account of form, invention, and production. Was it not meant in part to re-center writing around the student by appealing to our students' interests and care? And yet, today instead we encounter the emergence of what Hayles calls "hyper attention" alongside increased distraction, disaffection, and carelessness. As I'll argue, this new age of distraction and disaffection demands a specifically *neurological* account of affect and affectability, and a renewed recognition of the role technologies (including writing) have in giving shape to our brain and our society.

Towards the Uses and Limits of a Neuro Foundationalism

I should clarify at the outset that what I mean by neuroscience might better be termed "neurophilosophy," which is a capacious interdisciplinary effort to think the humanities in terms of the biological, and vice versa. Further, some of the insights in this book draw from a burgeoning cognitive neuroscience—that is, work that begins in research on cognition in order to interpret (and often re-interpret) neuroscientific discoveries. But while Della Sala and Anderson similarly hedge at the beginning of their 2012 edited collection on the intersection of neuroscience and education, arguing, as have many others that have done work at this intersection, that it is cognitivism that does the "heavy lifting" for pedagogy—mildly reproaching the 90% of teachers that "consider knowledge about brain functioning relevant for the planning of education programmes"—I'll try to demonstrate neuroscience's increasing relevance, arguing that works such as theirs have missed what's most revolutionary about neuroscientific discovery to education. While Della Sala and Anderson question if the applicability of neuroscience to education was reducible to "where in the brain . . . learning happens" (3), against their "locationism," I'll emphasize the significance of the neurophilosophical concept of *plasticity*. As I began to argue above, the most responsible, sophisticated, convincing, neuroscience no longer dabbles in correlational accounts of the brain and behavior.

The main chapters in this book will attempt to move us towards a pedagogy informed by contemporary accounts of neuroplasticity. Additionally, across this book in special breakout chapters titled "Pedagogy Breakout" (Appendices 1.5, 3.5, and 5.5), I will suggest practical techniques for applying neurorhetorical insights—at the intersection of contemporary neuroscience and rhetorical theory—to the writing classroom, with the goal of advancing what I'm calling a "plastic pedagogy." To accomplish this, I'll first need to assert the potential for science to address problems traditionally addressed by the humanities; more specifically, I'll need to show how the biological enables a more radical deconstruction of the Cartesian (student) subject than even the affective turn has allowed for, bridging affect and emotion studies while giving a stronger account of both. This will be no mean feat. For one, there are the very compelling critiques of neuroscience from the humanities, many of which point out neuroscience's starting point in reductive models of social phenomenon. For instance, above, I argued that our field has, despite the affective turn, continued to privilege the symbolic, even in accounts of embodiment. But one might reasonably retort that neuroscience reduces the symbolic to the material. This is what Daniel Gross argues in his "interpretive social theory" of the value of apathy to ancient Greek politics, stipulating that emotions "cannot be exhausted by [their] description in biological, physiological, or any other natural-scientific terms . . . without a dramatic reduction of the phenomena at hand" (67). However, while this is doubtlessly true, contemporary neuroscience is *not* reductive, and indeed, as I'll demonstrate, represents a more radical deconstruction of the subject than either Heideggarian destruction or Derridian deconstruction.

Nevertheless, the critiques of neuroscience are clearly substantial enough to be taken seriously here. Daniel Gross, again, finds in the otherwise important contributions of neuroscientists like Antonio Damasio to our understanding of emotion the vestiges of 19th-century-style racism, as when Damasio views "trustworthiness" as universally identifiable in facial features. As Gross states with regard to this disturbing normalization of social and historical constructs, "When the social model used to analyze a brain damaged patient's abnormality is so impoverished, a host of new problems are thereby introduced into the experiment and beyond, into both its interpretation and its application to theories of a larger social world" (31). That is, neuroscience frequently lacks developed models of the social and historic contingency and complexity of human behaviors. Furthermore, much has been written about epistemic and methodological problems and the public overstatement of neuroscientific findings (e.g., McGinn; Rose & Abi-Rached; Satel & Lillienfeld)—including by neuroscientists themselves—and also specifically about the limitations of neuroscience to education (Willingham) and writing studies (Jack & Appelbaum). Again, following critiques from continental philosophy, the humanities has long defined itself through its resistance to the bio-reduction of the social and symbolic; philosophical empiricism, it argues, leaves the "soul" of metaphysics to the side, failing to explain how we can get from the physical brain to conscious experience.

Below, I've grouped the critiques of neuroscience into three major categories:

Epistemological problems, including but not limited to:

The non-reciprocity of laboratories with lived experience: a modeling problem that results from the limitations of transference from the abstracted laboratory to real life situations.

The non-reciprocity of animal testing: a modeling problem that results from the lack of conservation between the structures and functions of animal biology and human biology (Rose & Abi Rached 94–95).

The problem of "reverse inference": reasoning backwards from neural activation to subjective experience (Satel and Lilienfeld 13).

The "circular analysis problem": the result of inferring statistically significant correlations from massive datasets of tens of thousands of voxels through single experiments.

The problem of image aggregation: neuroscientists pinpoint regions responsible for different functions by overlaying multiple brain images. This poses some problems, including the problem that such aggregations may not tell us anything about a specific individual.

Confusing correlation with causation: a problem in all sciences but especially significant in neuroscience, where it's not clear if neural activation precedes behavior or *vice versa*.

Variable construction problems: neuroscientists often rely on naïve or underdeveloped definitions of complex mental functions, such as memory.

Mental inference fallacy: inferring an inner mental state based on one's own concepts and observations—for example, a "freezing" behavior in a rat, triggered by matching a loud noise with a shock, becomes a sign of "fear" (Barrett 272). Can also be a form of anthropomorphizing.

Discursive problems, including but not limited to:

Discursive non-correspondence (or "level of analysis") error: using language suited to describing one system to describe another with different properties. For instance, although cars are made of atoms, we wouldn't want to turn to particle physics to answer the question of "how does a car run." The properties of consciousness are of a different order than the properties of the brains, and must be described in different terms.

Mereolological or Homunculus fallacy: another level of analysis problem. Related to Wittgenstein's observation that "Only of a human being and of what resembles (behaves like) a living human being can one say: it has sensations; it sees, is blind; hears, is deaf." By speaking of the brain in anthropomorphic terms we shift the problem of experience from the individual to the brain by evoking a "little man" in the brain that acts. See especially Bennett and Hacker.

Technical versus ordinary language: while neuroscience promises a more scientific language to replace how we discuss our experience, it's unclear that this language will prove better than others, including the "folk psychology" derived from our immediate experience.

Media hype: the tendency of the media to privilege simple solutions to complex problems and especially to trumpet neuroscientific research as "findings" rather than as unresolved problems.

Ontological problems, including but not limited to:

Qualia: the problem that even though neuroscience might be able to decode human behavior, it can never describe the experience of what it's like to be human.

The "looping effect" on the empirical subject: once the human subject has a knowledge of neuroscience, the subject of study has effectively shifted, becoming "subject with knowledge of neuroscience."

Medicalization: the tendency of the neuro-reductive ontology to privilege drugs as a solution to human problems.

Subjectification: the problem of the relation of the subject to neurological knowledge as a form of bio-power that governs behavior.

Locationism or "biological fingerprint" error: the error that presumes complex processes like emotions have a singular "fingerprint" and universal manifestation (for instance, emotions correspond to specific bodily states and facial expressions). This extends from the classical neuroscientific model that views mental phenomenon as corresponding to a specific location in the brain.

Related to these critiques of neuroscience, some have questioned the value of writing pedagogies rooted in affect. As Julie Nelson argues, theories of affect in our field—as opposed to emotion—have possibly become too diffuse to be useful to rhetoricians: "When affect is studied only as an unnamable force or ungraspable excess, it is useful only in demarcating a dimension we can never access, except very indirectly or after the fact . . . This false binary has contributed to almost exclusive bodies of affect and emotion scholarship in rhetoric and composition." Even a scholar as sympathetic to the study of affectivity as Daniel Gross has quipped, "critics who depend on affect as pre-ideological, pre-subjective, and pre-linguistic now are starting to sound mystical since they aren't left with much to talk about" (Langdon).

With all of these problems and questions to consider, one might reasonably ask, why neuroscience? Do we really need an account of affectivity and our disciplinary subject at the level of neurons? This is a question that I take very seriously, one I'll return to throughout the book. Nevertheless, along with skeptical critics from other disciplines—including prominent theorists such as Paul Rabinow, Nikolas Rose, Andy Clark—we must now recognize the recent neuroscience is conclusive on some topics, that certain debates have been settled, and that, contra Gross, the neuroscientific account of affect leaves us with much to talk about. As I'll argue throughout the book, the moment has come for a consideration of the transcendental—which in the philosophical tradition is the original synthesis of subject and world, irreducible to materiality—in terms of the biological, one that will enact a transformation within the transcendental without becoming "mystical." In short, we can no longer maintain a division between the humanities and the biological sciences—we can no longer leave the social-biological binary undeconstructed—and writing studies and pedagogy must once again turn to the cognitive sciences in founding the subject of our discipline. As Walter Pater put it, what's in us "rusts iron and ripens corn" (217).

Nevertheless, composition and rhetoric has long accepted an essential opposition between foundational and anti-foundational theories, reflecting in many ways the epistemological distinction in philosophy between empiricism and metaphysics. This opposition between the material and the symbolic, the scientific and the humanistic, the natural and the rhetorical, the body and consciousness, the affective and the emotional, is evident especially in composition theory's epistemic division between cognitive and social theories of process. While foundationalist approaches to composition have been derived from cognitive and linguistic sciences, anti-foundationalism, as Gary Olson stipulates, "is most closely associated with those often called social constructionists—and, lately, with those advocating for a 'post-process' paradigm" (46). Let's take these in order. First, the social epistemic pedagogy was meant precisely to upset the tradition of the "classical" Cartesian subject in our field, a tradition dominated by formalist approaches to language, intelligence, structured systems of classification, and the pedagogy of "mental discipline." Theorists like James Berlin were frequently responding specifically to the foundationalist, cognitivist process pedagogy that unwittingly conserved this tradition in its computational view of cognition; instead of teaching critical thinking, the current-traditional writing pedagogy, so the argument went, taught students to be workers in a capitalist economy.

However, as many postprocess theorists have argued, the social epistemic pedagogy itself conserved the classical subject. Byron Hawk described this situation early on through the example of the critical pedagogy of Ira Shor, one of Pablo Freire's interlocutors. In pushing his students towards a "political subjectivity" through processes of critique, Shor generalizes his pedagogy, making the mistake of assuming "that certain methods will lead to specific results" (Hawk 211). He is therefore surprised when, in the name of a critical pedagogy that forefronts resistance, his students "rebel."[5] As Hawk points out, Freire understood his critical pedagogy as pertaining specifically to the conditions in South America, and did not mean for his "critical" method to always result in political subjectivity. Shor, on the other hand, made the mistake of turning his pedagogy into something every bit as deterministic as any prescriptive current-traditional method. As a result, he discovers that "Establishing a pedagogical method as a universal law simply produces its own resistance" (Hawk 210). Instead of making critique an open process of questioning the rules or code, Hawk argues that the social epistemic pedagogy privileged a version of questioning *as* a stable rule, guaranteed by a transcendental political subjectivity. For this reason, the social epistemic pedagogy fails in the same way that the various attempts to found writing and rhetoric in scientific materialism have—it is ultimately characterized by a rationalized code and closure to difference. In the years after Hawk's *A Counter-History of Composition*, attempting to get around the problem of the subject, postprocess and new materialist theories (as we began to see above) have sought to deconstruct the distinction between foundationalism and anti-foundationalism around its basis in the rational, transcendental subject, theorizing instead an ecological complexity or vitalism that rediscovers an element of the spiritual, symbolic, or intellectual in the biological. What neuroscience adds to this deconstruction of the foundational/anti-foundational binary is a thoroughly materialist rhetoric and pedagogy, a radical decentering of the subject that does not require vitalism or panpsychism.

Finally, the neuroscientific theory of affect will enable a more rigorously materialist approach to our field's "affective turn," and a more complete response to our field's privileging of the symbolic and reason. For one, as we'll see through a crucial distinction made across this book, neuroscience discovers affect as a rhetorical intensity at the level of the body, distinguishing it from the social and intentional structure of emotion—that is, affect is a pre-conscious, non-signifying grammar, while to an entirely different order of conscious meaning. Where affect is (to use Deleuze and Guattari's term) an "emergent assemblage" of embodied intensities, emotion is social and conceptual—and neuroscience further explains (pointing to the limits of Brian Massumi's theory, which tends to view affect and emotion as metaphysically distinct) how these two different orders interface. While a complete review of the affective turn is beyond the scope of this chapter, I'd like to focus on the fact that, even following the affective turn, affect continues to be viewed as secondary to reason and epistemic composition; indeed, emotion is still frequently viewed as precisely *irrational*. As Julia Prebel claims, in writing pedagogy, "Emotion has been viewed as an irrational response that should be restrained in the classroom and privatized in our individual lives," to the extent, she points out, that students resist including emotional appeals in their writing. But furthermore, as Joddy Murray recognizes, *even within recent composition theory that emphasizes emotionality,*[6] affect is often viewed as supplemental; as equally significant to but separate from reason; or worse, as the cause of unreason and error. Our failure to recognize that emotions are in fact a condition of *all* meaningful communication has resulted in "false dichotomies, such as mind/body and emotion/reason, that often drive many of the debates in rhetoric and composition" (Murray 84–85). Failing to theorize emotion at the level of embodied affect leaves pedagogy following the affective turn as vulnerable as the social epistemic pedagogy to student disaffection.

Neuroscience Today: Beyond Locationism

While a vigilant skepticism remains in order concerning certain correlational neuroscientific accounts of human behavior and learning, it's clear that neuroscience has advanced our understanding of cognition significantly from the days when Patricia Bizzell rightly criticized the Flower-Hayes model of cognition—characterized by the homunculus fallacy[7] that elided the decision-making process of the writing subject through its displacements. And clearly, neuroscience has moved far beyond the right-brain/left-brain locationism that characterized Janet Emig's "Hand, Brain, Eye: Some Basics in the Writing Process." Today, new understandings of the role of emotions in brain functioning paint a more complicated picture of reason and the writing process. It is now no longer sufficient to cite the indeterminacy of the play of traces and symbols, accuse neuroscience of determinism, and move on. As this work will demonstrate, such strawman arguments ignore the fact that neuroscience, in offering a materialist account of the trace, represents a critique of reason and meaning more radical than deconstruction or new materialism.

For one thing, developments within neuroscience have undermined the early picture it painted of locationism and biological determinism, a vision that drew heavily on computation metaphors to depict the brain as a processor of bottom-up sensory information.[8] Indeed, contemporary neuroscience discards the computational account of the brain and even the idea that brain regions are dedicated to specific activities. For instance, important figures in the study of cognition, such as Michael L. Anderson, Lisa Feldman Barrett, Andy Clark, Karl Friston, and many others, have challenged the classical account of the brain through a "predictive processing" model, viewing the brain as involved in active and emergent meaning making based in past knowledge and ongoing calculations. From the perspective of this model, instead of building an image of the world based on incoming sensory information, it appears that the brain actively *simulates* the world; that is, instead of passively processing sensory representations, the brain actively represents the world. If this theory is correct, the brain creates its own evolving, *ad hoc* predictive models based on modifications made in response to "prediction errors." Relatedly, neuroscience has embraced "a fundamental principle of 'neural reuse,'" the self-organizing recruitment and repurposing of brain regions for different tasks. For example, across his work, Michael L. Anderson argues for a version of plasticity that involves not only the ongoing formation of connections between neurons (the Hebbian insight that neurons that "fire together wire together"), but the *ad hoc* formation of "long distance partnerships" across entire regions (3). Therefore, just as the famous Broca's language area is involved in forms of cognition other than language, language use is "scattered" across regions. This discovery refutes the Chomskian generative grammar and other classical linguistic accounts that posit deep grammatical *a priori* structures, internal systems for processing symbols (like a computer).

In addition to undoing the naïve locationism that seeks to discover a kind of one-to-one correspondence between brain locations and behaviors, a stable interface between brain and behavior (or cognition and perception), the predictive processing theory challenges the classical evolutionary account of an atavistic emotional, animal brain surrounded by a neocortex devoted to reason. Indeed, neuroscience has discovered that processes of reason and emotion are bound together across the brain. For neuroscience, as we'll see, emotions are bodily manifestations of symbolic experiences. They are the cartographers of experience, mapping our symbolic, conscious experiences in physical, neural connections. These neural maps are therefore viewed as forming *in between* the material and the symbolic, as existing at the points where the brain encounters the mind, and as *reducible to neither*.

In the ongoing effort to maintain homeostasis in the face of external stimulation and perturbation, neuroscientists argue, the brain *maps* the embodied condition of the organism. This underlying neural map is the "protoself," a "nonconscious collection of representations of the multiple dimensions of current organism state" (Damasio *Feeling* 199). It represents in the working memory not only external objects, but also the *affective response*[9] of the organism to the external and the overall processes of change itself. Or again, the protoself maps the body's affective-physiological response to the external, registering changes to the stasis of the organism. In this way, the mind is said to be "about" the organism's embodiment in the world—*the brain maps the body's encounter of difference*. The brain is in this way a complex, Gestaltian, and emergent system—which is to say, plastic—through a process of ongoing self (re)presenting.

Neural maps take shape at the points of encounter between brain and mind, the biological and symbolic. And it is affects that work to inscribe these maps, joining physiological and symbolic experience. As famed neuroscientist Antonio Damasio theorizes, the "emotional thought," emerging first as an embodied response to situations, comprises the automatic production of the basic images of conscious representation:

> The brain of a normal, intelligent, and educated adult reacts to the situation by rapidly creating scenarios of possible response options and

> related outcomes. To our consciousness, the scenarios are made of multiple imaginary scenes, not really a smooth film, but rather pictorial flashes of key images in those scenes, jump cut from one frame to another, in quick juxtapositions.
>
> (Damasio, *Descartes Error* 170)

And again, many neuroscientists now argue that these images are *predictions* made by the brain about the world (as opposed to computations of incoming sensory information). But there's an overwhelming amount of possible response options made available by the brain to consciousness: "a diverse repertoire of images, generated to the tune of the situation you are facing, entering and exiting your consciousness in a show too rich for you to encompass fully" (170). This is in part because, upending classical neuroscientific and cognitive theory, these images are not being monitored, as projections on a unified screen, by a homunculus (as critics often suggest), but rather are distributed throughout the interrelated regions of the brain, united by the broader tendency towards homeostasis and survival (84). Damasio therefore needs to explain how certain images are recommended to consciousness while others are suppressed.

Damasio's "somatic marker" theory is his account of how emotions delimit (or bias) these images so that we are not overwhelmed by the proliferation of the brain's predictions. In his theory of the somatic marker, following Spinoza's theorization of the *conatus*—the innate will to persist—Damasio argues that these images are "marked" with either "joy"—which increases the power to think and act—or "sadness"—which decreases the power to think and act. These emotional marks are gained through experience and allow the subject to make *automatic* predictions about the world. In this way, somatic markers recommend images, or not, either for immediate action (this is the automatic act of "intuition") or to conscious attention for further deliberation and reflection (reason): "A preselection is carried out for you, sometimes covertly, sometimes not. A biological mechanism makes the preselection, examines candidates, and allows only a few to present themselves for a final exam" (189). Emotions for Damasio (he uses the word "feelings") are in this way mental representations made *about* affects.

To prove his theory of the somatic marker, Damasio turns to organic pathology. His research provides multiple examples of subjects with brain lesions that disrupt emotional response, incapacitating the subject's ability to make decisions (perhaps even more famously, neurologist and best-selling author Oliver Sacks, in works like *The Man Who Mistook His Wife For a Hat*, presents many such case histories). What these case histories show is that, even where reason is conserved as a capacity for abstract thought, we require emotions to function socially. Many of his insights are based on a brain damaged patient named Elliott, a former businessman who, having part of his orbitofrontal cortex removed in surgery, lost his capacity for emotion despite retaining full capacity to reason. However, as opposed to being able to reason more perfectly, without emotional interference, Elliott was left unable to make even basic decisions. The protoself damaged, patients like Elliott are able to function normally on tasks of reasoning, but unable to, for example, select from among the myriad options for ketchup at the grocery store. Such decisions, as advertisers well know, are aided by our spontaneous emotional bias. Patients like Elliott suffer greatly in both business and in life, yet remain indifferent to (unaffected by) this suffering. As we'll see, it's these neuropathological subjects that gain us insight into the broader social phenomenon of disaffection described above.

Ultimately, what's most important to understand in Damasio's somatic marker hypothesis is that it theorizes the fundamental priority of the affective over the cognitive, of affect over reason. Understanding this neuroscientific discovery—strongly supported by the study of pathological organic lesions, the gold standard of medical science—radically challenges the classical Cartesian subject.[10] From this perspective, emotions represent an "animal" response distinct from reason, an atavistic nervous response beneath human dignity, "like a toddler in a china shop, interfering with the orderly rows of stemware on the shelves" (Immordino-Yang & Damasio 4). Still, even despite neurobiology's strong account of a decentered subject, those of us working and teaching in the humanities might be wondering at this point, what's the big deal? There are myriad anti-foundational theories in our disciplines that decenter the subject, undermining the primacy of reasoned intentionality. We can, of course, see that our own field came to similar conclusions long ago. So allow me to emphasize what's important here, a theme that I'll develop more extensively in Chapter 1. What neuroscience finally demonstrates, beyond the epistemological threshold, is that our deconstructions are in fact material reality: *neuroscience discovers deconstruction in nature itself*.

Again, while a certain tradition within rhetoric has long speculated about the role of affect in relation to reason, we can now assert with some certainty, beyond the epistemological threshold, the primacy of affect. Grounded in pathological anatomy, this discovery is as close to capital "t" Truth as we can get. It's time for compositionists and rhetoricians to take notice. Neuroscience decenters reason not only in its relation to discourse but at its biological root. And therefore, although his work is an explicit rejection of the biologization of emotions, contemporary neuroscience puts us far closer towards Daniel Gross' account of the social-historical "emotional economy" than his work admits. Far from ignoring the social and rhetorical in favor of the biological, neuroscience upsets their distinction.

Neural Reuse and the Affordances of Writing

But what does any of this have to do with writing pedagogy? As I've already begun to argue, and as I'll argue across this book, neuroscience points to the significance of care and the emotional experience of writing. In fact, reading and writing are fantastic examples of the neuroscientific deconstruction of the affect–reason binary and the principle of neural reuse; appearing too late in human history to be understood in evolutionary terms, both reading and writing reuse and reorganize evolutionarily old parts of the brain, giving shape to human cultural experience by causing "widespread changes in human neural organization" (Clark *Surfing Uncertainty* 281). From the perspective of neuroscience, language is "a form of action and social coordination" (Anderson 249) that "reuses" already existent neural potentials; and perhaps unsurprisingly, language uses parts of the brain associated with other forms of social action. For example, "words such as 'lick,' 'pick,' and 'kick' activate regions in the primary motor cortex involved in mouth movements, hand movements, and leg movements, respectively" (Anderson 252). More generally, language reuses regions associated with motor control and social interaction. Again, these discoveries radically undermine locationist accounts, demonstrating the imbrication of sensory, motor, affective, and cognitive functions.

To further understand this, consider how neural reuse underlays writing as an "affordance" of cognition extended into the environment. As an external cognitive affordance, language enhances embodied and cognitive functions, allowing subjects to reuse neural connections for entirely novel purposes; and "This is especially so in the case of *written* language" (249), which is an external system for solving complex problems. For example, a sensorimotor awareness of fingers can support mathematical ability; in short, the neural representation of fingers affords an enhanced ability to count:

> the idea is that this neural circuit, originally developed to support finger awareness, is offering some functionally relevant resource in the domain of numerical cognition. . . . Fingers provide children a useful physical resource for counting, with the neural result that the supporting structures for finger awareness and magnitude representation now overlap, and . . . the circuit in question might itself offer useful resources (such as a storage array).
>
> (Anderson 23–24)

In other words, in learning math we reuse earlier-forming sensorimotor neural networks. This holds intriguing potential for writing pedagogy, suggesting the significance of the relationship between embodiment and various external affordances. For instance, compositionists know that we discover new ideas and arguments by moving units or chunks of text around; it would not be surprising to find that in discovering arguments, we are reusing parts of the brain associated with spatial tasks (similarly, we now know Broca's area is recruited in a variety of tasks beyond language). Through affordances like this—which are in fact sensorimotor skills—writing as a system of extended cognition may itself be understood to "speak," composing us as we compose it at an embodied, sensorimotor level. Looked at this way, as some rhetoricians have long speculated, invention—like other dimensions of rhetoric—does not originate in the self-reflecting subject. As Andy Clark puts it, reflecting certain tenants of process pedagogy, textual products do not "spring fully developed from inner cogitations." Instead, reasoned compositions are the result of manipulating external textual resources, "a sustained and iterated sequence of interactions between my brain and a variety of external props" (Clark *Magic Words* 171). Furthermore, this two-way relationship between the forms and technologies of writing and consciousness raises significant ethical and pedagogical questions concerning recent calls to abandon received forms of academic writing that will be explored in the final chapters in this book.

Learning to write, from the perspective of neural reuse, entails understanding the various affordances that different forms of composition allow, affordances that extend and amplify cognitive ability, enabling humans to act into the world in different ways, beyond the limits of our "inner cogitations." At the same time, neuroscience allows us to better understand how we are in turn written or composed by these affordances. This moves us as far as possible from the classical representational view of writing and cognition, and "The assumption is that the end product of perception is an inner world that fully reproduces—that in its elements and their relations is appropriately homologous to—the outer" (Anderson 282). The classical approach emphasized a reflective, "mirror like" contemplation—including the famous phenomenological introspection and "critical thinking" that would be so important from the social epistemic perspective, and the "metacognition" theorized by the cognitivists. Contemplative thought—the educative ideal—was understood as the manipulation, computation, and processing of both sensory data and "inner objects," representations of the world that language (and writing) were understood to both shape (originally through "mental discipline" and then through critical thinking) and express. Instead of a Cartesianism that asks how the mind is organized to represent the external world, again, neuroscience posits a brain actively engaged—before cognition—in *simulating* the world, predicting sensory data, and drawing on affordances to act into the world within embodied contexts. What neuroscience discovers is not a mind representing the world, but a mind representing the body's preconscious, affective interface with the world. It is in this way that neuroscience allow us to understand the primacy of affective embodiment in the work of composing and rhetoric. This will be the focus of Chapter 1, which will return us to the pedagogical problems raised above concerning writing, embodiment, and affectivity in the digital age.

Notes

1. Relatedly, Joddy Murray argues, "Rhetors throughout history have often addressed the emotions, but in rhetoric and composition—a discipline that, at least in part, derives itself from this tradition—scholars have largely ignored the work on the affective domain" (85).

2. Malabou is a primary inspiration for this book, which I envision as, in part, an introduction of her work to our field. The definition of plasticity I advance in this book—and more besides—is hugely indebted to her thinking; indeed, Chapter 1 will explain her fascinating account of plasticity and its relevance to writing pedagogy.
3. This is also what likeminded philosopher Bernard Stiegler, another student of Jacques Derrida, calls "I-don't-give-a-fuckism" (je-m'en-foutisme)—the tendency towards short-term interests over long-term responsibilities.
4. For similar reasons, I strongly disagree with DeStigter that social justice and resistance will require turning away from reason and the argumentative form.
5. While Shor famously allowed his students to help design the curriculum, asking them to then sign the syllabus, they rebelled because they knew the teacher could not, in fact, abnegate his power—he was an authority figure whether he liked it or not. Hawk comments, "One thing liberatory pedagogy tends to sidestep is the fact that students can and do see teachers as embodying the power of law, no matter how much the teacher may genuinely want to help them. Help can be patronizing when distributed downward from a point of authority" (211). As teachers, Hawk argues, we can't sidestep these power relations—Shor finds no Archimedean point outside of the power dynamics of the pedagogical relationship, no metacognition above the embodied dynamics of the classroom; instead, his abnegation is reinscribed as patronization.
6. It's not difficult to find examples of affect's diminished role in our field, even within scholarship on emotion. Take, for example, Christine Martorana's recent work, "The Real/Ideal Research Project: Fostering Students' Emotional Literacy," a pedagogical recommendation inspired by emotions studies and the affective turn. Martorana defines "emotional intelligence" as an ability to make the right choice between *logos*, *pathos*, and *ethos* in challenging a political order rooted in "inequity." But, as promising as her pedagogy is, Martorana has bracketed the question of the student's embodied, emotional disposition towards writing itself, determining at the outset that students will or should *feel* connected to the critique of unequal conditions regarding "gender, race, religion, family, class, and/or physical appearance/ability." But what if they are not? Even in the strongest accounts of affect, there is always—more or less—this residue of the symbolic. For instance, in *Doing Emotion: Rhetoric, Writing, Teaching*, Laura Micciche's overarching interest was in emotions as *symbolic performances*. This subtending of affective embodiment to its ends in conscious, social performances is present as well in Lynn Worsham's early call for the "reeducation of emotions." Relatedly, this body of scholarship has had little or nothing to say about the embodied relation between emotion and the embodied act of writing—an important oversight following the explosion of new media and technologies in the attention economy.
7. The gist of Bizzell's critique of Flower and Hayes was that their "monitor" exhibited the homunculus fallacy. By imagining the brain as a screen that is monitored, they displaced the problem of the writing subject by simply moving it back a level.
8. As Immordino-Yang & Damasio argue, this classical account of the subject long dominated neuroscientific research: "Well into the 1980's, the study of brain systems underlying behavior and cognition was heavily dominated by a top-down approach in which the processes of learning, language, and reasoning were understood as high-order systems that imposed themselves upon an obedient body" (117). This rationalist model informed a massive amount of neuroscientific research that sought to discover "localized" brain functions, the correspondence of synaptic regions to behaviors and other outcomes.
9. It's important to note that Damasio uses the word "emotion," as distinguished from "feelings," to denote what composition theorists usually mean by affect.

I will attempt, with some awkwardness I'm afraid, to get around this confusion by using the word affect where Damasio would use the word emotion.

10. To further understand the relation of reason and emotion in the classical account of the subject, it's instructive to consider classical economics, rooted in the premise that humans are rational actors—*homo economicus*. If it were true that humans were rational actors, making choices based in reason, then, as mathematical models demonstrate, free markets would be the ideal economic system. But we're not, and they're not, as any number of global financial crises have revealed. And just as in economics, classical neuroscience (and much in contemporary composition theory) is modeled after the myth of the rational actor: "The model begins with ancient subcortical circuits for basic survival, which we allegedly inherited from reptiles. Sitting atop those circuits is an alleged emotion system, known as the 'limbic system,' that we supposedly inherited from early mammals. And wrapped around the so-called limbic system, like icing on an already-baked cake, is our allegedly rational and uniquely human cortex . . . an animal brain gift-wrapped in cognition" (Barrett 81).

Works Cited

Anderson, Michael L. "Neural Reuse in the Organization and Development of the Brain." *Developmental Medicine & Child Neurology*, vol. 58, 2016, pp. 3–6. Web.

Banks, Adam. "2015 CCCC Chair's Address: Ain't No Walls Behind the Sky, Baby! Funk, Flight, Freedom." *College Composition and Communication*, vol. 67, no. 2, 2015, p. 267.

Bennett, M. R., and Peter Hacker. *Philosophical Foundations of Neuroscience*. Blackwell Pub, Malden, MA, 2003.

Berlin, James A. *Rhetorics, Poetics, and Cultures: Refiguring College English Studies*. Parlor Press, Anderson, SC, 2003.

———. "Rhetoric and Ideology in the Writing Classroom." *Cross-Talk in Comp Theory*. 2nd ed., pp. 717–737.

Bizzell, Patricia. *Academic Discourse and Critical Consciousness*. University of Pittsburgh Press, Pittsburgh, PA, 1992.

Barnett, Scot, and Casey A. Boyle. *Rhetoric, through Everyday Things*. The University of Alabama Press, Tuscaloosa, 2016.

Brand, Alice G., and Richard L. Graves. *Presence of Mind: Writing and the Domain Beyond the Cognitive*. Boynton/Cook Pub, Portsmouth, NH, 1994.

Carr, Nicholas G. *The Shallows: What the Internet Is Doing to Our Brains*. W.W. Norton, New York, 2010.

Clark, Andy. "Magic Words: How Language Augments Human Computation." *Language and Thought: Interdisciplinary Themes*. Eds. Peter Carruthers and Jill Boucher. Cambridge University Press, Cambridge, 1998, pp. 162–183.

———. *Surfing Uncertainty: Prediction, Action, and the Embodied Mind*. Oxford University Press, New York, 2016.

Cooper, Marilyn M. "Rhetorical Agency as Emergent and Enacted." *College Composition and Communication*, vol. 62, no. 3, 2011, pp. 420–449.

Damasio, Antonio R. *The Feeling of What Happens: Body and Emotion in the Making of Consciousness*. Harcourt Brace, New York, 1999.

———. *Descartes' Error: Emotion, Reason and the Human Brain*. Random House, London, 2008. Print.

Davis, D. Dianne. "Identification: Burke and Freud on Who You Are." *Rhetoric Society Quarterly*, vol. 38, no. 2, 2008, pp. 123–147. Web. March 15 2014.

———. *Inessential Solidarity: Rhetoric and Foreigner Relations*. University of Pittsburgh Press, Pittsburgh, PA, 2010.

Della Sala, Sergio, and Mike Anderson. *Neuroscience in Education: The Good, the Bad and the Ugly*. Oxford University Press, New York, 2012.

DeStigter, Todd. "On the Ascendance of Argument: A Critique of the Assumptions of Academe's Dominant Form." *Research in the Teaching of English*, vol. 50, no. 1, 2015, p. 11.

Dewey, John. "Whitehead's Philosophy." *The Philosophical Review*, vol. 46, no. 2, 1937, pp. 170–177.

Dobrin, Sidney. *Postcomposition*. Southern Illinois University Press, Carbondale, 2011.

Emig, Janet. "Hand, Eye, Brain: Some 'Basics' in the Writing Process." *Research on Composing*. National Council of Teachers of English, Urbana, IL, 1978.

Gross, Daniel M. *The Secret History of Emotion: From Aristotle's Rhetoric to Modern Brain Science*. University of Chicago Press, Bristol, 2007.

Haraway, Donna J. *Manifestly Haraway*. Universrity of Minnesota Press, Minneapolis, MN, 2016.

Hawk, Byron. *A Counter-History of Composition: Toward Methodologies of Complexity*. University of Pittsburgh Press, Pittsburgh, PA, 2007. *ProQuest ebrary*. Web. 8 June 2016.

Hayles, Katherine. "Hyper and Deep Attention: The Generational Divide in Cognitive Modes." *Profession*, vol. 13, 2007, pp. 187–199. *JSTOR*. Web. 19 February 2015.

Immordino-Yang, Mary H., and Antonio Damasio. "We Feel, Therefore We Learn: The Relevance of Affective and Social Neuroscience to Education." *Mind, Brain, and Education*, vol. 1, no. 1, 2007, pp. 3–10.

Jack, Jordynn, and L. G. Appelbaum. " 'This Is Your Brain on Rhetoric': Research Directions for Neurorhetorics." *Rhetoric Society Quarterly*, vol. 40, no. 5, 2010, pp. 411–437, doi:10.1080/02773945.2010.516303.

Jackson, Brian. "Neuroscience and the New Urgency of Emotional Appeals." *JAC*, vol. 31, no. 3/4, 2011, pp. 473–496. Web.

Langdon, Lance. "The Passions of Rhetoric and Composition: An Interview With Daniel M. Gross." *Composition Forum*, vol. 34, *Association of Teachers of Advanced Composition*, 2016.

Lanham, Richard. *The Economics of Attention: Style and Substance in the Age of Information*. University of Chicago Press, Chicago, IL, 2006. Print.

Malabou, Catherine. "Emotional Life in a Neurobiological Age." *Youtube*, uploaded by Cornell University, 9 August 2013, www.youtube.com/watch?v=H4oFump89W4.

———. "From Sorrow to Indifference." *Youtube*, uploaded by Stony Brook University, 14 November 2013, www.youtube.com/watch?v=KoAd1lQ1bXM.

Martorana, Christine. "The Real/Ideal Research Project: Fostering Students' Emotional Literacy." *Composition Forum*, vol. 34, *Association of Teachers of Advanced Composition*, 2016.

McGinn, Colin. *All Machine and No Ghost?*, vol. 141. New Statesman Ltd, London, 2012.

Micciche, Laura R. *Doing Emotion: Rhetoric, Writing, Teaching*. Boynton/Cook Publishers, Portsmouth, NH, 2007.
Muckelbauer, John. *The Future of Invention: Rhetoric, Postmodernism, and the Problem of Change*. State University of New York Press, Albany, 2008.
Murray, Joddy. *Non-Discursive Rhetoric: Image and Affect in Multimodal Composition*. Suny Press, Albany, NY, 2009.
Pater, Walter. "Conclusion." *Walter Pater: Three Major Texts*. Ed. William E. Buckler. New York University Press, New York, 1986.
Prebel, Julia. "Engaging a 'Pedagogy of Discomfort': Emotion as Critical Inquiry in Community-Based Writing Courses." *Composition Forum*, vol. 34, *Association of Teachers of Advanced Composition*, 2016.
Reid, Alex. "Composing Objects: Prospects for a Digital Rhetoric." *Enculturation*, vol. 14, 2013. Web. 1 April 2013.
Rice, Jenny. "Para-Expertise, Tacit Knowledge, and Writing Problems." *College English*, vol. 78, no. 2, 2015, pp. 117.
Richmond, Kia J. "Repositioning Emotions in Composition Studies." *Composition Studies*, vol. 30, no. 1, 2002, pp. 67–82. Web.
Rickert, Thomas. *Ambient Rhetoric: The Attunements of Rhetorical Being*. University of Pittsburgh, Pittsburgh, PA, 2013. Web.
Rose, Nikolas, and Joelle M. Abi-Rached. *Neuro: The New Brain Sciences and the Management of the Mind*. Princeton University Press, Princeton, NJ, 2013. Print.
Satel, Sally L., and Scott O. Lilienfeld. *Brainwashed: The Seductive Appeal of Mindless Neuroscience*. Basic Books, New York, 2013.
Shipka, Jody. *Toward a Composition Made Whole*. University of Pittsburgh Press, Pittsburgh, PA, 2011.
Stiegler, Bernard. *Taking Care of Youth and the Generations*. Stanford University Press, Stanford, CA, 2010. Print.
Willingham, Daniel. *When Can You Trust the Experts? How to Tell Good Science From Bad in Education*. Jossey-Bass, San Francisco, CA, 2012.
Worsham, Lynn. "Going Postal: Pedagogic Violence and the Schooling of Emotion." *JAC*, vol. 18, no. 2, 1998, pp. 213–245. Print.

1 Neuroscience and Neuroideology

Plasticity, Flexibility, and the Emotional Architecture of Experience

As Daniel Gross argues, against the biologization of emotions, emotions "were once treated by everybody as externalized forms," but have today been "sucked, as it were, into the brain." By examining the "irreducibly social" circulation of (for example) anger and apathy in antiquity, their relation to power discrepancies in a culture's "emotion economy," Gross argues that "scientific terms would be, in fact, thoroughly inappropriate." Doubtlessly, rhetoric will remain essential in our understanding of the constructedness of emotions and their political and ideological circulations. It's certainly true that many neuroscientists lack adequate theorization of the social; where this is the case, neuroscience becomes ideology.

However, is contemporary neuroscience indeed guilty of reducing emotion to biological terms? As we'll see, the answer is no. Instead, far from bio-reductivism, neuroscientific discovery concerning the primacy of affectivity allows us to understand *constructivism* from a more thoroughly materialist perspective. As a result, as I'll argue here and across this book, contemporary neuroscientific theories comprise a more radical deconstruction of the classical subject than other contemporary rhetorical, posthuman, and new materialist accounts. Rhetorical analysis alone, divorced from a biological foundation, will not be sufficient to theorizing and addressing the psychological and sociological construction and circulation of affect and power.

To be clear up front, I can't claim (and would not want to) that neuroscience offers, once and for all, any determinate pedagogical program.[1] Pedagogy—even when it is constructed on objective biological foundations—necessarily entails subjective interpretation and theorization. Yet, far too often, neuroscience as it's relayed through popular culture offers facile solutions to very complex problems. Looked at one way it seems to suggest *this*, and another it seems to suggest *that*. Nevertheless, as we'll see, what the most compelling neuroscience *does* do, objectively and profoundly, is demonstrate *the limits of all rational determinisms at the level of materiality itself*. This has vast pedagogical consequences, as, for instance, neuroscientific objectivity *does* enable us to reject much in received writing pedagogy while providing the foundations for a more consistently materialist approach to writing and learning.

In order to understand how neuroscience offers a materialist (deconstructed) foundation for rhetorical affectivity and writing pedagogy, without reducing learning to mechanistic or automatized accounts of the subject, this chapter will explore emerging intersections between neuroscience, philosophy, and composition and rhetoric around the nature of plasticity. Having raised the question of emotions and indifference in the writing classroom in the Introduction, I intend here to further establish the objective neuropathology and theoretical neurophilosophy behind a thesis I began to argue for in the Introduction that I will return to in different ways across this book: the contemporary subject is characterized by an increasingly pervasive indifference—and in the classroom, an absence of wonder and care—a situation that is exploited by bio-power today. This situation is best described in the terms of contemporary neurophilosophy, which allows us to understand the pedagogical, ethical, ideological, and political significance of our students' embodied and emotional experiences with writing, entailing both creative and destructive experiences of *failure*. At the same time, as we'll see, often under the pretense of care, much received writing pedagogy—especially in overemphasizing positive and flexible productivity—far from resisting disaffecting power, reinforces ideology.

As we saw in the Introduction, with Damasio's groundbreaking "somatic marker hypothesis," neuroscience demonstrates that reason itself emerges from our primary affectivity: "It is as if we are possessed by a passion for reason, a drive that originates in the brain core, permeates other levels of the nervous system, and emerges as either feelings or nonconscious biases to guide decision making" (*Descartes's Error* 245). Indeed, by speaking of reason's "passion," Damasio is subtly arguing against the tradition that centers the subject in reason. As we'll see, understanding the relations between affect and consciousness in terms of neuroscience moves us past the classical essentialist model of emotions; but—offering a stronger deconstruction of the subject than other posthumanist theories—it also does so in thoroughly materialist terms. To further demonstrate this, I'll explore two major insights from contemporary neuroscience that, at this point, we can label facts established beyond the epistemological threshold. The Introduction began to establish the first: *affect precedes reason*. Below I'll further develop the pedagogical significance of this discovery by turning to the groundbreaking neuroscience of Lisa Feldman Barrett. The second major insight, which I'll explore below through the neurophilosophy of Catherine Malabou, is that through neuroplasticity, neuroscience discovers *deconstruction in the materiality of form itself*. What the humanities can add to these discoveries is an understanding of the political and ethical dimensions of these discoveries, as they suggest the biological significance of the practices Foucault called the "care of the self and other."

Barrett's Emotional Intelligence and the Predictive Process Model

To further understand how neuroscience deconstructs the subject around the false binary between the biological and the social, affectivity and consciousness—and to further establish the theoretical significance of neuropathology to theories of emotions and consciousness—I'll turn here to Lisa Feldman Barrett's work on emotions. Challenging the classical neuroscientific subject, Barrett's theory shows that emotions are *predictions* made by the brain—but also, at the same time, that emotions originate not in some primitive area of the brain, or in universal brain locations, but rather in *society*. The classical model of the brain theorizes emotions as emerging through natural selection to their current seats in distinct brain regions. Incoming sensory data "trigger" these regions, which result in their identifiable physiological appearance (or "fingerprint") in the face and body. As the famous Silvan S. Tompkins "emotional recognition" tests postulated, by having subjects look at pictures of various actors displaying different emotions, we are quickly able to recognize emotions in their registers on the face. When we are "happy" we smile. When we are "angry" we scowl. So too do we attribute embodied states to different emotions: when in love we sense butterflies in our stomach, when we're excited our pulse quickens. Universally, when we see a snake, our pulse quickens, we tense up, and our face takes on a telltale wide-eyed expression that denotes "fear" in any culture. Or so the story goes.

The classical theory of emotions has the advantage that it conforms to our everyday experience. When we see a snake, it's easy to image that our body is *reacting* to the snake, tensing up and going into flight or fight mode in the same way as our human and even animal ancestors. In this way too, snakes seem somehow *naturally* scary. But Lisa Feldman Barrett's "Conceptual Act Model" tells a different story, challenging the linear cause-and-effect narrative of how emotions are made. While we may believe experientially that outside sensory input influences how we feel, in fact, the opposite is generally the case: what you feel alters what you see, hear, and think.

Furthermore, according to Barrett, the physical sensations we experience as emotions have *no essential or universal meaning*; instead, embodied sensations, or affects, are given meaning only within specific situations, such that the same sensations underlay radically different mental experiences. To wit, while we might recognize a smiling friend as happy, this meaning is hardly universal—in many cultures (such as ancient Greece and Rome) there's simply no relationship between a smile and being happy. We might experience a quickened pulse in both happiness or sadness, or these sensations might not occur to us as an emotion at all. Barrett tells the story of going on a date with a man she was previously unattracted to: "As we sat together in a coffee shop, to my surprise, I felt my face flush several times as we spoke. My stomach fluttered and I started having trouble concentrating. Okay, I realized, I was wrong. I am clearly attracted to him" (*How Emotions Are Made* 30). However, an hour later Barrett became ill, and spent the next week in bed with the flu. The point? "An emotion is your brain's *creation* of what your bodily sensations mean, in relation to what is going on around you in the world" (30). In fact, when we experience an emotion, we will perform it differently each time—will display different behaviors—in Barrett's words, "depending on what works best in the situation" (35).

This is because the brain is constantly running *simulations*, which is to say, constructions or representations of the world. These simulations take our past experiences—like our knowledge of snakes and where and how they may appear in relation to us in a given situation—and gives meaning to the cacophony of incoming sensory information: "simulation lets your brain impose meaning on the noise, selecting what's relevant and ignoring the rest" (27). The brain draws on *concepts* in making its simulations—that is, information about things in the world as well as their context (information both about what snakes are and where they are, for example). Concepts work to make meaning of the world by sorting and categorizing sensory experience, "Construction treats the world like a sheet of pastry, and your concepts are cookie cutters that carve boundaries" (28). While the classical view holds that there is a kind of one-to-one correspondence between our embodied state and emotional experience, the same emotional experience (e.g., "happiness") can be comprised of entirely different—even conflicting—affects:

> Inside your body, your heartbeat, blood pressure, breathing, temperature, and cortisol level fluctuate throughout the day. . . . Your muscle movements and bodily changes become functional as instances of emotion *only when you categorize them that way*, giving them new functions as experiences and perceptions. Without emotion concepts, these new functions don't exist. They are only moving faces, beating hearts, circulating hormones, and so on, just as without color concepts, "red" and the sound of a falling tree would not exist. There'd only be light and vibrations.
>
> (133)

This too is why, when we lack a concept for a thing (or emotion), it appears to us without meaning. If we encounter a new form of music, we will try to make sense of it in terms of the music concepts we already possess, but it's always possible that—lacking a concept for it—we'll just hear it as nonsensical *noise*. In other words, it's perfectly conceivable that in your life you might encounter a form of music so unfamiliar that your brain won't even categorize it (make meaning of it) as music at all. Thus, the familiar generational battle over musical taste.

Our brain uses concepts to simulate the outside world, but it also uses this same process to make meaning of bodily sensations. Bodily sensation, after all, is just more sensory data from the brain's perspective. Therefore, "If you feel an ache in your stomach while sitting at the dinner table, you might experience it as hunger. If flu season is just around the corner, you might experience that same ache as nausea. If you are a judge in a courtroom, you might experience the ache as a gut feeling that the defendant cannot be trusted" (30). With regards to the latter, it's been shown that criminals coming up for parole are treated more leniently later in the day, after lunch.

In this way, "You are not a passive receiver of sensory input but an active constructor of your emotions" (31).

Furthermore, emotions have no distinct brain region. Even Damasio's somatic marker hypothesis retains something of a neurological "fingerprint" that Barrett's theory disproves. Barrett challenges us to think of the brain as being like a kitchen, where we can use the same ingredients to create diverse foods; that is, the brain creates different emotions out of the same physiological regions, synaptic pathways, or "ingredients." Variation is the norm, rather than the exception, and each particular emotional experience is marked by difference (this is called "degeneracy" by neuroscientists). We therefore cannot work backwards from the emotional effect to a neurological cause, given that the neuronal interplay involved in the appearance of an emotion involves emergent properties, just as bread accrues properties like "crustiness" and "chewiness" that aren't themselves properties of the ingredients. Therefore, "An instance of fear has irreducible, emergent properties not found in the ingredients alone, such as unpleasantness (as your car skids out of control on a slippery highway) or pleasantness (on an undulating rollercoaster)" (37). And perhaps most interestingly, just as the difference between a muffin and cupcake is entirely social—depending largely, for instance, on what time of day they are eaten—so too are emotions. We make meaning of essentially the same sensory data in different ways in accordance with cultural concepts—we don't simply "recognize" or "detect" emotions in others, but construct them through our concepts. Again, there are no emotional fingerprints either in the body or the brain.

Simulation, Interoception, and the Predictive Process Model

We can, however, universally distinguish between the basic categories of feeling: pleasant and unpleasant. This basic distinction is marked in the body's *interoception*, which is "your brain's representation of all sensations from your internal organs and tissues, the hormones in your blood, and your immune system" (Barrett *How Emotions are Made* 56). Interoceptive activity is the entire background of embodied feeling constantly churning through us—even more fundamental than affect, however, it's a system for the distribution of energies in the body in general—and we make meaning of it variably but always, one way or another, along the spectrum of pleasure. This general affective state in the body has two features, *valance* and *arousal*, representing the quality (pleasure and displeasure) and the quantity (high or low) of an affect. The brain runs its simulations, awash in this intrinsic interoceptive activity, in order to form *predictions* about body and world, which are "your brain's best guesses of what's going on in the world around you, and how to deal with it to keep you alive and well" (59). The brain makes "millions and millions of nonstop predictions" about what's happening around us, selecting what is most *probable*, "simultaneously in every moment, in a storm of probabilities" (122). The most probable match between predictions and incoming sensory information comprises our meaningful consciousness experience.

Reading offers a strong example of how neurological prediction works: "right now, with each word that you read, your brain is predicting what the next word will be, based on probabilities from your lifetime of reading experience. In short, your experience right now was predicated by your brain a moment ago" (*How Emotions Are Made* 59). The key here again is that the brain does not just *react* to sensory data, but anticipates and meaningfully *constructs* it. It may *seem* like we make decisions and then act upon them, but in fact "your brain issues motor predictions to move your body well before you become aware of your intent to move" (60). This is the "efficiency" of the brain; from within the cacophony of sensory data, the brain carves out what's important relative to your *goals* in a specific situation, drawing on your concepts—which is to say, your past experiences.

In this way, when we see a thing in the world, as opposed to interpreting sensory data we are constructing it according to predictions, rooted in experience, that the brain then confirms or revises. For example, when we are presented apple sauce in baby diapers as opposed to on a plate, we are likely to gag—our brain has made a prediction based on past experience. Barrett gives another interesting example of this related to reading, "Right now, as you read these words and understand what they mean, each word barely perturbs your massive intrinsic activity, like a small stone skipping on a rolling ocean wave" (62). While we might believe that reading is a kind of reaction to the text on the page, such that we interpret text after experiencing it, in fact we are constantly *predicting and constructing* meanings that our experience of the text merely confirms or denies. In reading, we are attuning ourselves to the language and ideas in an ongoing process. Our brain is constantly predicting and correcting, creating and revising our affective map of the world, such that "You might think that your perceptions of the world are driven by events in the world, but really, they are anchored in your predictions, which are then tested against those little skipping stones of incoming sensory input" (62). Therefore, when we read a sentence like "Once upon a time, in a magical kingdom far beyond the most distant mountains, there lived a beautiful princess who bled to death" (to use Barrett's example), we are jarred by the *prediction error* that failed to anticipate those last words. However, as we read, we compare our brain's automatic prediction to the actual language, rapidly attuning ourselves to the situation. Whereas classical linguistics and Chomskian transformational grammar view grammar largely only as a vehicle for content, when we view language in terms of predictions made by the brain—as in the "once upon a time" sentence example above—it's clear (as rhetoricians have long known) that even minor differences in the rhetorical form of a sentence create substantial difference.[2]

Prediction error also explains the so-called "outfielder problem"; that is, if you were to ask an outfielder in baseball to predict where a ball will land, she'd not be able to tell you. However, in practice (and with practice), she'd easily make the play: this is because the predictions happen below the level of cognition as opposed to resulting from reasoned contemplation. Through simulations, outfielders make immediate predictions about where the ball will land not only prior to conscious contemplation, but exclusive of it. The received intentionalist account would entail a cognitive predictive process that involves a conscious estimate of the ball's trajectory registered in relation to an internal model, resulting in a mapping that informs motor function, finally allowing movement toward the ball. In this computational model, the mind processes sensory input, yielding action. But as the embodied predictive processing perspective demonstrates, there is no need for an internal cognitive model. Instead, Andy Clark and others argue that the outfielder only requires the ability to perceive the ball and experience. When an outfielder moves to the ball, they run towards it to keep a stationary image of it, canceling the perception of its acceleration to keep it within a stable visual boundary.

According to the predictive processing theory, perception and action work according to this same mechanism. In perception, the brain attends to predictive errors by creating simulations, or hypotheses, that will predict the input. On the other hand, in action, the brain is not predicting sensory input, but canceling out prediction error until its predictions become correct; that is, the brain isn't predicting what's real, so much as registering motor commands, moving body the around, *until the brain's predictions become true*. By predicting that the ball will remain stable in the field of vision, every time the ball moves within that field (a prediction error), the outfielder makes a motor adjustment. In doing so, the outfielder may employ a model (knowledge) of the outfield terrain, the weather, and so on, which (less efficiently) registers at every level of the system all the way down to sensory input. Sensory data is not feeding into a cognitive model, but providing just enough information to get to ball in the most frugal way. In this way, *the brain makes the world conform to its predictions*. This reverses the computational metaphor; the brain is not just passively processing and modeling a bunch of incoming sensations; instead, it actively issues predictions about what it's likely to discover in the world.

Here we can link back to Barrett's account of the relation between embodied emotions and meaning. As Barrett explains, we usually experience interoception only in general terms along the gamut of pleasure. However, we experience emotions as interoceptive *intensities*, applying emotional concepts to the underlying affective experience and "budgeting" energy resources (according to the brain's predictions) to different parts of the body (as in quickening our heart rate or releasing a hormone), making that interoceptive sensation *personally meaningful*. In this way, the interoceptive network "controls your body, budgets your energy resources, and represents your internal sensations, all at the same time" (*How Emotions Are Made* 70). This happens even when we are not physically active, but just imagining stimuli (like a snake) and simulating scenarios, which we do constantly.

Furthermore, we must understand emotions in relation to *cultural* concepts (and language) and their performance within specific contexts. Interoception, while an important ingredient of emotion, cannot explain it: "An emotion category like anger or sadness is far more complex than a simple feeling of unpleasantness and arousal" (83). Our overall affective state is one part of an emotion, but it's in making that state meaningful, in relation to experiences categorized within *culturally constructed* concepts, that we actually experience and perform emotions. Interoceptive sensations, the predictions our brain makes about the world and the energies it budgets, are "categorized" through the concepts the brain employs to interpret those sensations. Barrett illustrates how concepts work to make meaning out of the chaos of sensory information:

> Without concepts, you'd experience a world of ever-fluctuating noise. . . . All sensory information is a massive, constantly changing puzzle for your brain to solve. The objects you see, the sounds you hear, the odors you smell, the touches you feel, the flavors you taste, and the interoceptive sensations you experience as aches and pains and affect . . . they all involve continuous sensory signals that are highly variable and ambiguous as they reach your brain. Your brain's job is to predict them before they arrive, fill in missing details, and find regularities where possible so that you experience a world of objects, people, music, and events, not the 'blooming, buzzing confusion' that is really out there.
>
> (85–86)

Concepts enable your brain to *categorize* "objects, actions, and events" according to some *purpose*; a concept is a "mental representation of a category" (87). Finally, it's important to understand that we don't conceptualize categories of things, as held in the classical view, within "firm boundaries"—as if things possess an underlying prototype or fingerprint that transcends their *variation* in reality. Otherwise, we'd require a concept for every *specific* bird we encounter—not to mention each specific feeling.

Barrett and Recategorization of Emotion: Towards Emotional Intelligence

Understanding neuroscience's deconstruction of the subject along the lines of affect, emotion, and reason, allows us to return to the question of a neurorhetoric posed in the Introduction and above. Further following Barrett, I would like to explore the significance of emotional intelligence to composition pedagogy as a disruption of blockages, interferences, and bad writing habits. Emotional intelligence is essential for the dialectical advance of learning and self formation. My argument therefore is that emotional granularity is important not only in neurorhetoric—in commanding affect to persuade others—but also in forming a set of tools for dealing with the inevitable disruption, destruction, and failure that characterizes the plasticity of learning, the structural leaps entailed in breaking habituated and automated response.

As we've seen, emotion concepts are constructed—"no emotion concept is universal" (Barrett 145). And because of this, we are in fact able to *create new emotions*, which is to say, new *concepts*, to regulate our interoceptive activity: we are architects of our experience. In these creations, we can rewrite our brain to make new predictions, predictions that better allow us to manage our body budget. Indeed, this is the definition of "responsibility" for Barrett—the deliberate adult choices we can make to change our emotional concepts.[3] Again, this all may seem counter-intuitive, given that we experience emotions as if they were physical and natural phenomena; however, as we saw above, before becoming hardwired in the brain, our emotion concepts are cultural constructions. And emotional intelligence is a function of our conceptual granularity—our ability to form concepts to best regulate our body budget.

To put this all somewhat differently, there are many ways to better regulate one's body budget (like exercising, or changing one's environment). But where we lack emotional intelligence, our body is more likely to make *bad* predictions that waste energy: "Your body-budgeting circuitry . . . doesn't respond quickly to counterevidence (prediction error) from your body. Once predictions have been off-base for long enough, you will feel chronically miserable" (Barrett 177). Emotional intelligence is *not* about being able to accurately "detect" the emotions of others, as the classical model would imply, but about "getting your brain to construct the most useful instance of the most useful emotion concept in a given situation" (Barrett 179). This may all sound like New Age bromides—as Daniel Gross' quip in the Introduction about affective "mysticism" would suggest—but what we are really dealing with is a radical challenge to the conventional and classical account of the mind–body relationship. As Barrett argues, "This is not magic; it's what happens when you leverage the porous boundary between the social and the physical" (Barrett 181). Or as Pierre Bourdieu (an unlikely ally, perhaps) already knew, "We learn bodily. . . . As much in everyday pedagogic action ('sit up straight', 'hold your knife in your right hand') as in rites of institutions, this psychosomatic action is often exerted through emotion and suffering, psychological or even physical" (141).

Indeed, as Barrett demonstrates, even the "Self" that we experience is the progressively formed concept that we have of our overall embodied, affective experience. As we know, babies are born without this concept; the "Self" emerges only as the child learns to more efficiently categorize their multi-sensory experiences. That is, if we did not form the rudimentary concept "Self," the child would remain trapped within a meaningless, swirling chaos of sensations, unable to efficiently regulate energy in order to purposefully act into the world. Consider Barrett's explication of concept formation:

> The visual system represents a straight line as a pattern of neurons firing in primary visual cortex. Suppose that a second group of neurons fires to represent a second line at a ninety-degree angle to the first line. A third group of neurons could *summarize* this statistical relationship between the two lines efficiently as a simple concept "Angle." The infant brain might encounter a hundred different pairs of intersecting line segments of varying length, thickness, and color, but conceptually they are all instances of "Angle," each of which gets efficiently summarized by some smaller group of neurons. These summaries eliminate redundancy. In this manner, the brain separates statistical similarities from sensory differences.
>
> (115)

Each concept successively becomes itself a part of other concepts; for example, "Angle" becomes a part of the concept "Eye" which becomes part of the concept "Face." Although we haven't yet gotten into the specifics of brain function, this, in a nutshell, is the basis of the neuroscientific account of *learning*.

What's important to understand here is that the brain learns by grouping together *similarities* (similar concepts) in progressively forming more efficient summaries of sensory data, such that it can efficiently *elide* the concept "Line" when we encounter an "Angle." And as the brain forms its predictions about the world, it learns to select those that are most statistically relevant to the specific meaningful context we dwell in. Learning therefore *begins* in meaningfulness, our thrown-ness into the world (which will be explored more thoroughly in Chapter 3 in considering Heidegger's account of care), as opposed to being a cognitive "add on" to sensory data. And remarkably, "Any given concept is not represented in the information flow among one single set of neurons; each concept is itself a population of instances, and these instances are represented in different patterns of neurons on each occasion" (117). In other words, neuroscience now knows that concepts *aren't reducible to specific locations* in the brain—as reductive locationist neuroscientific theories once argued—but are constructed each time anew on *an ad* hoc basis relative to the meaningful contexts into which we are thrown. From a rhetorical perspective, this means that the "mental images" that comprise concepts and ideas need to be understood not only in relation to what they *mean* in a given situation, but also what they *do*—both socially in the world and physically in the brain. For Barrett, concepts cannot be exhausted in terms of language or critique. Beyond the classical understanding of concepts as representing the world, Barrett shows that concepts are in fact unfolding rhetorical events. Just as rhetoricians like Laurie Gries now understand text and images in terms of the changes they undergo in their unstable rhetorical circulation across forms and media, we can also understand mental images as events within emerging ecologies. In these ways Barrett's theorization of the concept extends ecological theories of meaning, and points to the psychological complexity of concept transfer. However, again, as opposed to rhetorical theories, neuroscience also demands that we account for the traces of these events upon the brain, somewhat complicating, as we'll see, the ecological de-prioritization of the subject.

But Barrett's most profound discovery is that emotion concepts work the same way. Our brain can only issue predictions based on the concepts that we possess. Thus, in order to experience the emotion of "*gigil*," a Filipino concept that we lack in Western culture, meaning "the urge to hug or squeeze something that is unbearably adorable," you will need to "combine other concepts that you do know" (Barrett *How Emotions are Made* 147). Filipinos possessing this emotion concept, on the other hand, *automatically* predict with it—their brains have learned to predict their embodied and sensory data through this meaningful concept before cognition. So when some Filipinos encounter a cute puppy, their brain will interpret the experience as *gigil* before they are consciously aware that they have seen a puppy.

It is in this way too that we can literally invent emotions. Barrett gives her own example of "Chiplessness," defining the feeling of disappointment in an empty bag of potato chips, combined with relief that you won't be taking in more calories, combined with guilt for having eaten an entire bad, along with hunger for more chips. *Even the description of this emotion, as Barrett points out, creates the experience*—reading this, your brain likely simulated it even without having a concept for it (a form of emotional telepathy that itself has an important payoff for rhetoric, as neurorhetoric has already begun to understand). But now that you do possess a concept for it, should you purposefully retain it as a concept, your brain will automatically form predictions about the feelings of this experience that previously would have remained an unrecognized, subtle discomfort. Having a concept for these affective experiences is what is meant by emotional intelligence; and a remarkable thing about the brain is that, simply by giving these experiences names, we've created a transferable concept for making predictions. Both our "Self" and our emotions are in this way examples of "collective intentionality"; that is, just as "Chiplessness" is a social construct whose reality is no more than a cultural agreement (just like other concepts, from "Cash" to "School"), so too is Self. Finally, if people agree that this emotion is real—or your Self or your money—than it is. These concepts need not have a psychological, social, or neurological fingerprint.

Tacking towards the pedagogical payoff of these neuroscientific discoveries, we can see that creating new emotion concepts doesn't *immediately* change your experience, but making changes will "influence your *future* emotional experiences, to sculpt who you will be tomorrow" (176). Once a new emotion concept has taken hold—once the brain begins to make sense of embodied data within specific social situations—new predictions will become *automatic. In other words: our emotional concepts change our affectability.* And through repetition, a disposition is formed, resulting in new patterns of prediction.

This phenomena is what Jenny Rice intuits in describing how AIDS activists were able to "disarticulate" and "rearticulate" the meaning of AIDS. By rearticulating AIDS in relation to positive emotions in public discourse, the public became affected by AIDS in new (more positive) ways (Edbauer Rice). Rice's example points to the potential for neuroscience to ground a public rhetoric. But here I would like to consider the pedagogical potential of a plastic pedagogy at the individual level.

I discussed this idea with a good friend, who, without knowing it, had suffered from severe anxiety—to the point of agoraphobia—when he was young, such that he frequently wanted to skip school. It wasn't until later in his life, having gained the concepts of "social anxiety" and "agoraphobia" that he was able to make sense of those feelings and categorize them appropriately—this recognition in turn enabled him to work on solutions. For instance, instead of merely believing that he felt "bad" enough that he wouldn't be going to school that day, he learned strategies for dealing with his anxiety when it came upon him. Better still, he learned to predict his bad feelings as anxiety before the full weight of his stress and agoraphobia could set in. And while he doubtlessly still often felt the need to retreat socially, he was also able to socialize more (and better), predicting his "bad" feelings as mere *discomfort* as opposed to true physical *suffering*.

But moreover, further granularity would have allowed him to better parse all of those experiences of anxiety in *positive* ways: for instance, as "excitement" about his attraction to a classmate (as opposed to "fear" of socializing), or as "pride" in his desire to do well on a test (as opposed to "despair" over his performance). This is an example of what Barrett calls *recategorization*, the "tool of the emotion expert" (Barrett *How Emotions are Made*, 189). Recategorization is especially important given that dwelling (without emotional granularity) in negative affects hardwires us to fail. As Barrett argues, "Rumination is a vicious cycle: each time you dwell on (say) a recent breakup of a relationship, you add another instance to predict with, which expands your opportunity to ruminate" (183).

As we'll see, this ability to recategorize emotions has special relevance to writing instruction, which necessarily involves frequent *failures*. And we can see that when students are stymied by "bad" emotions in experiencing failures and blockages, they begin to predict accordingly, hardwiring a pernicious and disempowering affective response to writing, increasing the potential for writer's block, procrastination, and other forms of disaffection and disengagement. Indeed, in addition to blockage, recent research suggests that bad feelings correlate with a lack of transference. Furthermore, it's been shown that student's emotional experiences with writing directly impact the transference of knowledge about writing and overall development (Driscoll & Powell). I'll further develop this pedagogical significance in Appendix 1.5, but before doing so I need to explain the *ethical* significance introduced by neuroscientific deconstruction of the biological and social. As we'll see, what the humanities offers to neuroscience's special and weird account of *form*—that is, neuroplasticity—is an analysis of its relevance to language, nature, objects, and ethical and bio-political relations beyond the subject. As we'll see, understanding these ethical relations is necessary for articulating a non-reductive rhetoric and writing pedagogy informed by neuroplasticity.

Catherine Malabou's Neurophilosophical Plasticity: "The Heart of the Brain"

The second major discovery of contemporary neuroscience, a deconstruction of the biological and social around the nature of *form*, is that *the brain is plastic*. You've no doubt heard this before, but perhaps without recognizing the radical significance of this discovery, much less its importance for writing pedagogy. To develop this significance, I'll turn to the work of Catherin Malabou, the great contemporary thinker of plasticity, whose important work remains, to my knowledge, completely absent from our field. A determined materialist, Malabou—whose thinking is essential to each of the main arguments advanced in this book—nevertheless avoids the kinds of facile correlationalism and reductionism that too often characterizes both popular and academic accounts of neuroscientific discovery. This is important because, above all, we'll require a theory of the *translation* between brain and mind that avoids the automatization implied by the classical account. Furthermore, as I'll argue, Malabou's theorization complicates not only contemporary rhetorical accounts of affect and emotion (including neurorhetoric), but also supplements Barrett's theorization of emotional intelligence and recategorization by introducing the question of power and ideology.

Malabou's goal is to incorporate findings from the material sciences into contemporary continental philosophy, while at the same time providing the sciences the critical theorization—the work of the humanities—that they often lack. Her core concept, plasticity—the property of form that joins its dimensions of suppleness and fixity, its flexibility and solidity—is derived from her re-reading of Hegel. By reading Hegel through the lens of plasticity—a concept hidden in plain sight that arises, Malabou demonstrates, at crucial points across his work—she emphasizes qualities of openness, emergence, and transformation in Hegel that Heidegger that others have since ignored or denied. Ultimately, by establishing plasticity as a hinge between the material and the symbolic, Malabou recuperates the Hegelian dialectic as a strategy to move beyond their opposition. Neuroscience has long suggested that it could replace introspection with a more precise scientific language. Malabou is not suggesting this. Instead, she is recommending a "consciousness" or self-critique, more closely aligned with Michel Foucault's late-career theorization of the care of the self and other, in which self care always passes through the other. But as opposed to the external other of discourse, Malabou argues that the brain is a kind of internal-other, the otherness of the singularity that comprises our essence. Here she is strictly dialectical: the self emerges out of a conscious relationship to the brain. One might say that this is a kind of Cartesian formulation, preserving a fundamental difference between brain and consciousness, even in their synthesis. However, it is the plastic "openness" of the materiality of the brain, the first term, that complicates this assessment. That is, like Zizek, Malabou "opens" Hegel's dialectic by viewing its first term as plastic. It is in this sense that she theorizes against a reductive scientism that would totalize the workings of the brain, as if the "self" were merely its mechanical product.

Hegel's own dialectical analysis attempted to resolve Kant's problematic distinction between subject/object relationship (the mind/body problem), demonstrating that—through reflection—subjective consciousness (material *experience*) itself becomes an object, rising to the level of abstract thought. Malabou *introduces a difference into Hegel's contemplation of the difference* between brain and mind, asking what changes where consciousness is no longer consciousness of experience as classically conceived, but of the material brain itself? Such a consciousness cannot be, Malabou argues, simply an awareness of the brain as a pre-formed bio-chemical machine, but must also recognize, at this level of dialectical reflection, the brain's open, emergent, *plastic* capacity for self-transformation. Opposed to much of what has been called the "neurohumanities"—and aligned with much in Damasio, Joseph LeDoux, Barrett, and other key figures in contemporary neuroscience—Malabou's plasticity allows us to theorize the openness of the brain—the code, the "first term"—to difference, mutability, and essential freedom.

This has special relevance to conceiving of writing, rhetoric, and writing pedagogy in the wake of Derrida's "arche-writing." That is, following neuroscience, Malabou (a former student and interlocutor of Derrida's) shows that Derrida's conceptualization of writing is no longer able to account for the manner in which the brain is both *determined* by material "formal necessity" *and* capable of reforming or remobilizing formal essence. Malabou understands plasticity to be the "motor scheme" behind both the material (traditionally the domain of the scientific) and, through her compelling re-reading of continental philosophy, the symbolic (traditionally the domain of the humanities). While insistently pinning the neurological code to material essence, Malabou theorizes the essential *freedom* of plasticity to "displace, even nullify" its own code (*What Should We Do* 17). This description of the mind as emergent and extended—resisting the reductions of both cognitive determinism and intentionality—in many ways resonates with new rhetorical understandings of complexity, ecology, and ambiance, while at the same time offering a material foundation for "posthuman" or "post-writing" pedagogy.

Malabou's etiology of plasticity recuperates the ethical and political concept of resistance within esthetic form: plastic form is both supple *and* embodied. As Malabou argues, "The concept of plasticity has an aesthetic dimension (sculpture, malleability), just as much as an ethical one (solicitude, treatment, help, repair, rescue) and a political one (responsibility in the double movement of the receiving and the giving of form)" (30). So on the one hand, plasticity demands that writing teachers must reconceive the ethical relationship between writing, care, and otherness. We must understand, along with neuroscientist Maryanne Wolf, that "This plasticity at the heart of the brain's design forms the basis of much of who we are, and who we might become" (3). Plasticity, the "heart of the brain," is its formal openness to what is outside of it—we saw this, for example, in Barrett's theory of emotion, which emerges in the dialectical interplay of the affective and the social. And on the other hand, given the "double movement" of the brain, a plastic pedagogy must allow for *resistance* to forces of biological and social automatization.

Flexibility, Failure, and Ideology

Metis—the wise and skillful goddess—possessed the power to metamorphosize herself, to take forms ranging from a lion to flowing water. But like other shape-shifting gods, her polymorphism "comprises a vast but finite palette of identities" (*Ontology* 7). Metis' transformations form a circle in which she appears at the center, her changes in form representing no more than a trick, the adoption of a limited repertoire of masks. Cycling through various forms, Metis always arrives back at herself, and this is the limitation of her power, exploited by Zeus and the other gods. On the other hand, as Malabou argues, "If her metamorphic power were not limited, she would be invincible" (8). In this creative version of plasticity, the metamorphosing subject bends and stretches, but never breaks.

Creative plasticity, the kind Metis embodies, describes also the essential capacity of the brain to give new form to itself while preserving identity. The underlying map of the brain works to "maintain its homeostasis, which is continuously disturbed by intruding objects," meaning that in mapping its own condition the brain is "moment by moment" (Johnston & Malabou 67) formed and reformed through the relationship it has with external novelty. In Metis, however, we find a reduced account of plasticity, one that lacks a comprehension of the more radical openness of the subject to difference. The plasticity of Metis is, in fact, mere *flexibility*. And this reduced conception of plasticity, as we'll see, informs much in received composition theory and pedagogy, where plasticity is understood only in its (flexible) creative sense—this can even be true of the reasoned and "critical thinking" that we reward as intelligence. But where plasticity is reduced in pedagogy to creative and flexible reason, we demand that students flexibly adapt, like Metis, without a (plastic, formal) concept *resistance*. There is a long tradition here.

For example, this creative conception of plasticity is a guiding metaphor in the work of John Dewey, who defines the nature of learning in terms of the plastic ability of the pupil to cultivate new habits through inquiry and experience. One of Dewey's chief concerns is that in working "to impose the ways of acting they want to reproduce," education fails to realize "that plasticity also means power to change prevailing customs . . ." (*Human Nature* 64). Dewey imagines a liberating pedagogy of inquiry—rooted in our natural plasticity—that constantly questions dead habit and custom. For Dewey, plasticity characterizes learning as an ongoing habit of inquiry with no fixed ends other than flexible pragmatic action. As Dewey argues in *Democracy and Education*, "the acquiring of habits is due to an original plasticity of our natures: to our ability to vary responses till we find an appropriate and efficient way of acting." On the other hand, "bad habits," according to Dewey, close the individual to the environment: "They mark the close of power to vary." Importantly however, this closure signifies the detachment of the individual from reason: "Routine habits are unthinking habits: 'bad' habits are habits so severed from reason that they are opposed to the conclusions of conscious deliberation and decision" (47). Bad habits, that is, are a "hardening" of the student to experience, routines that mark intellectual closures; they are habits without reflective *intentionality*. Finally, the diminishment of plasticity for Dewey is the diminishment of the power of reason.

Because of this, Dewey's classroom must above all promote ongoing inquiry as an end in itself (as opposed to a means to attaining some final Truth). The classroom must therefore become a purified environment that "secures the full use of intelligence in the process of forming habits can counteract this tendency" towards the hardening of the flexible work of reason. Significantly for Dewey, "this fact only indicates the need of *persistent care*" (48, emphasis mine). Dewey's classroom is a space where *care* serves as the guarantee of plasticity as intelligence and growth. While future chapters will expand on this important relationship between plasticity and care, we also need to see the limits of Dewey's theory of learning as a habitus rooted in flexibility.

For Dewey, "cumulative movement of action toward a later result is what is meant by growth" (40). Growth is above all characterized as the active and flexible capacity for the continuous conscious integration of new experiences by the cohesive, reasoning subject. Conventional pedagogies have long been informed by this "student-centered" progressivist template, which privileges a habitus of productivity and self management, envisioning learning as an incremental and continuously connected process—and, significantly, an open, ongoing process (in opposition to the classical pedagogy Dewey was responding to)—of mastery and conscious symbolic integration. Instead of theorizing reason as a unified, progressive, and indestructible capacity for confronting disequilibrium, I argue a consciousness of the ethical dimension of plasticity demands that we theorize writing as both habit and *event*, a foundation for self-creative "insistent accidents."

That is, a plastic writing pedagogy must recognize the *indeterminate*, *spontaneous*, and *accidental* particularization of social and biological codes. It must recognize intelligence and learning as a response to prediction error, accident, disruption, and *failure*—as opposed to linear (social) progression or the elaboration of foundational (biological) codes. From the perspective of plasticity, intelligence is not simply a linear accumulation, but also an ability to respond, repair, and reorganize following accidents and failures. Failures and accidents are therefore not the outside other of intelligence, but characterize the plasticity at the center of intelligence as formal excess that enables both difference and growth. Indeed, Malabou's plasticity demands that we theorize growth not only in terms of Dewey's linear "modifications," but in accordance with the explosive and traumatic potential for the brain to re-form and repair itself through the various encounters with Otherness (including the encounter of the self-as-Other) that writing introduces (I'll return to Malabou's theorization of destruction in Chapter 3). Through persistence in habits born of responses to accidents and failures, intelligence both requires and gives shape to *plastic dispositions* capable of growth and difference.

Learning, far from linear and flexible accumulation, is also therefore significantly characterized by the *destructive* dimension of plasticity discovered, as we saw in the Introduction, through neuropathology (e.g., patients like Eliot). For neuroscientist Jean-Pierre Changeux, neurons match with "reality" to form "resonances," or mismatch to form "dissonances," working to reinforce or weaken neuronal circuits. As Changeux famously argued, "to learn is to eliminate," and while the brain remains plastic in the creative sense throughout life, learning also involves a destructive process where certain synaptic connections are reinforced while others are pruned ("selective stabilization"). In short, the brain maps experience by creating and reinforcing some synaptic connections while eliminating others.

And as we'll see further in Chapter 3, Malabou builds on Changeux and others to theorize an adaptive excess in the neurological system, the explosive quality of the brain to become radically other than itself. Malabou therefore argues that we must "accept exploding from time to time," adding, "this is what we should do with our brain" (*What Should We Do?* 79). We can do this precisely because, unlike the automaton, the human organism has the plastic potential to not only adapt, but to (explosively) transform the (brain's) code. It is in this way too that learning is not the linear, cumulative, flexible process we've long imagined, but instead requires a plastic disposition capable of greeting and accommodating otherness. This utterly transformational, explosive relation between the brain and consciousness—having the character of an accident or event—could never be mere flexibility, because in explosions the stored energy of the brain becomes something totally other than itself, resisting reduction to itself through its (destructive, explosive) contacts with Otherness (the social symbolic). In this way, there is nothing automatized about brain function.

Above all, flexibility, or "plasticity minus its genius" (12), emphasizes only the organism's ability to *receive* form. And as Malabou theorizes, any definition of plasticity must conceptualize an "agent of resistance" that refuses form as it takes shape:

> From the Greek, *plassein*, to mold—the word *plasticity* has two basic senses: it means at once the capacity to receive form [think clay] . . . and the capacity to *give form* [think plastic surgery]. . . . From this perspective, to talk about the plasticity of the brain means to see in it not only the creator and receiver of form but also an agency of disobedience to every constituted form, a refusal to submit to a model.
>
> (5–6)

Neither the creativity nor receptivity of plastic form can be thought in accordance with a fixed (political or biological) model. Or, in other words, consciousness entails a self-creative capacity that emerges in dialectical relation to—in an *explosive*, disobedient relation to—the underlying neural map.

"Paradoxically," Malabou stipulates, "if we were flexible, if we didn't explode at each transition, if we didn't destroy ourselves a bit, we could not live. Identity resists its own occurrence to the very extent that it forms it" (*What Should We Do* 74). That is, if life were flexible, if it lacked destructive, explosive powers, it would in fact be incapable of adapting. Just as stem cells are recruited into novel, creative purposes, life both destroys and reuses form in order to survive. The learning subject must be able to respond to failure and disintegration; the subject must have the emotional tools—supplemented as I'll argue, by teacher care—to give shape to their brain and their self as an "insistent accident." Giving shape to this plastic disposition is what we must view positively as a plastic writing intelligence: the creative response to difference, Otherness, and failure.

Learning and the Reduction of Plasticity

Counter to Malabou's plasticity, Dewey's plasticity always first involves an essential self preservation in the face of difference: "It lies near the pliable elasticity by which some persons take on the color of their surroundings while retaining their own bent." Ultimately for Dewey, plasticity is the ability to "learn from experience" and to *intentionally* adapt to the environment, as needed; it's a "power to modify actions" (*Democracy and Education* 43) in an ongoing but essentially cohesive, incremental, and linear process governed by intentionality and transcending reason.

In this way, while offering an essential critique of the automatization of knowledge and learning, Dewey's plasticity remains nevertheless a capacity governed by the *centrality of reason* (I'll explore this further in Chapter 4). Further, Dewey's plastic ideal lacks resistance, such that flexible docility is itself synonymous with learning: "To be truly docile is to be eager to learn all the lessons of active, inquiring, expanding experience" (*Human Nature* 64). In short, Dewey's plasticity is Metis-like in its insistence that learning involves flexible, linear, and incremental changes around an intentional "center."

Beyond Dewey, much in our received composition pedagogy reflects this diminished account of plasticity, one characterized by the primacy of a transcendental rational agency made present through reflective attention, the monitor, or "metacognition." And even where our field has turned to emotion as a disciplinary subject, we can often find this privileging of rational flexibility. But we don't need to dig very deep to discover the reduced sense of plasticity that informs contemporary writing pedagogies, often tied to socio-political demands (like employability). Take for example the WPA's position statement on the flexible skills of "experienced writers": specifically, "how to be curious, attentive, engaged, open to new ideas, persistent, flexible, reflective, and creative" (Miller & Juerecic 8). "Flexibility" is one of the eight WPA "Habits of Mind," and other entries similarly emphasize qualities of attention (e.g., "Engagement," "Persistence")—or "Metacognition"—as habits of cognitive, flexible rhetorical awareness. When "Writing Processes" are later elaborated upon in the document, they appear under the heading "Developing Flexible Writing Processes."

Similarly, the NCTE position statement titled "NCTE Beliefs about the Teaching of Writing" begins, in the first sentence, with this claim: "Just as the nature of and expectation for literacy have changed in the past century and a half, so has the nature of writing." It is quickly made clear that what is "natural" now involves preparing students for "complicated social relationships" by "[moving] them toward greater *flexibility*" (my emphasis) (NCTE Executive Committee "NCTE Beliefs"). The "Framework for Success in Postsecondary Writing" also explicitly emphasizes flexibility as one of its eight habits of mind ("Flexibility—the ability to adapt to situations, expectations, or demands") (Behm, Rankins-Robertson, & Roen). Endorsing the inclusion of multimodal compositions in writing pedagogy, Elizabeth Wardle argues that we need to view writing as "flexible and not static" (662). A recent essay by Patrick Sullivan celebrates this inclusion of flexibility as part of a grouping of habits of mind that value *creativity*: "Curiosity, openness, flexibility, and metacognition can all be grouped together within a suite of dispositional characteristics that feed and nurture creativity" (16). Sullivan argues that we need to understand intelligence in terms of flexible creativity in a contemporary world that requires and rewards it, citing "important business writers" and seeing an "important opportunity to embrace common cause with our colleagues in the business community." Of course, from the perspective of neuroscience, creativity is massively important. But so is *destruction*. And any pedagogical account of creative productivity must recognize this (I'll develop Malabou's account of destructive plasticity further in Chapter 3).

From a somewhat different angle, consider for instance our conventional account of "writer's block." The title of Mike Rose's classic work says it all: "Rigid Rules, Inflexible Plans, and the Stifling of Language: A Cognitivist Analysis of Writer's Block." The link between writing performance and flexibility is so engrained that writer's block is conceived of as a "stifling" or diminution of powers. And yet, as Malabou reminds us, "plasticity ought not to be confused . . . with the mere capacity to act" (*What Should We Do* 48). In these (and other) foundational expressions of our discipline, a constructive, networked vision of mind, brain, and society is at the center, and is used to justify the socio-political requirement of flexibility. And the same holds true, as we'll see, of recent cutting-edge ecological and new materialist theories of rhetoric.

On the one hand, in moving towards recommending "habits of mind," these disciplinary positions reflect an admirable desire to combat what Miller & Juerecic call "recipe-driven" writing in favor of something more plastic in Dewey's sense of the word. However, while plasticity has long been an important disciplinary concept, where it is read as an injunction to remain constantly supple or elastic, to constantly modify the self as an exchange or transfer point for information in the neo-liberal economy, to retreat from all centers, it is reduced to mere flexibility. And as Abraham argues, the requirement of flexibility—and the "conceptual indeterminacy" to which it speaks (70)—reduces writing itself to an act of following orders.

Malabou notices, following Luc Boltanski and Eve Chiapello's *The New Spirit of Capitalism*, that the "network" is the "master term" of a neo-liberal ideology that "rests on a redistribution of centers and a major relaxation of hierarchies." Flexibility characterizes the *formless* movement of neo-liberal markets that requires constant circulation without local investment. Employability becomes *synonymous* with flexibility, while, as Malabou's survey of management literature reveals, management now facilitates, inspires, connects, and enhances. Like the decentered, non-hierarchal brain, the boss "transmits, distributes, and modifies connections by potentiating or depressing them according to circumstances and needs, without being identifiable with or assigned to a fixed post" (*What Should We Do* 44). This all leads Malabou to ask, "How could we not interrogate the parallelism between the transformation of the spirit of capitalism (between the sixties and the nineties) and the modification, brought about in approximately the same period, of our view of cerebral structures?" (*What Should We Do* 41).

From this perspective, just as we must critique recipe-driven pedagogy, we must remain suspicious of all "network" theories of subjectivity, which tend towards valuing flexible dispositions precisely in terms of employability, production, and political economy. As Gross and Alexander argue in critiquing the "Framework for Success in Postsecondary Writing," a pervasive focus on a flexible and productive positivity leaves no room for recognizing the productive potential of failure and resistance. In fact, metaphors that tie rhetorical flexibility to productivity are so engrained in our field that a recent special edition of *College Composition and Communication* set out to critique the relationship between political economy and composition pedagogy. In the edition, Matthew Abraham speaks of his concern for the tendency towards making our field "*flexible* and responsive to changing economic contexts and circumstances" (71, emphasis mine). Similarly, Tony Scott argues that our field too often seeks legitimation in the terms of the "crises" that sustain neo-liberalism, as opposed to the terms of our own scholarship, in turn placing our field itself in "perpetual crisis" (13).

As Abraham argues, the scope of our discipline's commitment to neo-liberal flexibility is greater than is generally understood: "Composition's place in the corporate imaginary is significantly larger than perhaps imagined, as it weds the concept of the academic skill set with the pragmatic desire to obtain an identifiable marker of 'employability.'" And reducing the development of plastic disposition to employability, Abraham argues, reduces writing intelligence to a flexible responsiveness to corporate and social demands, making the writer a "producer and shaper of texts who can follow orders without reflecting on whether those orders are ethical or consistent with one's personal code" (87). Even recent rhetorical and postcomposition theory (e.g., Sydney Dobrin), Abraham argues, measures success according to the student's persuasive abilities in the marketplace (78). In short, where employability in the neo-liberal economy becomes the justification for disciplinary practices, writing pedagogy becomes *ideology*. And as we'll see in Chapter 3, the ideology of flexibility requires and produces a *disaffecting power*.

The First Form of Neuronal Ideology and the Social Epistemic Pedagogy

By discovering plasticity at the heart of the transcendental, and without resorting to the mysticism of other posthumanist theories, neuroscience has replaced problematic models of cognition—such as the computation model—with metaphors of flexible assemblage, population, and network. In doing so, as Malabou argues, it has revealed a political—and potentially liberating—dimension of the ethics of plasticity. And while neuroscience is the central place where these new metaphors of the subject have emerged, they are also, of course, increasingly familiar to compositionists versed in complexity and ecological theory. But while these metaphors offer a potentially liberating perspective of our understanding of writing and learning, these same metaphors, where they work to naturalize what is essentially political (i.e., the neo-liberal capitalist system), become ideological.

Neuroscience is, of course, itself a cultural product; and because science, like all knowledge, is a cultural product, we must turn rhetorical analysis and humanistic inquiry back onto it. In doing so, we realize the value of the humanities in accounting for plasticity. The reduced account of plasticity as flexibility results in the first form of "neuronal ideology" that I'll consider here, one that that has held great sway over contemporary thought. Where neuroscience hypostasizes plasticity, it essentializes the healthy, homeostatic subject in the socio-political terms of the neo-liberal economy. In this mode, as we've seen, there is an ideological convergence between plasticity and economic and management literature that emphasizes networks and flexibility. That is, where neuroscience hypostatizes the brain, it rediscovers in the brain the neo-liberal demand that we become self-adapting, supple, productive and entrepreneurial subjects—*homo-economicus*. And as we saw in the Introduction, much in our own discipline—at least in part due to the direct influence of neuroscience[4]—reflects these same ideological tendencies.

In Malabou's words, "the scientific description of brain plasticity produces, while taking its inspiration from, an extremely normalizing vision of democracy, in that it accords an overly central role to the absence of center, a too rigid prominence to flexibility, that is to say, to docility and obedience" (*What Should We Do* 53). To theorize "*writing pedagogy* ideology," we can revise Malabou's quote to say: "the rhetorical and neuro*compositional* vision of plasticity produces, while taking its inspiration from, an extremely normalizing vision of democracy, in that it accords an overly central role to the absence of center, a too rigid prominence to flexibility, that is to say, to docility and obedience." Through a consciousness of the brain as an object, we must both realize its material essence, its *resistant form*, but reconcile this vision with the brain as a non-identity, an object always taking shape. However, much in our received process pedagogy has worked to inculcate flexible identification, even theorizing resistance itself in terms of the flexibility of intentionality and reason.

Byron Hawk argues exactly this point in his critique of James Berlin, identifying the ideology in social epistemic theory through its rationalized, intentionalist conceptualization of the subject. In *A Counter-History of Composition*, Hawk shows that social epistemic pedagogy fails to teach critique as an open process that questions rules and codes precisely to the extent that it privileges a certain mode of questioning *as a rule*. As a result, "Berlin attempts to construct a heuristic that is structured around emphasizing, if not imposing, his politics" (211), leaving students no room to resist the code in the balance.[5] Relatedly, while one may abstractly believe in the value of community service, the reality of one's embodied, emotional experience in performing it may preclude their commitment. Julie Prebel notices this in examining the discomfort some of her students experienced doing social work in her service learning class: "For some students, this discomfort with their emotions took the form of guilt, embarrassment, or shame, and they either resisted emotion or interpreted their emotions as evidence of what Ellen Cushman describes as a "'liberal savior' stance." Or, again, as the 2016 presidential election again reminds us, we cannot distinguish the emotional from the political, and we cannot achieve justice through reason alone.

In other words, in critiquing cultural codes, the social epistemic perspective too easily valorizes its own rigid code of critique, rendering the student docile. This kind of political imposition, the imposition of the code, is in this way a fetishization of the symbolic, another determinism on the flipside of biological reductionism. The result, Hawk demonstrates, is that students *naturally resist the conclusions Berlin demands they come to*. In other words, precisely where it has been ignored, emotion creeps in through the back door. In this way, I submit, we might also understand the academic focus on disembodied reason as giving rise to our student's too frequently *overzealous* pursuits of sports, parties, sex, and drinking. As Alfred North Whitehead advised educators, "you will come to grief as soon as you forget that your students have bodies" (50). Berlin failed to allow his students their own emotional response to knowledge; as a result, Berlin's students resisted the forms of social and political engagement he assumed they would adopt in the spirit of equality and resistance.

The Second Form of Neuronal Ideology: Lost in Translation

In order to understand the *second form of neuroideology*, and how it relates to writing pedagogy, we need to return to Barrett's theorization of the brain's primary affectivity, and the groundbreaking significance of Antonio Damasio's somatic marker hypothesis. Here we encounter the question of how the body's affectivity is *translated* into conscious experience. As Patricia Bizzell argued concerning the rules describing the "translation" of ideas into writing, cognitivism assumed that "the rules we can formulate to describe behavior are the same rules that produce the behavior" (404), reducing the social and the contingent to automatized, biologically determined categories. Is the situation any different in the once-more-removed translation from brain to consciousness?

In a significant way, things are very different. The reductionism that Bizzell identifies does not apply to Damasio's theory. Nevertheless, Damasio's somatic marker theory describes a "biological precedence" that "leads directly to that of the continuity between the neuronal and the mental. . . . Core consciousness and autobiographical consciousness are formed from, and emerge from, the proto-self in a progressive manner, without rupture or leap" (*What Should We Do* 59). Neuroscientists contend that the brain seamlessly maps itself, yielding images ("second-order maps") in a succession moving from the protoself, to the "core self," to "core consciousness," to the "autobiographical self" and final "extended consciousness" (60). Between the protoself and consciousness, they assert, there is a progressive "translation of neuronal patterns into mental patterns," forming the "images" of conscious representation (61).

And yet, conserving something of Bizzell's critique, Malabou points out that the account of this metabolism is "insufficient on many points" (62). As fascinating as Damasio's theorization of the translation process is, it remains precisely that: a theory. The translation process will almost certainly never be able to be deduced empirically; understanding *translation* will always require *interpretation*, and therefore there is always room for ideological slippage. Indeed, Malabou argues that Damasio imports a Darwinian account of change and transformation that privileges the brain's homeostasis over and against its potential for productive and destructive difference: "Only those neuronal configurations capable of survival, thus those capable of being the 'best,' the highest 'performing,' would be converted into images" (65). "Mature" individuals, Damasio argues implicitly, are those best adapted to "harmonious" function in the social domain—indeed, those who are the most flexible.

Daniel Gross makes a similar argument about Damasio's reduction of the social emotion "trustworthiness" to the "fingerprint" model that discovers it as universally recognizable. Damasio and other neuroscientists are indeed sometimes guilty of what Gross terms the "paradox of the observer"; as Gross argues, "how can one adequately characterize an abnormal emotional brain when one's study might be designed within a sick culture or at least in a culture affected by maladaptive biases inherently unidentifiable and therefore uncontrollable from within the scientific study?" (37). Importantly, the tendency in neuroscience (and popular culture influenced by neuroscience) to ignore the fundamentally constructed nature of emotion by normalizing its performance and recognition introduces ideology.

For Malabou, by privileging the "harmonious" subject defined in terms of productivity and homeostatic self-sufficiency, neuroscience repeats neoliberal ideology, writing it into "natural" human development. The valuation of images and ideas according to their efficacy in survival describes only how identity *receives* form, reducing the order of consciousness to the neuronal. It does not account for the *explosive* metamorphic potential latent within the order of consciousness. After all, "Only an ontological explosion could permit the transition from one order to another, from one organization to another, from one given to another. The neuronal and the mental resist each other and themselves, and it is because of this that they can be linked to one another" (72). This is not merely the same thing as saying, as many critics of neuroscience have, that we require different *levels of analysis* to know the brain and mind, that mind is irreducible to the brain, that we cannot know a fish by counting its ribs. Of course, it is no doubt true that these two levels "do not speak the same language" (72). But more than this, the relationship between the two levels is characterized by the hinge of a plasticity that resists reduction to either.

Finally, we must view Barrett's account of emotional intelligence through the prism of Malabou's critique. While our potential for recategorizing negative feelings into positive ones is certainly pedagogically significant—as I'll explore in Appendix 1.5—just as we must value the role of destructive plasticity in learning, we must also recognize a value in "bad" feelings. One reading of Barrett might view her as endorsing a conservative agenda of self-responsibility and productivity. However, while I believe this reading of Barrett is indeed available given her overarching concern with self control and rational determination, I think the better part of Barrett's work is rather a reminder that we require what Foucault termed *care for self and other* in a society increasingly devoid of it.

Conclusion: Flexibility and Trauma in the New Attention Economy

What, ultimately, is at stake in the question of this distinction between plasticity and flexibility for pedagogy? How do ideologies of flexibility matter for our students? As Malabou argues, a lack of flexibility is increasingly understood in the normative terms of bio-power, such that "the frontier separating psychical suffering from social suffering is thin" (*What Should We Do* 47). Those suffering from social and political disorders and traumas—ranging from AD/HD to PTSD—present the same symptoms, marked by inflexibility and disaffection, as those suffering from biological disorders (such as Alzheimer's) and head trauma. The depressive and the socially disaffiliated both suffer from "a lack of 'employability' and adaptability" (47). The depressed, like everybody who is inflexible, are viewed in the same way, and both are advised by the forces of bio-power to "rewire" their brain to better conform to flexible networks. "In effect," Malabou states sarcastically, "anyone who is not flexible deserves to disappear" (46).

Later in this book, I'll follow Malabou in arguing that students increasingly "present" with a lack of flexability, as *disaffected* in ways that parallel the symptoms of neurological trauma—the exponential increase in AD/HD students over the last 30 years is a clear example of this. Malabou locates the increased presentation of distraction and disaffection precisely in the increased demand for flexibility. I'll build on Malabou's insight by arguing that there is a relation between the neo-liberal demand for flexibility and the "attention economy" exploited, above all, by new technologies and media. In this way, affect and attention are essentially linked, as the ability to be affected requires attention and *vice versa*. And just as Gross points out that emotions function within "emotion economies" that link emotion variably to power, so too, as we'll see, do different forms of attention in "attention economies."

Finally, whatever a plastic pedagogy is to become, it cannot simply settle on the formation of a flexible, critical, or metacognitive awareness, nor the inculcation, through affective accumulation, of "positive" dispositions likely to succeed in today's markets. It must instead begin in an awareness of plasticity itself—a recognition of our potential to resist all models, our potential for explosive difference. After all, both metacognitive awareness and epistemic critique posit centers, a faith in special forms of reason that will deliver us outside of our society, our politics, our body, our selves. In claiming that we can attain a knowledge of things from an external, Archimedean point, both try and fail to get around our logocentrism; as Derrida argued, the *difference* that makes the categorization of reality and identity "impossible," the excess within any system of reason that defies its reality, at the same time makes "knowledge" and categorization inevitable in any particular rhetorical situation. That is, we cannot know thought directly or critically from its outside, because to think thought from the outside is always already to have begun from a point on thought's inside. This is not at all to say that we cannot have a useful awareness of our cognition, but rather that such an awareness gives us no final purchase over actual situations—metacognition is a cognition formed from what is internal to cognition as opposed to a position outside of it. The affective relation of our nervous system to our own mind and to others, on the other hand, suggests a more radical self-difference—the difference internal to the self that is plasticity. This is why *plasticity*, inasmuch as it characterizes the materiality of the formal excess within any system, is the best term. Plasticity is not what is excluded from the systems of difference but is the material reality of difference as such; what we require therefore is a knowledge of plasticity.

As we'll see, recognizing the value of accidents and failures, a plastic pedagogy demands relationships of *care*—between teachers, students, and other affective bodies (especially, as I'll argue, writing and other media)—given the explosive potential for *disaffection*, increasingly manifested as a pervasive *carelessness* that characterizes both neo-liberalism and neuropathology alike. But in order to arrive at these key themes, in Chapter 2, I'll first consider alternative posthuman theories of subjectivity that have been influential in our field—Speculative Realism (SR) and Object Oriented Ontology (OOO). What we'll find is that while these theories have reintroduced the significance of wonder to pedagogy, in turning to the *object* as the privileged site of ontological inquiry, they've failed to grasp the "weirdness" that neuroscience introduces on the side of the subject, and relatedly, the significance that plasticity brings to pedagogical accounts of emotion and wonder.

Notes

1. Although, a burgeoning "neurorhetoric," including significant works by Brian Jackson and Jordynn Jack and Gregory Appelbaum, suggests the intriguing potential for cataloging rhetorical effects as brain effects. "With science as ally," Jackson argues, "perhaps we no longer have to operate exclusively under the Aristotelian

faith in rhetorical devices theoretically conceived and theoretically taught" (475). However, I'm concerned that this theorization to date fails to fully account for neural reuse and plasticity.

2. While I'll save my more substantial links to pedagogy for Appendix 1.5, I'd like to point out here that prediction error has significant ramifications for understanding rhetorical grammar that have only barely begun to be developed. In Chomsky, differences in linguistic "output" are subtended to the underlying generative model—it is this universal grammar that generates meaning. But in the field of neurolinguisitcs, Benjamin Bergen has begun to trace the overlap between grammatical form and embodied simulation.

   Against the Chomskian model, there is "ample evidence," perhaps most famously associated with the work of George Lakoff, that the brain mentally simulates the content of sentences, such that when processing a sentence like "You are giving Andy a slice of pizza," there is a corresponding motor simulation by the brain of what it would be like to move one's hand to offer pizza (Bergen & Wheeler 150). And in addition to this, Bergen argues across his work—through his extensive research and experiments—that there is evidence that changes in grammatical form *also* impact the content of the simulation; help determine what kind of contribution content words make to the simulation; and, most significantly, modulate a "second-order" of mental simulation that "Given a scene to be simulated . . . specifies what part to focus on" (Bergen & Wheeler 155). For example, given the sentence "John is closing the door," Bergen discovered that the brain simulates motor performance of the "core" action. However, by making slight alteration to this "progressive" sentence (describing a motor action) to make it a "perfect" sentence that focuses on the "endstate" (e.g., "John has closed the drawer") results in *no* motor region activation. This leads Bergen to conclude that grammar has a "quantitatively different" effect on mental representation at a "second-order" beyond linguistic content, linked to pre-existing neural systems dedicated to perception, motor action, and affect. That is, different grammatical markers will trigger different simulations, creating different *embodied* rhetorical effects leading (as Barrett shows us) to prediction.

   While Bergen demonstrates that there is no simple correspondence between grammatical markers and these embodied rhetorical effects—while the processing of language is context dependent—what his work makes clear is that grammatical difference is *physically* tied to differences in meaning. And given that these simulations are distilled into meaningful predictions made before conscious awareness, rooted in probability (i.e., the chances that sentence will unfold in an expected way), neurolinguistics allows us to understand rhetorical effect in relation to a knowledge of possible outcomes. In other words, possessing diverse experiences leading to concepts representing different grammatical forms will decrease prediction error, resulting, literally, in a better physical experience, more harmonious emotions about writing. Similarly—and this should come as no great surprise to rhetoricians—an enhanced conceptual understanding of rhetorical form will enable the writer to have a stronger command over the emotional experience of readers. For instance, grammar can be deployed to purposefully create prediction error and create different effects (as in our "once upon a time" example). And further, Bergen's research suggests the potential to purposefully calibrate grammar to prompt the creation of different simulations in the reader's brain, creating different affective responses (for example, the motor response described in the progressive sentence above).

3. Further, as I'll argue in Chapters 4 and 5, we must view *intelligence* in terms of these creative and destructive dimensions of plasticity.

4. See for example Patrick Sullivan's "The UnEssay: Making Room for Creativity in the Composition Classroom," which explicitly makes the connections between creative plasticity and productivity in today's business world.
5. Lynn Worsham offers a similar critique.

Works Cited

Abraham, Matthew. "Rhetoric and Composition's Conceptual Indeterminacy as Political- Economic Work." *College Composition and Communication*, vol. 68, no. 1, 2016, pp. 68–97.

Anderson, Michael L. "Neural Reuse in the Organization and Development of the Brain." *Developmental Medicine & Child Neurology*, vol. 58, 2016, pp. 3–6. Web.

Barrett, Lisa F. *How Emotions Are Made: The Secret Life of the Brain*. Houghton Mifflin Harcourt, Boston, MA, 2017.

Behm, Nicholas, Sherry Rankins-Robertson, and Duane H. Roen. *The Framework for Success in Postsecondary Writing: Scholarship and Applications*. Parlor Press, Anderson, SC, 2017.

Bergen, Benjamin, and Kathryn Wheeler. "Grammatical Aspect and Mental Simulation." *Brain and Language*, vol. 112, no. 3, 2010, pp. 150–158.

Bizzell, Patricia. *Academic Discourse and Critical Consciousness*. University of Pittsburgh Press, Pittsburgh, PA, 1992.

Boler, Megan. *Feeling Power: Emotions and Education*. Routledge, New York, 1999. Print.

Boltanski, Luc, and Eve Chiapello. *The New Spirit of Capitalism*. Verso, New York, 2005.

Bourdieu, Pierre. *Pascalian Meditations*. Stanford University Press, Stanford, CA, 2000.

Changeux, Jean-Pierre. *Neuronal Man: The Biology of Mind*. Princeton University Press, Princeton, NJ, 1997.

Clark, Andy. *Surfing Uncertainty: Prediction, Action, and the Embodied Mind*. Oxford University Press, New York, 2016.

Cushman, Ellen. "The Rhetorician as an Agent of Social Change." *College Composition and Communication*, vol. 47, no. 1, 1996, pp. 7–28.

Damasio, Antonio R. *The Feeling of What Happens: Body and Emotion in the Making of Consciousness*. Harcourt Brace, New York, 1999.

———. *Descartes' Error: Emotion, Reason and the Human Brain*. Random House, New York, 2008. Print.

Dewey, John. *Human Nature and Conduct*. New York: Henry Holt, 1922.

———. *Democracy and Education*. Dover Publications, New York, 2004.

Edbauer Rice, Jenny. "The New 'New': Making a Case for Critical Affect Studies." *QJS*, vol. 94, no. 2, 2008, pp. 200–212. Print.

Gross, Daniel M., and Jonathan Alexander. "Frameworks for Failure, or What Happened to the Social Turn in Writing Studies?" *Pedagogy*, vol. 16, no. 2, 2016, pp. 273–292. Print.

Hawk, Byron. *A Counter-History of Composition: Toward Methodologies of Complexity*.University of Pittsburgh Press, Pittsburgh, PA, 2007. *ProQuest ebrary*. Web. 8 June 2016.

Immordino-Yang, Mary H., and Antonio Damasio. "We Feel, Therefore We Learn: The Relevance of Affective and Social Neuroscience to Education." *Mind, Brain, and Education*, vol. 1, no. 1, 2007, pp. 3–10.

Jack, Jordynn, and L. G. Appelbaum. "'This Is Your Brain on Rhetoric': Research Directions for Neurorhetorics." *Rhetoric Society Quarterly*, vol. 40, no. 5, 2010, pp. 411–437, doi:10.1080/02773945.2010.516303.

Jackson, Brian. "Neuroscience and the New Urgency of Emotional Appeals." *JAC*, vol. 31, no. 3/4, 2011, pp. 473–496. Web.

Johnston, Adrian, and Catherine Malabou. *Self and Emotional Life: Philosophy, Psychoanalysis, and Neuroscience*. Columbia University Press, Columbia, 2013. *eBook Collection (EBSCOhost)*. Web. 19 August 2015.

Malabou, Catherine. *What Should We Do With Our Brain?* Trans. Sebastian Rand. Fordham University Press, New York, 2008. Print.

———. *The Ontology of the Accident: An Essay on Destructive Plasticity*. Trans. Caroline Shread. Polity, London, 2012.

Meillassoux, Quentin. *After Finitude: An Essay on the Necessity of Contingency*. Trans. Ray Brassier. London: Continuum, 2008. Print.

Miller, Richard E., and Juerecic, Ann. *Habits of the Creative Mind*. St. Martin's, Bedford, 2016.

NCTE Executive Committee. "NCTE Beliefs About the Teaching of Writing." *National Council of Teachers of English*, 2004.

Piaget, Jean. "Piaget's Theory." *Piaget and His School*. Springer, Berlin Heidelberg, 1976, pp. 11–23.

Reid, Alex. "Composing Objects: Prospects for a Digital Rhetoric." *Enculturation*, 14, no. 2013. Web. 1 April 2013.

Rivers, Nathanial. "Tracing the Missing Masses: Vigrance, Symmetry, and Public Rhetoric Pedagogy." *Enculteration*, 2014.

Rose, Mike. "Rigid Rules, Inflexible Plans, and the Stifling of Language: A Cognitivist Analysis of Writer's Block." *College Composition and Communication*, vol. 31, no. 4, 1980, pp. 389–401.

Sacks, Oliver W. *The Man Who Mistook His Wife for a Hat*. Duckworth, London, 1985.

Scott, Tony. "Subverting Crisis in the Political Economy of Composition." *College Composition and Communication*, vol. 68, no. 1, 2016, pp. 10–37.

Stiegler, Bernard. *States of Shock: Stupidity and Knowledge in the 21st Century*. Polity Press, Cambridge, 2015. Print.

Sullivan, Patrick. "The UnEssay: Making Room for Creativity in the Composition Classroom." *College Composition and Communication*, vol. 67, no. 1, 2015, p. 6.

Tomkins, Silvan S., and Robert McCarter. "What and Where are the Primary Affects? Some Evidence for a Theory." *Perceptual and Motor Skills*, vol. 18, no. 1, 1964, pp. 119–158.

Whitehead, Alfred N. *The Aims of Education and Other Essays*. Williams and Norgate, London, 1950.

Wolf, Maryanne, and Catherine J. Stoodley. *Proust and the Squid: The Story and Science of the Reading Brain*. Harper, New York, 2007.

Worsham, Lynn. "Going Postal: Pedagogic Violence and the Schooling of Emotion." *JAC*, vol. 18, no. 2, 1998, pp. 213–245. Print.

Appendix 1.5: Pedagogy Breakout 1

When Writing Explodes: The Relations Between Emotional Intelligence, Transference, and Blockages

In *Doing Emotion*, Laura Micciche suggested that students play at "inhabiting" the emotions of others. This idea was quickly adapted by many others, but her own examples are strong. For instance, in another work, she offers one example of how writing pedagogy can engage the trauma of discontinuity. As Micciche argues, "we use language not just to describe or reflect embodied realities; we also use it to work against constraints imposed upon our bodies" ("Trouble" 273). Micciche recommends therefore that first year students study critical theorists, such as Judith Butler, writing about their emotional involvement in their own writing, the intellectual and emotional pain involved in pushing against normative thinking; as she argues, "This 'pain' or trouble calls for sacrifice of sometimes what one holds dear (concepts of gender, selfhood, sameness, and so on) for the goal of scrutinizing what's embedded, and often what's violent or hurtful in these holdings" (274). However, from the perspective of a plastic pedagogy, I'm skeptical; cannot we see here, too, even in Micciche, the privileging of critique and the symbolic? Better would be to have students reflect on their embodied, affective experience reading Butler and other difficult academic writers—and I mean this literally and not cynically—naming the painful emotions (but also, of course, the pleasure) this experience involves. Similarly, instead of having students practice "critical empathy," or play the "believing game," or engage in Rogerian listening, a pedagogy rooted in embodied affectivity might have students attempt to imagine what it *feels like* to occupy another position.

Following the contemporary neuroscience on emotional intelligence, this will be my main contention in this first pedagogical breakout chapter. However, I need to first address a possible critique of this approach, one I mean to take seriously. Pedagogies that emphasize emotion and affect—much as those that emphasize politics and social critique—have long been criticized for turning away from writing itself (infamously, by Stanley Fish). The expressivism of Peter Elbow was called too "soft," while the emotional pedagogy of Kia Jane Richmond, Micciche, Rice and others following the affective turn is still called "impractical." What each have in common is that they only (or seem to only) address the fundamental concepts and skills young writers require *indirectly*. But unlike these authors, I'm not arguing for a pedagogy of care aimed, in the first instance, at enriching our students' overall emotional lives, so much as their emotional life as it relates *specifically to development and writing*. In response to the valid concerns of the critics of the affective turn, my goal here is to advance a pedagogy rooted in plasticity—one that emphasizes, among other things, emotional intelligence and a consciousness of the brain—that nevertheless always points back to writing "practicalities" and the composition discourse in which they are established.

But being "practical" about teaching writing cannot only mean a simple focus on positivity, productivity, and linear development, because neuroscience shows that this is not how most learning works. Following from Malabou's and Barrett's accounts of the relations between affectivity and plasticity, we require new ways to think about the emotional, embodied experience of composing, and the affective work of both writing and teaching. We require a pedagogy capable of inculcating plastic dispositions, and to do this we must recognize the primacy of our students' affective embodiment in both the learning and transference of writing skills and concepts. Let's consider the significance of neuroscientific accounts of affective support to two fundamental dimensions of student performance—transfer and blockage—keeping in mind Silvan Tomkins' maxim that "the absence of the affective support of interest would jeopardize intellectual development no less than the destruction of brain tissue" (343).

Emotional Intelligence and Transfer

The conventional account of the transference of writing proficiency reflects our disciplinary privileging of reason over embodiment and a limiting concept of "writing expertise" rooted in conceptual and metacognitive awareness. For example, Anne Beaufort's scholarship argues that transference is most likely to occur where students have a metacognitive, conceptual command of the writing process, the subject matter, rhetoric, and genre—in short, the discourse community. As Chris Anson puts it, "A foundational principle of writing transfer equates ability with various forms of conscious awareness" (532). However, following Lisa Barrett's neuro-constructivist theory, we know that when students are stymied by "bad" emotions when they write, they begin to predict accordingly, hardwiring a pernicious and disempowering affective response to writing, increasing the potential for writer's block, procrastination, and other forms of disaffection and disengagement.

For example, it's been shown that students' emotional experiences with writing directly impact the transference of knowledge about writing and overall development (Driscoll & Powell). Following 13 college writers over five years, Driscoll and Powell reveal that emotions impact writing performance across discrete writing tasks, and furthermore that "emotional states or traits" have a "tremendous long-term impact that persisted over a period of years and that directly impacted students' ability to transfer as well as their writing development." Simply put, in addition to whatever other benefits might accrue, learning is more likely to transfer to new situations if students *care about the work they are doing.*

Overall, Driscoll and Powell find that while "disliking" a writing situation is always disruptive (leading to procrastination or poor performance), these dispositions are important in determining whether "circumstantial" negative emotions—experienced by all students—will be generative or disruptive for learning. These findings empirically substantiate Lynn Worsham's early deconstruction of the "distinction between public and private and between reason and emotion" (220), underscoring the import work of inculcating "emotional dispositions" in composition courses. For their part, Driscoll and Powell specifically advocate for the pedagogical value of an emotional metacognitive awareness.

Furthermore, they argue that "Faculty members play a major role in helping students to foster generative emotions towards writing and to learn how to better handle the inevitable negative emotions that occur." And they found that: "When a student in this study had a positive emotional experience with a faculty member, then that student was very likely to have a short- (and possibly) long-term generative experience that positively impacted his or her overall development." This leads the authors to offer practical pedagogical advice, such as including positive comments in feedback, and avoiding a tone that gives "students the perception that their instructor did not like their writing." However, their focus on monitoring and controlling emotion, and one of their proposed pedagogical solutions—a turn to critical pedagogy—reflects the conventional bias that still privileges conscious reasoning over the biological, embodied understanding of emotion in our field.

Emotional Intelligence and Writer's Block

Synaptic connections are dynamic and changing, never fixed; and what contemporary neuroscience has discovered is that, as with stem cells that are capable of metamorphosing into entirely new roles, through neural reuse (described in the Introduction), the brain recruits across synaptic connections and entire regions, and different cognitive functions make use of different regions, *ad hoc*, relative to the organism's goals and the overall rhetorical situation or ecology. Learning involves both the ongoing creation *and destruction* of these connections through experience; for example, "synaptic pruning" works to increase the predictive efficiency of the brain, eliminating redundancies (of mental models we already possess) and thereby improving generalization—the "ability to use what you know in a wide range of superficially distinct (but fundamentally similar) cases" (Clark 272). The plasticity of consciousness entails the repair and reorganization of the subject following errors, accidents, and failures. And, as I'll argue across this work in light of the neuroscientific account of affect, learning entails destructive experiences where predictive error, accidents, and failure lead to novel formations, and therefore should ideally occur within careful (with high emotional granularity) relations of intergenerational transmission and dispute.

We can understand the *ad hoc* relation between neuronal formations and cognition in relation to "Interference." Interference describes blockages to learning and action where different tasks rely on the same neurons. There are many examples of this in the literature, where neural usage in a given task makes the same neurons less available for usage in another. For example, we know that the visual cortex of newly blinded subjects is activated when they read Braille. This should not be terribly surprising, given that vision and Braille literacy both involve spatialization, the perception of shapes, and so on. But here things get more interesting. An experiment blindfolded sighted patients and taught them Braille over five days, demonstrating that in these subjects, brain regions associated with vision were activated more often than non-blindfolded subjects. But when the blindfolds were removed, there was no difference between the treatment and control groups. Although the previously blindfolded subjects could still read Braille, they ceased to involve the visual cortex given that their vision was now again *in use*. Sightedness posed an interference to usage of the visual cortex in reading Braille. Nevertheless, *the brain recruited new regions* so that the treatment group could continue to read. This is a strong example of neural reuse, a form of plasticity (Anderson 55).

Can the principle of neural reuse help us better understand other blockages, such as writer's block? I suggest that it can. Anderson also gives the simple example of the interference caused by being trained to play tennis while trying to play squash. While one might think that the two sports are similar, given differences in spatial and motor coordinates between the two games, the ability to learn squash is interfered with where we have learned tennis. Extrapolating from Anderson, we can understand how interference would cause a student trained extensively in, for instance, writing five-paragraph essays, to struggle when they encounter new rhetorical situations. In such cases, a knowledge of the five-paragraph form will actually work against the student's success; and it is in these cases that *failure* stimulates learning. When the brain uses the five-paragraph essay as a predictive concept, students will fail to rise to the rhetorical challenge. Given that the brain, in a given writing situation, will automatically recruit neural pathways associated with five paragraph-related concepts, these concepts will *interfere* with success in the new task. Indeed, it is only through the *destruction* of the brain's predictive networks that new ones can form on top of the old. Learning in this way entails destruction.

Writer's block too can be understood in relation to affective response and emotional intelligence—exploring the relationships between writing, emotion, and various blockages are addressed across this book. While cognitivists have traditionally understood these phenomena in terms of cognitive overload (e.g., Crosswhite 271–272; Pinker), recommending increased planning—consistent with the linear conceptualization of learning—again, we should also realize that from the perspective of plasticity, *failure can also represent growth*. This further suggests that we cannot reduce the problem of writer's block to a lack of motive, where motive is defined as a "natural" and automatic capacity rooted in desire, presuming the universal and indestructible presence of care. Instead, we need to take into account affective accumulation and emotional intelligence. From this perspective—although, clearly, affect isn't the only factor in blockage—an embodied, emotional intelligence will help convert negative feelings into positive ones, enabling the writer to name the specific emotions associated with their block and to seek productive solutions for unblocking.

As Piaget recognized, growth occurs through accommodation and assimilation, but also through *gaps* and *leaps* that cannot be understood in terms of symbolic mastery or the linear accumulation or development of skills and knowledge. For Piaget, the changes and differences that characterize learning entail *exploding* into new structures of thought. Indeed, for Piaget, much as we saw with neural reuse, development and intelligence mark a difference or excess in which the subject is first unable to reconcile new problems in relation to old dispositions. Therefore, the explosive moment of learning will appear as a kind of "blank" space in which the learner may seem to have *regressed*. In these "blank" moments between stages where the previous stage is interrupted, Piaget theorized that intelligence, as an *excess within the system*, was in fact working to "accommodate" failure, no longer able to "assimilate" new experience according to previous schema. In fact, for Piaget, it is the margin of indeterminacy between schema that enables our sensitivity to the external other, enabling growth. We can understand this excess, this overdetermination, this margin on indeterminacy as plasticity. Emotional intelligence can help students negotiate these blank spaces, these moments of failure, where exposure to new experiences and writing situations will require that they break through (destroy) entrenched habits and overlearned concepts.

Towards Pedagogical Applications of Emotional Intelligence

In both transference and writer's block, we'll need to think about the value of failure and destructive plasticity to learning. Fortunately, I believe much in recent scholarship on affectivity (e.g., Davis; Rice; Cooper; Micciche) as well as much in postprocess theory (e.g., Dobrin; Hawk; Rickert) already allows us to conceptualize the value of failure and indeterminacy in writing pedagogy. After all, as Kristopher Lotier argues, postprocess theory has gone a long way in theorizing the subject's openness to the accidental and external: "In foregrounding contingency, profound uncertainty, randomness, and openness, and in learning how to enable, channel, or direct forces beyond one's direct control, the writer allows himself or herself to be rewritten, rewired, re-paired" (375). We can see this "foregrounding" of indeterminacy, for instance, in Byron Hawk's "lines of flight." There are many ways in which postprocess theory recognizes contingency, ways to break out of the habituation and automatization of intelligence, the potential for sudden, dramatic, explosive *leaps* in ability.

This project of rethinking the humanities through the biological and the biological through the humanities—of transgressing transcendental reason—will require and reward experimentation by both teachers and students. To help our students develop new writing concepts and affordances—to increase writing intelligence—will require that we challenge their embodied habits. But it will also require that our students have the emotional intelligence required to meet these challenges in order to overcome *failure*, recognizing that failure characterizes the plastic excess of intelligence required for growth, the subject's ability to repair and reorganize following a breakdown or failure.

At this point I'd like to share an assignment that I've piloted in my freshman composition course (WRTG 100), rooted in my understanding of the neuroscience of emotion, meant especially to empower students that associate writing with negative feelings:

1. **Background:** Students read and discuss some basics of neuroplasticity, with the goal of giving students a consciousness of their brain. I've begun by assigning a single, brief but clear essay by Barrett on emotional intelligence.
2. **A Consciousness of the Brain:** As we know, writing is a very emotional experience for our students. They frequently feel high levels of anxiety when writing, for reasons that go well beyond procrastination, to the point of writer's block. Students often find that the only way they can complete writing assignments is to emotionally divest—that is, to fall back on completely unsatisfying routines and formulas that in the past have allowed them to finish assignments, but without (more or less) any sense of their personality invested. At the same time, some students take feedback about their writing personally, becoming emotionally attached to their writing as a sign of their intelligence or self-worth. How can we help them to make sense of these debilitating feelings? Learning to identify emotional experience, following Driscoll and Powell and Perkins and Salomon, is required for the "transfer of most complex academic tasks, including writing" (Driscoll & Powell). Towards this end, I've asked students to work together on *naming* some of these feelings and share their results. They begin by contemplating an experience that resulted in "bad" feelings about writing; I instruct them to think of a *specific* moment in the writing process where things broke down—for instance, in trying to connect ideas, in writing an introduction, in

making use of their research, in revision, in crafting sentences, and so on. With a list of emotion words in hand, they find the most appropriate labels for those bodily feelings (affects), settling on a handful of emotion words to describe common writing experiences. They then share in small groups, and the group selects one to present to the class. Finally, the ones that the class as a whole accept as most characteristic of their experience are selected for further work. (I also do a similar version of this assignment in relations to debilitating feelings with regard to academic reading.)

3. **Categorization:** Having connected bodily feelings to emotion words, we then give these experiences their own original names (one fun part of this assignment is that the names can be anything). Although some might be rudimentary, students have no trouble coming up with all sorts of examples. For instance, one group described a group of emotions ("disappointment," "tired," "impatient," "shame," "resignation," and "uneasy") they sometimes feel when they can't seem to find the right words to express themselves, when their writing feels flat or lifeless, as "voicelessness." Voicelessness, they agreed, was distinct from "disappointment" in that that it also involved a touch of "impatience" as well as a dash of "shame," "resignation," and "uneasiness." Voicelessness, they stipulated, didn't feel as intense as any singular feeling listed—it has its own essence. Identifying the list of associative "bad" feelings with precision is not nearly as important as arriving at this new emotion concept, which allows them to give a name to what was, for the most part, previously only vaguely experienced as an underlying tension, anxiety, or uneasiness. Finally, I have each student in the group write about this experience, where they've experienced it, and what the result was.
4. **Emotional Intelligence:** Next, we discuss productive ways to *respond* to the emotion once it has been predicted. In Driscoll and Powell's terms (discussed in Chapter 1), we need to move students from "metacognitive monitoring" to "control," given that students might be capable of monitoring disruptive emotions but unaware of how to resolve their problem. For instance, in the case of voicelessness, I recommend readings from our field about voice, which I in turn have them write about as part of a larger portfolio project. To take another example, students that identified an emotion they called "franudated"—related to the blockage they experienced in writing the first paragraph of an essay—next discovered an essay on writingcommons.org that suggested that that there's no reason to begin at the beginning when you sit down to write. Students found this idea liberating, and reported that by associating this simple strategy with being franudated, it had reduced both anxiety and blockage in future projects. And moreover, there was evidence that they were learning to disassociate from their negative feelings.

5. **Recategorization:** Next, I prompt students to recategorize negative feelings about writing as positive emotions. For example, in both class discussions and through a short writing assignment, I work towards associating the shame and hopelessness students feel in voicelessness to an understanding of the "pride" they take in their writing, education, and future. Once they begin to predict voicelessness in terms of "pride," some students have reported that they feel better about the writing experience, turning their energies towards solutions as opposed to dwelling in—and thereby hardwiring—unpleasantness, leading to writer's block.
6. **Resisting Flexibility:** Finally, I ask students to consider negative emotions in relation to failure without recategorizing. That is, in relation to their new emotion concept, I prompt students to consider how assignments they've struggled with in the past (or present) have conflicted with their own values. They consider how the bad feelings they have about writing are not "their fault," how they might represent a natural resistance to classroom power dissymmetry, schooling, and problematic or unfair pedagogical demands. For example, in the case of "voicelessness," students concluded that their high school emphasis on the five paragraph form worked explicitly against cultivating voice; the negative feeling that they had about these experiences, they concluded, was in fact justified.

The Feeling of Saying "No" to Pedagogical Flexibility

One might argue that this strategy is no different than just teaching the concept voice (or grammar or process or audience or paragraphs) as we've always done. And indeed, there's interesting overlap here with certain received pedagogies of writing. However, I argue that there is a fundamental difference between writing pedagogies that teach concepts in the abstract, appealing to students' reason, and a pedagogy that aims directly at our students' *embodied experience*. Above all, developing an emotional intelligence about writing allows students to recognize that the bad feelings they have while they write does not mean that there is something physically (that is, intellectually) wrong with them. With this knowledge, they are better able, I submit, to focus on finding solutions as opposed to dwelling on their bad feelings, becoming caught up in a "vicious cycle" of prediction error.

While many of these ideas are taken directly from Barrett's account of emotional intelligence, asking students to consider embracing "bad feelings" in resisting marks a significant difference departure from her too. But even here, I've attempted to extend Barrett's insights into a pedagogical value, one that joins Malabou's account of destructive plasticity. That is, I'm suggesting that we help students to develop an emotional intelligence about learning with a specific focus on failure. Doing so, I submit, can give students increased control over their affective experience, in turn giving them more control over learning and performance. Take for example two student experiences detailed by (once again) Driscoll and Powell. Two students with different emotional dispositions, Alice (an "emotional interpreter") and Abby (an "emotional manager"), both experienced frustration with regard to a discreet assignment. Alice's frustration was disruptive, as she refused to persist in seeking help, giving in to her frustration; she was "unwilling to transfer her learning from one context to the next." Abby, on the other hand, was able to make her frustration generative, using it as an occasion to transfer strategies she'd learned to manage it. Failure, in a plastic pedagogy, becomes an opportunity for affective, material, and conscious difference.

However, as I've argued, it's not always the case that bad feelings should be converted into positive ones. For example, what if Alice were intuiting something unfair about her situation; for instance, perhaps her frustration was not the result of a lack of emotional intelligence, but instead a poorly crafted assignment by an incompetent teacher? In such a situation, being flexible might help her get the good grade she wants, but would do little to reinforce her sense of justice. Relatedly, as Megan Boler's "pedagogy of discomfort" reminds us, re-adaptation can sometimes mean further submission and marginalization, and the negative feelings that accompany failure can sometimes be "re-claimed" to resist the power structures that produce them. Of course, owing to power dissymmetry in the classroom, students suffer injustices like these all the time. As a result, Micciche points out, students both identify with and resist the feeling of what it is to be a student, and for some students there is an important lack of identification that marks them as outsiders. But we don't necessarily need to push back against the performance of resistance by students that don't fully identify as such, as one would in what Erving Goffman called a "total institution." As teachers, we know that the most successful students are not necessarily endlessly flexible and docile, but those capable of both productivity *and* resistance—that is, those with plastic dispositions.

In answer to the question, "what should we do with our brains?," Malabou responds that we must "visualize the possibility of saying no to an afflicting economic, political, and mediatic culture that celebrates only the triumph of flexibility, blessing obedient individuals who have no greater merit than that of knowing how to bow their heads with a smile" (*What Should We Do* 78–79). That is, we must "visualize the possibility" of resisting neuroideology and realize, in this visualization, the potential of the brain to be disobedient to all codes and programs (including the biological). While it's clear that our disciplinary emphasis on flexibility has served as a bulwark against various determinisms, we must also recognize how the demand for constant, systematic flexibility becomes itself a linear, rationalized code or program.

At worst, flexibility becomes a requirement for a "polymorphism" that requires students to move fluidly from form to form, justified by the purchase reason or metacognition supposedly gives over this flux. Yet, as Malabou argues, "polymorphism, open to all forms, capable of donning all masks, adopting all postures, all attitudes, engenders the undoing of identity." This is because "One is formed only by virtue of a resistance to form itself" (*What Should We Do* 72). Like Gregor Samsa who persists in his being through an inner monolog that preserves his familial role, polymorphism preserves a limited vision of form (and style) as "skin, vestment or finery" (*The Ontology* 17) supplemental to essence. And as we've seen, this vision, which, despite important lessons from rhetorical theory concerning the primacy of form over content, is at the center of the "conceptual indeterminacy" (Abraham) of composition pedagogy. In other words, the resistance internal to Malabou's account of plastic form points to its value in understanding the relations between writing pedagogy, affectivity, and the creative and destructive dimensions of development and self formation.

Works Cited

Abraham, Matthew. "Rhetoric and Composition's Conceptual Indeterminacy as Political- Economic Work." *College Composition and Communication*, vol. 68, no. 1, 2016, pp. 68–97.

Anderson, Michael L. "Neural Reuse in the Organization and Development of the Brain." *Developmental Medicine & Child Neurology*, vol. 58, 2016, pp. 3–6. Web.

Anson, Chris M. "The Pop Warner Chronicles: A Case Study in Contextual Adaptation and the Transfer of Writing Ability." *College Composition and Communication*, vol. 67, no. 4, 2016, p. 518.

Cooper, Marilyn M. "Rhetorical Agency as Emergent and Enacted." *College Composition and Communication*, vol. 62, no. 3, 2011, pp. 420–449.

Crosswhite, James R. *Rhetoric of the Human Sciences: The Rhetoric of Reason*. University of Wisconsin Press, Madison, WI, 1996.

Davis, D. Diane. *Inessential Solidarity: Rhetoric and Foreigner Relations*. University of Pittsburgh Press, Pittsburgh, PA, 2010.

Dobrin, Sid. *Postcomposition*. Southern Illinois University Press, Carbondale, IL, 2011. Print.

Driscoll, Dana Lynn, and Roger Powell. "States, Traits, and Dispositions: The Impact of Emotion on Writing Development and Writing Transfer Across College Courses and Beyond." *Composition Forum*, vol. 34, *Association of Teachers of Advanced Composition*, 2016.

Hawk, Byron. *A Counter-History of Composition: Toward Methodologies of Complexity.*University of Pittsburgh Press, Pittsburgh, PA, 2007. *ProQuest ebrary*. Web. 8 June 2016.

Lotier, Kristopher M. "Around 1986: The Externalization of Cognition and the Emergence of Postprocess Invention." *College Composition and Communication*, vol. 67, no. 3, 2016, p. 360.

Malabou, Catherine. *What Should We Do With Our Brain?* Trans. Sebastian Rand. Fordham University Press, New York, 2008. Print.

———. *The Ontology of the Accident: An Essay on Destructive Plasticity*. Trans. Caroline Shread. Polity, London, 2012.

Micciche, Laura R. "The Trouble With Affect." *JAC*, vol. 26, no. 1/2, 2006, pp. 264–276. Web. 4 June 2015.

———. *Doing Emotion: Rhetoric, Writing, Teaching*. Boynton/Cook Publishers, Portsmouth, NH, 2007.

Piaget, Jean. "Piaget's Theory." *Piaget and His School*. Springer, Berlin Heidelberg, 1976, pp. 11–23.

Pinker, Steven. *The Sense of Style: The Thinking Person's Guide to Writing in the 21st Century*. Viking, New York, 2014.

Rice, Jenny. "Pathologia." *Quarterly Journal of Speech*, vol. 101, no. 1, 2015, pp. 34–45.

———. "Para-Expertise, Tacit Knowledge, and Writing Problems." *College English*, vol. 78, no. 2, 2015, p. 117.

Rickert, Thomas. *Ambient Rhetoric: The Attunements of Rhetorical Being*. University of Pittsburgh, Pittsburgh, PA, 2013. Web.

Tomkins, Silvan S., and Robert McCarter. "What and Where Are the Primary Affects? Some Evidence for a Theory." *Perceptual and Motor Skills*, vol. 18, no. 1, 1964, pp. 119–158.

Worsham, Lynn. "Going Postal: Pedagogic Violence and the Schooling of Emotion." *Journal of Advanced Composition-JAC*, vol. 18, 1998, pp. 213–245.

2 Composition's Correlationalisms
Objects of Wonder

Ian Bogost, a game designer more known for his contributions to Object Oriented Ontology (OOO), theorizes both a human experience and pedagogy rooted wonder. And this seems valuable to me from the perspective of a plastic pedagogy. Wonder, as we'll see, is an important component of dialectical accounts of learning, the affective relation of the subject to the world of objects and knowledge. Socrates said, "wonder is the feeling of a philosopher, and philosophy begins in wonder." Aristotle agreed, setting in motion a long philosophical tradition that has recognized wonder as the emotion that precedes reason. But Bogost's idea of wonder is not theirs, exactly. "To wonder is to respect things as things in themselves," Bogost argues, and wonder should therefore not find its ends in some larger social significance, purpose, or reason. "Unlike these old methods, which strive to illuminate," Bogost schematizes, "wonder hopes to darken, to isolate, to insulate. Perhaps this is one signal for the future: instead of roboticists and anthropologists, instead of biomedical engineers and medievalists, we will find alloyers and philopescetes and tacologists" (131). Bogost's theorization of wonder reflects an argument I made in the introduction, that writing curriculums based in rationalized and universalized programs can be emotionally—and therefore intellectually—deadening. But should we take seriously this suggestion that it may be in our students' best interest—indeed, that it may be our job—to develop a composition pedagogy that will better equip our students to become "tacologists"[1]?

To do so would be to follow recent paths forged in cutting-edge philosophy and rhetorical theory. In both, there has been a trend towards bracketing questions of epistemology and transcendental reason, working around (rather than directly engaging) the "linguistic turn" and poststructuralist accounts of language. This is an argument behind much in the "bring the funk" perspective on composition pedagogy, a line of thinking that has been further fueled by the successes and sudden rock-star-esque popularity of OOO. Abandoning the primacy of human subjectivity, from this perspective, rhetoricians need to understand new media and writing technologies—indeed, all objects—on their own terms. In short, OOO has argued that both philosophy and rhetoric should abandon the epistemological concerns that characterized much in poststructuralism and the linguistic turn—and therefore, of course, writing theory and pedagogy—and instead commit to *ontological* investigations (such as the being of tacos), recognizing the essential contingency of all knowledge.

It's not hard to see the appeal of OOO to cutting-edge rhetoricians and postcomposition theorists. In OOO, contingency replaces the *a priori* as the only satisfactory account of the universal. Each object—independent of human intent—has its own wonderful[2] adventure in the world, an adventure that can only be described through metaphor, indirect language, and other forms of *rhetoric*. And OOO theory clearly supports writing theorists' ongoing critique of conventional social epistemic and process accounts of writing—indeed, it calls into question the prioritization of epistemic writing in general, which is understood to be too "direct" in its approach to essences—arguing for a posthumanism in which relations between objects are on the exact same footing as relations between subjects and objects. However, the dalliance our field is having with OOO is not all wine and roses (or all footballs, hurricanes, eyebrows, candlesticks, shoemakers, and tacos). Without disallowing or negating the social, OOO can *also* be read as calling into question our disciplinary prioritization of the public and social work of writing and rhetoric. For OOO, inquiry into objects is self justifying; there is no need to explore the effects those objects (e.g., writing) realize in relation to the social. What do we do with *that?*

Still, there are intriguing points of overlap between OOO and rhetorical theory, and work is already well underway in both philosophy and rhetoric to trace them; in our own field, interest in an "object turn" goes back (at least) as far as a 2010 RSA panel featuring Scot Barnett, Robert Leston, Byron Hawk, and Rickert. More recently, Nathanial Rivers' video essay, citing recent OOO by Bogost and others, makes the case for teaching rhetoric as OOO-style ontological attunement. Following a line of thinking that passes through Latour and Vico, Rivers suggests the pedagogical and heuristical gains that will come from abandoning philosophical and political *critique* as our privileged modality, recognizing especially the relation between our disciplines' privileging of epistemic discourse and an increasingly untenable distinction between subject and audience. By shifting the focus of writing pedagogy to an ontological attunement, authors such as Rivers argue that our future as a discipline lays in the consideration of *ways of being* as opposed to *expertise* in the traditional fixed outcomes of composition pedagogy (e.g., mastering academic prose). From this perspective, given that it (potentially at least) privileges the indirect over the epistemic, tacology is viable—if dangerous to the teacher's career—in a composition course.

Relatedly, in de-emphasizing composition's human and social focus, Alex Reid argues from the interrelated perspectives of new materialism and Bruno Latour's actor-network theory (ANT) for the value of the "glitch"—for failures and accidents—as both a heuristic and point of entry for pedagogy. So, for example, where bad writing is viewed as a glitch in the system, rhetoric can turn to an analysis of the network, or writing pedagogy can address the writer as one actant in a technological network (that is, as merely one actant among objects that have their own agency): "We can treat those glitches as problems to be fixed by revising the compositional networks. Or we can investigate those glitches as compositional objections that might tell us something about the world we inhabit." For Reid, bad student writing too should be viewed as a glitch in the system; subsuming the subject into a network, he advocates for a writing pedagogy in which "we dislocate the perception of bad writing from . . . individuals and put it into the network."

If nothing else, many other ultra-contemporary theories of rhetoric—I think especially the work of Dianne Davis, Alex Reid, Laurie Gries, Byron Hawk, Thomas Rickert, Sid Dobrin, Jody Shipka—share much in common with OOO's de-prioritization of the subject and interest in objects. For instance, theories of rhetorical circulation and velocity—such as Laurie Gries' analysis of the cultural circulation and alteration of Shepard Fairey's Obama "Hope" image—represent significant contributions to the life of objects. As Gries states, by "writing about images and pictures . . . I most often use things, rather than discourse, in order to help reimagine the traditional boundaries of rhetorical scholarship." OOO also has obvious resonances with our discipline's recent interest in creativity (e.g., Patrick Sullivan). In short, there are clear connections between contemporary rhetorical theory and OOO—but do these affinities mask some underlying tensions? Also, does new materialism offer advantages over other posthuman accounts of learning and subjectivity, such as neuroscience? This is what I would like to begin considering in this chapter. After all, OOO is not without very vocal detractors in philosophy and literature departments (e.g., Andrew Cole; Malabou; Zizek), and we need to reconcile the substantial critiques of OOO with our own theorization.

So while I'm in no way against tacology as a hobby, interest, passion, or even a career, ultimately, I would like to consider the pedagogical trade-off that comes with the OOO vision of composing—a vision that, it must again be said, aggressively challenges the public and social (human) purposes of rhetoric. As we'll see, this bracketing has been somewhat obfuscated in the early embrace of OOO by compositionists. Ultimately, given that the new materialist response to the transcendental tradition in philosophy is its outright abandonment, I'll argue that it's important to remain skeptical of OOO's vision of learning, *especially*, perhaps, as it relates to the teaching of writing. However, I also believe that it's important to take the challenge OOO poses to the transcendental (the foundational Kantian tradition that Quentin Meillassoux terms "correlationalism") seriously, especially at this moment in which we are realizing the ecological extensions of rhetoric. But for reasons that I'll begin to develop here, while OOO and SR pose important challenges to both writing theory and pedagogy, the materialist, neuroscientific account of plasticity offers both a more radical deconstruction of transcendental reason as well as a more rigorous way to theorize wonder in writing pedagogy.

Eviscerations of Wonder and Rhetoric

Following Aristotle's theorization, Descartes, Hume, Kant, and Hegel all viewed wonder as ultimately a sign of ignorance, something to be overcome through philosophical or scientific inquiry. This is not what Bogost has in mind. From the perspective of OOO, a pedagogy rooted in wonder enables us to move beyond prescribed forms of reason and dialectical accounts of learning in order to engage with the profound mystery of objects that, in their beckoning, appeal to us more profoundly than our constructed social theories and uses of them. In some ways, this return to wonder reflects the work begun by rhetorician William Covino in the late 80's. Covino understood wonder as returning us to a "rhetoric as the elaboration of ambiguity" (2), tracing a tradition of "renegade advocates of open discourse" (3) ranging from Montaigne to Hume to Dequincy.

Bogost provides the example of his own youthful fascination with garbage trucks, a sense of wonder quickly coopted by teachers that wanted him to care about their social and scientific relevance. He offers that, "Perhaps, in [a] future world, versions of the younger me will smile as proud teachers tousle their hair over the wonderful garbage trucks they sketch at their grade-school desks" (131). Wonder is the pre-discursive medium through which this communication between humans and objects first occurs. As Bogost argues: "The act of wonder invites a detachment from ordinary logics, of which human logics are but one example. . . . To wonder is to suspend all trust in one's own logics, be they religion, science, philosophy, custom, or opinion, and to become subsumed entirely in the uniqueness of an object's native logics—flour granule, firearm, civil justice system, longship, fondant" (124). That is, its value is in its suspension of reason, which it makes socially "undesirable." Instead, Bogost claims, through a pedagogy of wonder we become "subsumed entirely in the uniqueness of an object's native logics."

As writing teachers, our folk wisdom—as well as Lev Vygotsky's theory of the zone of proximal development (ZPD)—emphasizes the developmental significance of beginning at the level of our student's own interests and abilities. So, it's no surprise that, over and over, research has demonstrated that teaching writing in terms of abstract rules and principles, or as a grammar divorced from lived experience, fails to transfer. Nor is it a surprise that, where we fail to create wonder, we too often resort to "wonder drugs," such as Adderall. In some sense at least, it's literally the job of writing teachers to inculcate or maintain wonder. Indeed, the *first two* "Habits of Mind" recommended under the WPA's position statement "Framework for Success in Postsecondary Writing" reflect a significant dimension of wonder: "Curiosity—the desire to know more about the world" and "Openness—the willingness to consider new ways of being and thinking in the world" (Behm, Rankins-Robertson, and Roen).

"Yet wonder," Bogost insists, "has been all but eviscerated in modern thought, left behind as a naive delusion" (124). And Bogost is right that in a political climate dominated by confirmation bias, a pedagogical climate dominated by measurement, and an intellectual climate that has witnessed reason's destruction and deconstruction, wonder seems in short supply among both teachers and students. Bogost challenges us to rethink how we ask students to approach their topics through writing. On the one hand, contemporary rhetorical theory (often drawing on Heidegger) offers us some interesting ways to think about invention in terms of wonder, such as Byron Hawk's emphasis on "lines of flight" or Thomas Rickert's emphasis on "attunement." Brown and Rivers have already specifically picked up on Bogort's challenge in order to rethink the composition classroom in terms of a "rhetorical carpentry," building on our discipline's traditional focus on making, production, and invention (29). In doing so, they emphasize moving beyond a pedagogy rooted in social epistemic *critique*—making rhetoric an alternate version of literary and cultural theory, "a reactionary mode of engagement with objects that too easily falls back on correlationalism"—to instead argue that an ontological study of rhetoric should enable students "to *invent* new ways of producing meaning through an attunement to the constraints and affordances of new media" (31).

Ultimately, as it pertains to our own field, it's not just the social epistemic pedagogy that Bogost's philosophy undermines. Following SR and OOO, his theorization, as we'll see, also discounts any writing pedagogy rooted in cognitivism, expressivism, critical pedagogy, discursivity, and public rhetoric, leaving it difficult for compositionists to be sanguine—despite interest by cutting-edge rhetoricians—about the potential of these theories. In short, Bogost argues that both humanist and scientific disciplines have failed in developing a pedagogy of wonder because of their stubborn insistence on human purpose:

> When we approach objects as social relativists, they bear interest only as products or regulators of human behavior and society. . . . But when we approach objects as scientific naturalists, the same prejudice applies. . . . Even though some scientists might try to deny the human-centricity of science itself, arguing that it seeks instead to uncover universal truths about the universe, the rhetoric of science is entirely and totally obsessed with human knowledge, action, and use.
>
> (124)

STEM is his main target here:

> even the more 'acceptable' professional goals like astronaut or chef speak less to a child's latent interest in astrophysics or chemistry and

> more to a state of natural wonder at the alien mystery of objects. But alas, common wisdom in STEM goals suggests that these moments of childhood opportunity must be captured and exploited.
> (126)

In the face of the commonly heard argument that science has "re-enchanted" the world, Bogost argues that both science and philosophy have equally failed to enchant by imagining the ends of wonder in human purpose:

> the real obstacle to youthful interest in science arises not from a distaste for mathematics or the natural world but from a latent dissatisfaction with the way science melts the shell of wonder around ordinary objects. Science, like philosophy, has assumed that wonder is always a type of puzzlement, an itch meant to be scratched so we can get on with things.
> (129)

One is reminded of Roland Barthes' analysis of toys as always serving to indoctrinate children into the closed order of adult discourse and reason. However, what can be the future of writing pedagogy's account of learning and development, and rhetoric's emphasis on public work, from this perspective?

From the perspective of OOO, in the dominant social epistemic pedagogy, conventional writing instruction becomes an obvious "capturing" of the wonder of students, directing it towards predetermined modes of critique around questions of social purpose. Again, it's easy to see how contemporary rhetoricians, linking invention to rhetorical attunement, are attracted to this perspective. Too often, as Bogost argues, pedagogical goals like correctness, process, metacognition, and invention are simply exploitative conversions of attention from the object itself towards the social. This is what Quentin Meillassoux terms "correlationalism," which I will explore here in some detail as a way to grasp the potential uses and limits of OOO theory in composition theory and practice. I believe that the best way to get at both will require that I walk us backwards into arguments between the realists and idealists about the nature of causation before turning to Meillassoux's response. Ultimately, my argument is that plasticity provides a stronger foundation for understanding of causation, as well as wonder as the experience of difference, of *becoming other*, that characterizes invention as it relates to both writing and learning.

Speculative Realism: Correlationalism, Contingency, and the Subject

For both OOO and SR, philosophy has been burdened by "correlationalism" ever sense Kant's transcendental synthesis. For Meillesoux, "correlationalism" describes "the idea according to which we only ever have access to the correlation between thinking and being, and never to either term considered apart from the other" (5)—an undeniable tendency in philosophy to view the world as if it were there *for* humans, as if the world were only knowable in relation to human usage and imperatives, as if the universe correlated with human purpose writ large. His point is that we should simply abandon this tradition—negotiation no longer being an option. Of course, critiques of the transcendental—by Heidegger, Foucault, and Derrida—have long been underway. Deconstruction, for example, views Kant's categorical imperative, like all transcendental systems, as existing outside of the thing (the "real") that it claims to make intelligible; the transcendental is in fact alien—abiding totally different laws—to the systems that it purports to describe. This is the basic deconstructive move: to reveal the absence, contingent, and supplemental at the center of (metaphysical) presence. Yet, even Derrida and Foucault (self-consciously) retain something of the transcendental in their analyses, preferring to negotiate their way out if it. And as Alex Reid points out, rhetoric too remains tethered to the transcendental: "Rhetoric operates within this correlationist frame, focusing conventionally on symbolic behavior with the premise that we do not have direct access to the world referenced by the symbols." Rhetoric, after all, traces the social and symbolic contexts in which meanings are made, unmoored to any pre-given blueprint. Both continental philosophy and rhetoric, in other words, share a concern with human meaningfulness given that, following the transcendental synthesis, meaning is always *irreducible* to thinking or being, materials or essences.

Kant's transcendental *a priori*—in an attempt to guarantee the stability of the universe, ensuring that the order of things today will remain the same tomorrow—always already discovers the original synthesis between subject and world. But for Meillassoux, there can be no *reason* available to us that could ground the transcendental deduction, and Kant's attempt to theorize the categories was instead a mere description of facts—that is, Kant circularly presupposes and *describes* what he claims to *deduce*. The transcendental itself appears a kind of residue, outside of and irreducible to thinking or being. But for Meillesoux, we cannot believe in *anything* irreducible to the real—the individual essences of things (including ideas and other abstractions) in the world. Indeed, nothing is irreducible for SR. Where Kantians would retort that we cannot know the "thing itself," and that SR is therefore ultimately *reductive*, SR would respond that all such claims are circular. Kant's *a priori* synthesis proposes an originary correlation between the subject and object (or the world), but the laws of the world are not the same thing as the laws of understanding—a failure of the logic of correlationalism. We are not correlated to the world—nature does not, through the transcendental synthesis, belong to us. While it's long been noticed that there is an all-too "convenient" relationship between the workings of Kant's categories and the workings of the world, such that the original syntheses presents the world and objects to us in a way that *just so happens* to be a way that those objects are easily engaged and used, SR does away with the necessity of this agreement.

Meillassoux instead argues that the world is in fact indifferent to our knowledge, characterized by an essential *contingency* and subject to constant change: "the only 'eternal principle' is the factuality of contingency" (59–60). This means not only that there is no correlation between thought and its object, but also that the workings of objects themselves are fundamentally mutable and contingent. In relinquishing the transcendental in favor of the contingent—that is, otherness—Meillessoux undermines the special status that it gives to human subjectivity, demanding that we think the world as totally indifferent to humans. He posits, as Malabou puts it, that: "the correlational structure cannot protect itself against what it is nevertheless supposed to prevent: the thesis of another possible world. A world in which it would not exist" (*Before Tomorrow*). Ultimately, Meillassoux argues that Kant is not able to answer Hume's skepticism about the potential that cause and effect are only related by *chance*, and that the world could become *wholly other than it is*.

However, even Hume's theorization of chance is insufficient to theorizing radical contingency. To theorize this potential for "another possible world," following Alain Badiou, Meillassoux turns to the set theory and the mathematical "transfinite," which distinguishes contingency from chance by arguing that a totalized, infinite set of probabilities is mathematically impossible. Radical contingency demands that we deconstruct *all* totalizations. That is, even if there are *infinite* possibilities given to chance, following Hume, even if our world might have been other than it is, the *concept of chance itself remains the same*. As Meillassoux conceives it: "Chance always presupposes some form of physical invariance—far from permitting us to think the contingency of physical laws, chance itself is nothing other than a certain type of physical law—one that is 'indeterministic' " (Meillassoux 99). The concept of infinite chance—even as it introduces innumerable potentials or possibilities, as in Hume's billiard ball example—relies on stable physical universe in which anything can happen, everything can become other, but only in accordance with stable physical laws that introduce all possibilities. Chance too is correlational. But the concept of the transfinite solves this problem, demonstrating that the totalization of possibility is itself impossible.

For Meillassoux, only this turn to mathematics can allow us to think beyond the chanciness of reality in accordance with its physics or otherwise in accordance with the transcendental principles that give us access to causation. As Malabou summarizes, for Meillassoux, "To separate the possible from all totality—from all the possibles (Hume) and from all the conditions of possibility (Kant)—is the work of the philosophy to come, which marks its rediscovered affinity with mathematics." Again, challenging the transcendental through the mathematical transfinite, Meillassoux wishes to introduce a difference or change into the very possibility of possibility itself. For Meillassoux, because everything is contingent, everything is possible—even the alteration of the mathematical set of possibilities. Chance too is contingent.

The contingency of chance—the impossibility of thinking beyond probability and possibility—is precisely what is *not possible* and beyond reason. However, this unreason "*is*, and can only *be*, the *ultimate* property of the entity. . . . Everything and every world *is* without reason, and is thereby *capable of becoming otherwise without reason*" (53). Contingency is the not possible, that which cannot be converted into any probability. It is a possibility radically other than what is possible, the *difference* within possibility, that is only thinkable through math (as opposed to correlationalism and reason) as a speculation. Finally, for Meillassoux, there is nothing but contingency, no conscious correlation—however variable or historicized (as it is in Foucault)—that ensures that *everything*, including both consciousness and nature itself, cannot be *completely different at any moment*. Therefore, as opposed to viewing "unreason" in terms of epistemic limit, we must rediscover it positively in the world of objects. Meillassoux says this all more clearly than I can, so allow me to rest his case by letting his words speak for themselves:

> we must grasp how the ultimate absence of reason, which we will refer to as 'unreason,' is an absolute ontological property, and not the mark of the finitude of our knowledge . . . the truth is that there is no reason for anything to be or to remain thus and so rather than otherwise, and this applies as much to the laws that govern the world as to the things of the world. Everything could actually collapse: from trees to stars, from stars to laws, from physical laws to logical laws; and this not by virtue of some superior law whereby everything is destined to perish, but by virtue of the absence of any superior law capable of preserving anything, no matter what, from perishing.
>
> (53)

And yet, and yet: things *do* remain the same. We awake every day to what appears to be, precisely, a superior law of stability; whatever system sustains trees and stars never collapses. So Meillassoux has a problem. And as Malabou argues, he tries to get around this problem by arguing that while radical contingency demonstrates that the world could indeed collapse, in order for things to be contingent and without correlation, they also cannot be "anything whatsoever." That is, while anything is possible, contingency means also that *nothing might happen* to things; things are their own facts, separate from human meaning, and therefore the contingent cannot be chaotic (otherwise, Meillasoux stipulates, his argument would be describing chaos as opposed to contingency). The world can't just become *anything* because otherwise contingency becomes chaos. But why, Malabou asks? Why is there no "empirical translation" of contingency? Why can't the world become anything whatsoever? Contingency remains only a mathematical possibility that, like Kant's transcendental, is merely *described* as opposed to *deduced* through empirical phenomenon. Therefore, in arguing against pure reason and the transcendental, against correlationalism, Meillessoux nevertheless makes an essentially transcendental distinction between an "inauthentic" contingency as chaos, and an "authentic" transfinitude that (like Kant's transcendental categories) is positively asserted without being discovered (Malabou "The Future").

Meillassoux's theory of causation and change, rooted in this idea of the contingency chance, is therefore ultimately unsatisfying. Plasticity, as I'll argue in Chapter 3, offers the stronger account, one more useful to understanding learning and writing. On the one hand, SR challenges us to think of writing beyond correlationalism and in terms that erase the boundaries between rhetoric and science. Again, in abandoning the transcendental, in prioritizing ontology, Meillassoux opens new problems for epistemology that we should take seriously in our discipline. For instance, we might consider what writing is in-itself, outside of transcendental subject, besides human purposes; I began with Bogost's theorization of wonder as an example of this (one that we'll return to both later in this chapter and in Chapter 3). However, following Catherine Malabou, I argue that any attempt to abandon the transcendental subject in our field must come through a *negotiation* with reason and the transcendental tradition—especially the work of Kant, Hegel, Nietzsche, Freud, Heidegger, and Lacan—as opposed to an outright *abandonment* (as we see in SR). In Chapter 3, I'll argue for a transgression of the transcendental from a different position—through an understanding of difference, otherness, and change in terms of plasticity.

Composition After OOO: Old Dog, New Tricks?

In order to know things from the SR perspective, as Latour argues, "specific tricks have to be invented to make [objects] talk, that is, to offer descriptions of themselves, to produce scripts of what they are making others—humans or nonhumans—do" (*Reassembling the Social* 79). But what does it mean to return to a mysticism in which we are able to answer to the call (or speech) of enchanted objects? It means, of course, returning to a pre-Kantian way of thinking, which is to say a pre-modern way of thinking. For Bogost, as we've already seen, this might mean, for example, careful investigations of the vicissitudes of how dough rises in different ways (bracketing edibility) to create different varieties and qualities of breads. For Meillassoux, it means adopting mathematics as an "indirect" knowledge of things. For Graham Harman, as we'll see, it means turning to metaphor and other indirect, poetic, and rhetorical ways of knowing. For all, it means a turn to the antithesis of both transcendental scientific empiricism and philosophical critique. Before turning to an extended critique of these and other "tricks," I'll explain Harman's theorization of indirect knowledge.

Bound in, among other things, their commitment to move beyond correlationalism, Meillassoux's SR and Harman's OOO share much in common—including, as we'll see, an unsatisfying account of causation and change. And Meillassoux's critique of correlationalism establishes a firm ground for understanding OOO. However, there are divergences too. In a nutshell, the biggest difference between the two approaches is that OOO maintains that we *cannot* know things-in-themselves through mathematics; after all, Harman maintains, the very moment we speak about a thing, we enter into the cognitive and the discursive which separates our knowledge from the thing. And relatedly, for reasons that I hope will become increasingly clear, Harman rejects Meillassoux's turn to set theory. That said, here I'd like to get at how it is that Harman posits we *can* know things, especially in light of his belief that *rhetoric* can serve as a form and model of the indirect knowledge he champions (a theorization already of interest to rhetoricians).

As opposed to the philosophical tradition that posits the subject and object in dualistic terms—each having their own essence—following Bruno Latour, OOO posits a "flat ontology." Harman explains that all objects—including subjects—possess the same ontological status and need to be equally understood; OOO "holds that the relation of humans to pollen, oxygen, eagles, or windmills is no different in kind from the interaction of these objects with each other" (*Guerilla Metaphysics* 1). As in this quote, Harman frequently punctuates his propositions with lists of diverse, colorful, and whimsical objects as a way of dramatizing this. Indeed, OOO critiques correlationalism by pointing out that humans are one among many objects in the environment, each undergoing its own adventure, bumping against each other, each according to its own intent.

And against the tradition of idealism that ignores objects—variably, following Socrates, in relation to some deeper, unchanging and indestructible reality—Harman unapologetically argues for realism. To accomplish this, he re-interprets Husserl (an obvious idealist), emphasizing his argument about the appearance of objects within intentions. For Husserl, we relate to objects through our intention towards them: "All perception, judgment, love, and hate is perception, judgment, love, or hate *of some object*" ("The Road to Objects"). Against both the metaphysical tradition and biological reduction, Husserl in this way reinforces an *intentionalist* tradition that informs the psychoanalytical, phenomenological, and cognitive psychologies that follow; in this tradition, mental states always have an intentional object (for instance, the emotion "fear" is always *about* some object, even if that object is repressed to consciousness). Harman argues, on the other hand, that objects are essences that precede our cognition of them, discovering—behind Husserl's idealism—a hidden essentialism unrelated to human intent. In this way, OOO, like neuroscience and other posthuman theories, understands *intent* as, somehow, distinct from or prior to symbolic consciousness. Harman argues that Husserl's "most important contribution to philosophy"—an argument with an *anti*-idealist thrust—is to recognize that objects have an essence that precedes cognition. For instance, we know an apple not by experiencing individual qualities—redness, crunchiness, tartness, etc.—compressed together. Instead,

> For Husserl, the experience of an apple is an object-giving act quite apart from the list of qualities it now seems to possess. We can toss the apple in the air, view it from numerous angles, observe it in various

> degrees of sunlight, describe it in moods of euphoria and in crippling depression, but for us it remains the same apple in all these cases.
> ("The Road to Objects")

For conscious experience, there is a "tension" between an object and its qualities. On the one hand, in Husserl we can see that the intentional object is not merely a totality of different empirical qualities, but rather an object that appears *within the envelope of intention*. Harman re-names Husserl's object the "sensual object" (he also calls it the "mediating object," among other terms) recognizing the unity or essence the object retains as it passes through a (sensual) mediation—that is, our conscious image of the object. Again, as opposed to being carved out of some singular lumpen clay by our cognition, objects appear to consciousness according to an essence that shines through their diverse sensuous qualities.

But there is a second kind of object that Harman is really after: the "real object." To understand the distinction, we need to turn to Heidegger, who famously demonstrated that our primary engagement with objects is not, in fact, conscious or sensuous. For example, when I enter a room, I am engaging with numerous objects (such as the floor I walk on, the air I breath, a chair I sit in) that I'm not representing consciously—or, in fact, paying attention to at all. Indeed, it is usually only when an object is *broken*—as Heidegger knew—that is, when it somehow upsets our preconscious image or prediction of the world, that it rises to the level of our attention. It's worth looking closely at what Heidegger's tool analysis means for Harman's theory.

Heidegger's Tool Analysis and the Real Object: What Does Fire Touch?

Across many articles and books, Harman builds on the Heideggarian account of tools. He begins with Heidegger's insight that the reality of objects withdraws from sensuous experience, such that we only ever encounter objects partially or "ready-at-hand." When we encounter a hammer, for example, we encounter it from within a specific situation—the intentionality of *Dasein*—that gives the object a presence or meaning that does not exhaust its possibilities. If I need to weigh down a pile of papers, a hammer will appear to me in a very different way than if I need to insert a nail into a piece of wood, which would be a very different way still than if I needed to defend myself from an attacker. In short, while the essence of the sensuous object is directly present to cognition, while we can touch the sensuous object, we *cannot* touch the real object. The real object is never directly present to us: it always *withdraws* from us.

Harman then expands on Heidegger's thinking on objects "present-at-hand," which is to say, the way objects are supposedly available to disinterested contemplation through different forms of empirical observation. Heidegger's greatest insight was, according to Harman, that "Our primary relationship with objects lies not in perceiving or theorizing about them, but simply in relying on them for some ulterior purpose" ("On Vicarious

Causation" 188). But more than this "first step," Heidegger recognized that, "If perception and theory both objectify entities, reducing them to one-sided caricatures of their thundering depths, the same is true of practical manipulation" ("On Vicarious Causation" 193). That is, both our use of objects (the way the object is "ready-at-hand") and thought about objects (the way the object is "present-at-hand") entail "distortions," the simultaneous revelation and withdrawal of the thing's essence.

Harman extends these insights about tools to emphasize a ramification of Heidegger's theory that Heidegger himself was seemingly only half aware of: objects have a reality of their own independent of—and perhaps indifferent to—their correlation to human cognition. Instead of emerging out of a lumpen, amorphous background, objects for Harman are entirely distinct, possessing their own unique (withdrawn) essence. They are therefore utterly separated: "Dogs do not make contact with the full reality of bones, and neither do locusts with cornstalks, viruses with cells, rocks with windows, nor planets with moons. It is not human consciousness that distorts the reality of things, but relationality *per se*" ("On Vicarious Causation" 193). The question then becomes, how do objects ever touch or affect each other—how do they cause difference and change?

Harman's answer is that objects only touch each other as a dog touches a bone—that is, in a way limited by intent, entailing therefore always a distortion of the object's real essence, a mere characterization of the object's entirety. In this way, Harman pushes Heidegger's tool analysis further by adding the insight that withdrawal characterizes not only human–object relations, but also *object–object* relations. That is, objects relate to each other exactly as humans relate to objects—indirectly, through a *translation*, *characterization*, or *image* of the real thing.

Harman's privileged example comes from Asharite occasionalism, an 11th-century (Islamic) philosophical reaction to Platonic philosophy. In Harman's paraphrase of the occasionalist argument, when cotton burns, the essence of the cotton, despite its obvious transformation, must in its essence remain untouched. This is because the flame has encountered only the *flammability* of the cotton—just one caricature or translation of its manifold essence. Just as humans only have finite relations with things, objects encounter each other only ever partially as caricatures or images of the thing-in-itself: "All real objects of every size now have the power to interact with all other things, at the price of turning them into images" (*Circus Philosophicus* 48). Harman's problem with the Kantian formulation of things-in-themselves, then, lays not in Kant's belief that we can have a knowledge of things, but in that objects too encounter each other only according to finitude.

Harman's "Vicarious Causation": Change, Learning, and the Touch of Objects

Again, just as the thing-in-itself is not present to humans and cannot be touched, things-in-themselves withdraw from each other and cannot directly touch, complicating Kantian causation. Nevertheless, objects do touch in some sense at least, and OOO therefore requires an account of this touch. Paralleling SR's theory of contingency, OOO's theory of the touch is especially important because it is also an attempt to explain causation, change, and emergence. And if OOO is going to have any relevance to writing pedagogy, it will, of course, need to explain how the differences that characterize learning occur. And furthermore, ultimately, it will have to offer a stronger account of learning than other theories, including neuroscience.

Harman calls his theory of the touch "vicarious causation." To better understand Harman's account of vicarious causation, let's look at another example of the touch, the oil rig. An oil rig encounters and touches other objects not directly, but vicariously through the intent of "fuel" (*Circus Philosophicus* 49). That is, the oil rig does not touch the entirety of the objects it encounters, but only a fuel-centric translation—it encounters and experiences *everything* through the lens of its translation, which Harman calls its *intent*. Objects therefore relate to each other, paradoxically, as both one and two ("Vicarious Causation" 197): the oil rig only touches other objects from the inside of the whole of an intent (fuel).

Further, Harman notices that there is an *asymmetry* to object relations: the oil rig is a real object, but what it touches is merely a sensuous translation. The real seabed that the oil rig touches recedes from this relationship, lying outside of the whole of the intentional relationship; for this reason, as opposed to an "equal and opposite reaction" or mutual affectivity, the causal relationship is asymmetrical. Again, the oil rig only relates to—and touches—the other object through the vicarious intermediary of fuel, such that the potential effects of the interaction between the sensuous "fuel-ness" of the seafloor and the seafloor as a real object exceeds the causal input (the oil rig). That is, the oil rig can cause *unexpected* changes to the seabed. From this insight, Harman argues that the Kantian transcendental, the guarantee of causation and knowledge, collapses:

> Let it simply be added that the withdrawal of objects from one another in causal relations turns causality into a serious philosophical problem. For if objects cannot touch directly, then how do they influence one another at all? There must be some third term, some medium through which they interact. Causation must be indirect or vicarious rather than direct and immediate.
>
> (174)

That is, causation, which can never happen directly because essences can't touch each other—objects simply cannot touch all of the qualities of another object—must happen from within the envelope of some vicarious "third term."

Having recognized that objects only touch indirectly, it's finally in response to Latour's theory of the touch that Harman formulates his own. He does this by calling into question Latour's reliance on a theory of systems or networks in which objects interact: "The real problem is not how beings interact in a system: instead, the problem is how they withdraw from that system as independent realities while somehow communicating through the proximity, the touching without touching, that has been termed allusion or allure." Latour gives the example of the discovery of neutrons, asking how the concept of "neutrons" could ever touch "politics" (neutrons after all are on their face entirely apolitical). This touch, Latour argues, required (not unlike Occasionalism) a third object—physicist Frédéric Joliot, who understood their political potential of neutrons in splitting atoms to create weapons. But Harman asks, if politics can't touch neutrons, then why can the subject touch either? Latour keeps pushing the problem backwards in an infinite regress. The nuclear scientist touches neutrons using an instrument, touches the instrument with his eye, touches the eye with the nervous system, touches the nervous system with the brain, and so on. But how do we know where to end? Latour offers the unsatisfying answer that we end where we become "bored." For him, there's no need to theorize the touch if we are simply trying to describe an actor network. But for Harman, he leaves the metaphysical question of the touch on the table (Lator, Harman, and Erdélyi *The Prince* 35). Left without a theory of the touch, as Harman points out, we'd enter into Zeno's paradox.

To resolve this problem, Harman returns to his distinction between the two *kinds* of objects: real and mediating. The touch, *always essentially incomplete*, is enabled through the intermediary object. Again, things never touch or affect each other completely because what they touch is an *image* of the thing. And given that we cannot know things directly in either their parts or in their use, only indirect discourses can explain this touch.

The Intent of Billiard Balls: Inside Husserl's Paradox

As opposed to philosophies where the paradoxes of ontological difference are resolved through appeal to a transcendental depth, all of the action here is on the surface: the only place in the cosmos where interactions occur is the sensual, phenomenal realm. In Harman's words, "Against philosophies that regard the surface as formal or sterile and grant causal power only to shadowy depths, we must defend the opposite view: discrete, autonomous form lies only in the depths, while dramatic power and interaction float along the surface" ("Vicarious Causation" 195). To illustrate this in another register, let's turn to the classical example of Hume's billiard balls. As Hume recognized, billiard balls do not possess within themselves the force to move each other, but rather require the vicarious causation of a third object. In Harman's words, "two entities influence one another only by meeting on the interior of a third, where they exist side-by-side until something happens that allows them to interact" (190). Because they always recede from each other, real objects cannot touch; one billiard ball causes another to move only from within the vicarious mediation or intent of a third object. Therefore, when I see one billiard ball cause another to move, I am not witnessing two "real" billiard balls directly touching. The first billiard ball touches the second, but *only as a sensuous characterization* (it does not touch its essence, after all) that appears on the *inside of an intent*.

For Harman, Hume was right that causation requires a third term: the *interior* of another object is the only place where two real objects can touch, and therefore real objects only ever touch indirectly. What is this intermediary? We know that it cannot be another real object, "or there would simply be an endless process in which the intermediary would need further intermediaries between itself and the other objects, with the result that nothing would ever succeed in touching anything else" (176). Returning to Husserl, Harman argues that the object must be an enveloping intent that joins together objects in its interior. As Harman argues:

> Husserl points out the paradox that intentionality is both one and two. On the one hand, in intentionality there is I myself and then there is the pine tree, not fusing together into a single lump, since the very fact that I am perceiving it proves otherwise. But on the other hand, the intentional relation between me and the pine tree must certainly be one, since we are joined together in the perception rather than being painfully and eternally separated. Given that perceptions are generally held to occur inside the mind, the easy conclusion would be that I and the sensual pine tree meet inside the mind.
>
> (177)

But this cannot be the case because "The sensual object and I cannot meet inside of me" (177). In other words, how can I myself be both the "one" (the meeting point of "I" and the tree) and one half of the "two"?

Following from this, there can be no transcendental synthesis at the level of the subject that joins it with the object. Rather, again, I only touch or relate to the tree indirectly, within an envelope of intent—that is, "on the interior of the relation between me and the real tree" (177). The relation between me and the tree occurs inside of a *new real object* in which we are joined: "So, what we have is the contact between me and the sensual tree on the interior of the relation between me and the *real* one" (177). And the same is true of non-human objects; objects themselves must be understood as intentional: "Intentionality is not a special human property at all, but an ontological feature of objects in general" (205). For Harman, we touch other things only as we might touch a ghost; we reach out towards real things from within the misty envelope of our relation with them. In this way, Harman reconceives the intentionalist tradition passed down from Husserl as existing outside of consciousness and the symbolic—that is, intent describes the way we touch the object without regard to meaning—and as somehow existing both between humans and objects and objects and objects.

So, as we've seen, things too can be said to have intent. Many have argued that this commits Harman to a panpsychism, such that objects themselves have consciousness. For what it's worth, while remaining committed to the intentionality of objects, Harman himself believes that this debate is important but unsettled. If objects do have consciousness, we might have a compelling explanation of the almost mystical experience we have with writing, which, in some sense, seems to write us. We might understand this transformative "touch" of writing in relation to language's own intent. But if we will refuse to embrace a panpsychism, from the perspective of writing theory and pedagogy, all of this raises some significant questions. First, is the distinction that Harman draws between real and sensuous objects really different than Kant's distinction between noumena and phenomena? Wasn't Kant's very point that there there's a world that withdraws from us, one we can't know in-itself, and a world we already know through sensuous experience? Does not Kant's idea of the unknowability of things-in-themselves falsify the OOO reading of correlationalism? And if not, given nothing but the deep isolation of objects, objects outside of relations, how can new objects be created? How can there be change? Finally, returning to pedagogy, how are we to understand writing outside of both (systemic) process and relationality? After all, while nobody would doubt that when we write much of what we do happens unconsciously, as in riding a bike or playing piano, this does not therefore mean that when we write we do so without conscious intent. *And as we'll see, it's precisely the nature of the interplay (the touch) between "unconscious" and conscious intent (between affectivity and meaning) that marks what's special about subjectivity.*

What Accounts for Learning and Change in OOO? Contemplation and Indirect Discourse

I take Harman's difficult essay "On Vicarious Causation," to contain an account of his position on this issue of learning and change: "Those who care only to generate arguments almost never generate objects. New objects, however, are the sole and sacred fruit of writers, thinkers, politicians, travelers, lovers, and inventors" (212). Harman makes clear here that argument, reason, or philosophical critique, "almost never" result in new objects. Critique changes almost nothing. However, Harman traces a mode of "contemplation" that *does* produce difference, a mode very similar to Bogost's wonder. On the one hand, as we've seen, the intention I have towards an object *contains me*, but it does not make me and the intention into a *new* object. Both myself and my intent are (disconnected) real objects, and to form a new object, there would need to be yet another mediation. On the other hand, "two vicariously linked real objects do form a new object, since they generate a new internal space" (207). What does this mean? Through *analysis of our intent*, another vicarious connection is created, and we are then enveloped, along with our intent, within a new intent.

That is, through my *contemplation* of my intent towards a sensuous object, I have created a "new internal space," a new mediating object through which real objects are able to touch in novel ways. In Harman's words: "I have converted that relation into an object for the first time. It has become a real object insofar as its exact nature recedes from view, inexhaustible no matter how many analyses I perform" (207). Our contemplation of intent meets the criteria for being a real object—a concept occupying new internal space. This is how Harman's theory accounts for change, pointing potentially to his understanding of how learning and development might occur. Interestingly, Harman describes this process in terms of the plasticity of the "internal space" of contemplation: "Unified objects can be molded at will from that clay-like interior. This already shows a way for sincere relations to be converted into real connections" (208). Through will—which he uses here a synonym for intent—we can create new connections, but always only from within the interior of another intent that we contemplate.

Harman has thereby outlined one way that new real objects can be created (and relatedly, that learning and development might occur)—that is, through contemplation. He seems, perhaps, to concede that contemplation is something special to human cognition, but hedges, "Whether it is the only such way, and whether this method belongs to humans alone, is still unclear" (208). Harman is now left to consider what, exactly, is the nature of this contemplation as it exists *between objects*, while also defining how it differs from the special techniques of "writers, thinkers, politicians, travelers, lovers, and inventors." In short, is contemplation a special human capacity for creating change, or is it not? Further, given that OOO demands that we think objects beyond their use and in their withdrawal, Harman must explain how, exactly, we can do this. That is, given the withdrawal of distortion of the object's essence as it is given to both thought and use, how can we ever know or use them? "For if objects withdraw from relations," Harman himself recognizes, "we may wonder how they make contact at all" (193). Finally, given that Harman agrees with Kant's famous dictum (which will be explored in further depth below) that we cannot know the *thing-in-itself*, what would a contemplative knowledge of objects in their withdrawal—one that does not refer back to the context-specific usage of the object, nor a transcendental subjectivity—look like?

Harman's surprising answer lays neither in scientific observation nor transcendental critique: "The world is neither a grey matrix of objective elements, nor raw material for a sexy human drama projected onto gravel and sludge" (211). Instead, in a general way, Harman recommends "eidetic variation" as a method to "strip away the noise and confetti of the accidental profiles of a thing, and move toward some sense of what the thing really needs in order to be what it is in the sensual realm." Through this method, we can pass from the sensual to the real of the object to discover the "enduring apple-qualities that the apple must retain for as long as we acknowledge it to be this very apple." In this way, a knowledge of the object also discovers that the "sensual object crosses into the underworld through its possession of *real* qualities as well" (175). Given that real objects too have qualities—such as the hardness or brownness of a wooden chair—they also must be able to affect the sensual. As I've already mentioned, it's when a tool *breaks* that we began to recognize its real qualities; a chair that lacks the quality of stability rises to our attention.

This does not mean, however, that a broken object gives us direct access to the real object. Again, objects don't exist *for us*, and each possesses its own "allure" that beckons to us from within the mysterious depths of the universe. That said, when something breaks, we do suddenly realize that there is a hidden reality to the object, one that that we have gained an indirect knowledge of:

> we are able to get a strange indirect sense of it anyway: our minds do not encounter it directly, but *allude* to it, or see the hammer without seeing it. The sensual qualities of the hammer no longer just swirl around the phenomenal hammer in the mind, but seem to be enslaved to a dark and hidden object that forever eludes our grasp despite its apparently obtrusive malfunction.
>
> (175)

In answer to the question, how do we contemplate essences, Harman's answer is, in short, "indirectly." Here, once again, Harman is close to Heidegger. But does it not also sound like Harman is describing a version of *prediction error*? The protoself also represents an "indirect" and preconscious knowledge of things, as well as the irreducibility of objects and experience to intentionality; however, as opposed to OOO, neuroscience is able to account for the "weird" relationality between unconscious *and* conscious intent. For OOO, the indirect "contemplating of intent" accounts for the production of new knowledge and objects; but lacking here is a satisfying account of how this touch between preconscious intent and conscious contemplation occurs. As we've already begun to see, while neuroscience allows us to understand intent in terms of the brain's affective surplus and active predictions, everything is complicated by the brain's fundamental relationality with the social, conceptual, and linguistic order of consciousness. A question is emerging: which, OOO or neuroscience, offers a stronger account of the touch?

Zizek's Critique of OOO: The Weirdness of Subjects

On the one hand, OOO offers an important critique of network and ecological theories as they have influenced composition and rhetoric. Following Husserl's phenomenology, OOO begins with the premise that things exist "out there" in their singularity as opposed to being carved out of some indiscriminate gray lumpen mass by conscious experience. One consequence of this is that objects have a reality that is relatively stable even as it withdraws. For example, although my hometown Washington, DC has undergone great changes over the course of its existence, OOO offers a plausible argument that it nevertheless retains a (withdrawn) unified essence. To argue otherwise, Harman believes, would be to theorize an impossible flux in which objects are constantly formed and reformed within networks, that an object is not identical with itself as the ecology changes. Such theories have the strange consequence that objects are both constantly composed and emerging, and also that they are indestructible—after all, a car that explodes in a given ecology has merely changed its relationship to that environment, taking on its new composition. Latour, for instance, argues that when we move a few feet to change our perspective on our environment, we are in some sense, given that we've altered the network, not the same thing we were before. In other words, for Harman, these network accounts of objects fail to envision the *surplus* in every system, the inherent potential objects to be more than their *image* in that system.

By insisting that we focus on objects in themselves as opposed to the relational "wholes" in which humans encounter them, OOO demands that any theory of networks account for emergence and change. This should be taken seriously. OOO itself claims to be able to theorize differences to the extent that objects always embody an *unactualized surplus* that *cannot be found in systems*. This surplus is the object's *allure*, the way objects beckon to each other in their concealment, the way we are affected by objects (and objects each other) that always contains the potential for novelty. This returns us to the question of wonder, which OOO places on the side of the object and its allure. And as we'll see in Chapter 3, neuroscience offers a radically different account of wonder in theorizing both affect and novelty. From the perspective of neuroscience, neural networks do indeed include an unrealized surplus. This surplus is of course the brain's *plasticity*, and given that our strongest understanding of plasticity comes from the neuroscientific study of the subject, as I'll argue, it appears that OOO and SR are working the wrong side of the ontological divide. Ultimately, neurobiology offers a stronger (and far clearer) account than does OOO or SR of the differences and changes entailed in learning.

But before turning to Malabou's own account of wonder, it's useful to understand Zizek's critique of OOO's critique of the subject ("Afterword: Objects, Objects Everywhere"), which at a few key points intersects with neurobiological theory. As we've seen, OOO rejects the subjectivist argument that we must reflect critically upon our cognitive apparatus before analyzing the real. But for Zizek, OOO's prioritization of the ontological comes at the cost of an epistemological displacement predicted in Kant's antinomies: "we reach the object in itself not by somehow seeing through these epistemological distortions but by transposing epistemological obstacles into the thing itself." In other words, Zizek argues that Meillassoux "transposes what appear to be transcendental partisans of finitude as the limitation of our knowledge . . . into the most basic positive ontological property of reality itself—the absolute '*is simply the capacity-to-be-other as such, as theorized by the agnostic*' " (178). While I've already begun to explain the limits of this theorization of the capacity of the world to be other than it is via Malabou above, Zizek further contends that OOO fails to account of the "weirdness" of the subject that only exists *in relation* to objects, somehow—as we've already begun to see relative to neuroscience, which understands the brain forming in between biological code and social-symbolic inscription—both within and outside of nature.

OOO theorizes the touch between objects in relation to a kind of "blind spot"; in their withdrawal, objects, as we've seen, always remain blind to something when they touch other objects: "each autopoietic system is self-enclosed in the sense that it selectively interprets external perturbations, so that the In-itself remains its inaccessible blind spot" (183). For example, a new electric razor that has fallen into a manhole retains the potential to shave only as a virtuality that will never be realized in its relations with other objects. The object is in this way divided between the totality of its reality (Levi Bryant's "volcanic core"), which constantly withdraws from it, and its surface relation to other objects. But Zizek asks, "in what sense can it be said that it implies the self-withdrawal of the object, not just the withdrawal of its virtual core for other objects which interact with it" (184)? Zizek contests the premise that essences withdraw, arguing that the electric razor's ability to shave remains—that, while its surface relations to other objects may withdraw, as opposed to the subject, the inner core never withdraws from itself. Indeed, "the object's inner virtual 'volcanic core' is withdrawn from the surface of its relations to other objects, but this inner core is still fully there, not withdrawn from itself in any sense" (184). In other words, in what sense is the object withdrawn to itself in the way the subject is? In what sense does the subject possess a self-essence to withdraw from in the first place?

For Zizek, OOO's theorization of withdrawal is shallow to the extent that it theorizes the Real precisely as the "blind spot" of objects withdrawing from our relation to them. However, the situation with the subject is essentially different: "the blind spot is not simply the mark of the inaccessibility of the transcendent In-itself, but the inscription of the perceiving subject itself into reality—the hole in reality is not simply the excess of the In-itself" (183). From Zizek's Lacanian perspective, on the other hand, the Real is not this withdrawal of objects in-themselves, but rather our "subjective excess"—the distorting *blot* through which we perceive reality. Ultimately, in order for there to be self-withdrawal, there has to be "a Self from which its own substance is withdrawn—and one cannot in any meaningful sense call the actual relations of an object to other object this object's Self" (184).

For Lacan, we see the world only from the interior of language—a limitation not visible to us from within. Is this the same thing as OOO's vicarious causation, where objects only encounter each other from within their intent, that is, on the inside of their own "constructing frame"? If this were the case, then we'd be a long way down the road towards Harman's theory that subjects encounter objects in the same way objects encounter objects, making writing and language but one object among others, complicating our conventional biases towards the symbolic and discourse. Taking Harman's position, Alex Reid argues, "If the hammer sees everything in the world as a nail, perhaps writing sees everything in the world as discourse." However, Zizek argues that the situation with language is different, that language and material reality exist at different levels, and do not ever touch. For Zizek, OOO and SR confuse Lacan's Real and real with Kant's thing-in-itself and its phenomenology. The thing-in-itself in Lacan is not "a brutal raw Real outside of or preceding the Symbolic" (185). Instead, Zizek argues that the thing-in-itself is a "weird thing" that is in fact "purely fantasmatic"; it is, "the absolute-incestuous object that would fully satisfy our desire or that would bring full *jouissance*." Therefore, *das Ding* is both radically external to the symbolic order and radically internal to it; or as Zizek puts it, "it is a specter of absolute Otherness generated by the distance from the Real introduced by the Symbolic." In other words, while material things are indeed "out there" and independent of us, the thing-in-itself "as the absolute point of reference behind and beneath these things is precisely what the subject adds to things, its fantasmatic projection/construction" (185).

Yet, Lacan claimed that we experience reality from within the frame of language—is he thereby making language a transcendental exception to the Real? To answer this, Zizek argues that language in its use and the formal linguistic structure behind it are both shaped by social antagonisms. Therefore, "When we conceive language as a mirror which is always already distorted/traversed by the pathology of social antagonism, we ignore *the way this mirror is itself included into the reality as a mode of its distortion*" (187). For example, we diagnose pathologies based on how subjects use speech; however, as Zizek argues, "at a certain key point, psychic turmoil itself is a reaction to the trauma of dwelling in the 'torture-house of language'" (187). That is, language is not just a distorted mirror onto reality, but is also inscribed into reality such that its distortions or antagonisms are themselves a part of it (posing an original trauma, which is the reality of our experience dwelling in language).

Therefore, for Zizek, as opposed to flattening the subject and object in reality, a materialist analysis must grasp that subjectivity, in addition to being limited by language, emerges through the traumatic experience of language as a "cut in the Real." In this way, the subject is not the same as substance; the duality or split in the subject is "much more radical" (187) than the withdrawal of objects. Where objects are split by the phenomenological appearance (qualities) to other objects and the withdrawal of their virtual "volcanic core," the subject is "divided between its appearance and the void in the core of its being" (188). This void is not some hidden virtuality, but rather that which is always in play on the surface of the subject, the "torture-house" of its composition. The subject is precisely the "cut in the Real," that which marks a gap or void or opening in the Real. The subject is in this way a special kind of object that Lacan called *object a*, an object that is not only withdrawn, but a "weird" embodiment of its own lacking, an anamorphosis.

As Zizek argues, the subject has no *substance*, existing only in its relations to other objects, objects that appear in the cut or gap in the real that characterizes the subject. The subject cannot just be another object with additional and distinctive qualities. Or again, objects in-themselves are what appear in the "cut in the Real" initiated by the desiring subject; and by the same turn, the substance of objects is what gives content to the desiring subject. Furthermore, given that the subject takes shape *in relation* to the objects of its desires, the critique of ideology has renewed importance as the specific nature of these desiring relations comes into question. Finally, for Zizek, any attempt to get around the subject in thinking objects in-themselves itself entails a transcendental vision of reality *that is itself subjective*.

The Brain as Weird Object: The Limits of OOO in the Study of Rhetoric

As we've seen here through Zizek's critique, in order for the self to withdraw from itself in the manner postulated by OOO, there has to be a Self *qua* "real object" for other objects to withdraw from. Significantly, however, Zizek points out that objects in their withdrawal from us (and from each other) cannot meaningfully be called their "Self." What neuroscience adds to Zizek's argument about the "weirdness" of subjective excess—the special way in which the subject is divided between the withdrawn unconscious and the appearance of the Self on its surface—is an enriched understanding of that weirdness. From the perspective of neuroscience, the "blot" that is our dwelling within language is our affective embodiment, the way our body registers—before meaning—its ongoing encounters with Otherness made meaningful by language (or what Lisa Feldman Barrett terms the "categorization" function of language).

Through neuroscience, we can witness Zizek's Lacanian decentered "Self" at the material level. Neuroscience presents us with a "Self" that is constantly formed and reformed within ongoing neuronal predictions; a "Self" that, as Zizek suggests, is more a "void" than "molten core"; a "Self" that is real only to the extent that its self-prediction continues to efficiently match both the embodied sensations that emerge in its relations to the Other, as well as the purposeful social contexts in which those sensations are conceptually interpreted. As we'll see, neuroscience has shown that neither need be the case. That is, one's concept of "Self" may no longer match one's affective experience. And further, one's concept of "Self" will need to be constantly revised in relation to social reality.

In a word, in learning as in self formation, neuroscience presents us with *plasticity*. In demonstrating that the subject's attunement, through attention to prediction error, *actively constructs* the world, plasticity presents a more compelling and strange account of the levels of causation OOO attempts to describe.

Recall from Chapter 1 that the "outfielder problem" demonstrates that in acting into the world, humans position the body to make the world conform to their predictions. The intention to act becomes self-fulfilling, as predictions don't precede but rather determine sensory input. But as I'll argue here, OOO suffers from a version of what neuroscientists term "affective realism"—that is, our projection of our "gut feelings" onto things in the world—the belief that "objects and people in the world are inherently negative or positive" (Malabou *How Emotions Are Made* 75). What OOO fails to realize, like the classical theory of emotions, is that our affective state—itself determined through a rhetorical relationality with external subjects and objects—determines both how we will perceive (predict) objects in the world as well as what we will see in the first place. That is, we hallucinate the world first and then confirm it; perception, as Andy Clark frequently points out, is "controlled hallucination."

Finally, important works in our field influenced by new materialism—such as Dianne Davis' *Inessential Solidarity* and Thomas Rickert's *Ambient Rhetoric*—are themselves theorizing rhetoric in terms of this material *relationality*, and this puts them at odds with Harman's OOO. Davis' theory is explicitly a theory of finitude and affective relationality, arguing that the social emerges out of fundamental, pre-symbolic affective engagements. Again, materialist theories—and this is why Harman is against materialism—reduce objects to their *relations* (e.g., neuroscience discovers the relations between brain and mind), such that the nature of the relationship is driven by the reduction that enables it. For instance, physics gives us the "spatio-temporal co-ordinates and tangible properties that can be measured, but all these features have meaning only in relation to other things" ("Intentional Objects"). Harman himself describes the difference between actor-network theory (ANT) and his own theory as follows: "rather than give objects their full independence, he defines them in terms of their *relations* . . . There are no objects in Latour's actor-network theory, at least not the kind we are looking for" ("Intentional Objects", my emphasis). ANT is essentially relational, and thoroughly materialist. In short: "there are no object [sic] in materialism" ("Intentional Objects").

Rickert is right to point out that rhetoric, reflecting the realist/idealist dichotomy, has long focused on objects only in either practical or theoretical terms. And it's true that Harman also shares this concern in his approach to objects. Like OOO, Rickert's ambient rhetoric offers one way of potentially getting outside of these perspectives. However, far from bracketing or flattening the significance of the social and public purposes of rhetoric, Rickert's ambient rhetoric—unlike Harman's OOO—is finally interested in how the ambient persuades at the level of public effects or meanings, forming the "background of intelligibility" (5). Or again, he's interested in how the ambient becomes salient: "Rhetoric may give priority to the expressly salient, but the salient must take part in and emerge from the ambient" (x). It is finally the *relation* between the ambient and the salient that Rickert is interested in. Rickert's concern here is important for writing pedagogy, especially as it pertains to the question of how writing technologies affect human beings:

> Today, as the digitization and externalization of information through networks and other media accelerate, and as ubiquitous computing

> (also called ambient intelligence, among other labels) comes into its own and promises further radical transformations of the built environment, we are confronted quite strikingly with the question of our relation to that technologized world—and its relation to us.
>
> (4)

It is doubtlessly given this concern that Rickert has always already conceived of his rhetoric in terms of materialism, relationality, and—perhaps most importantly—in terms of the causative "blowback" of things.

Notes

1. Tacology is the study of tacos.
2. It's worth noting here that the affect "wonder" is equally inspiring and horrifying, beautiful and sublime.

Works Cited

Barnett, Scott. "Toward an Object-Oriented Rhetoric." *Enculturation*, 7, 2010, p. 2. Barrett, Lisa F. *How Emotions Are Made: The Secret Life of the Brain*. Houghton Mifflin Harcourt, Boston, MA, 2017.

Barthes, Roland. *Mythologies*. Le Seuil, Paris, 2015.

Behm, Nicholas, Sherry Rankins-Robertson, and Duane H. Roen. *The Framework for Success in Postsecondary Writing: Scholarship and Applications*. Parlor Press, Anderson, SC, 2017.

Bogost, Ian. *Alien Phenomenology, or, What It's Like to Be a Thing*. University of Minnesota Press, Minneapolis, MN, 2012.

Brown, James, and Nathaniel Rivers. "Composing the Carpenter's Workshop." *O-Zone: A Journal of Object Oriented Studies*, vol. 1, 2013, pp. 27–36.

Covino, William. *Forms of Wondering*. Boynton, Portsmouth, NH, 1990.

Gries, Laurie. *Still Life With Rhetoric: A New Materialist Approach for Visual Rhetorics*. University Press of Colorado, Boulder, CO, 2015.

Harman, Graham. *Guerrilla Metaphysics: Phenomenology and the Carpentry of Things*. Open Court, Chicago, IL, 2005.

———. "On Vicarious Causation." *Collapse*, vol. 2, 2007, pp. 171–205.

———. *Circus Philosophicus*. John Hunt Publishing, Alresford, 2010.

———. "The Road to Objects." *Continent*, vol. 1, no. 3, 2011, pp. 171–179.

Hawk, Byron. *A Counter-History of Composition: Toward Methodologies of Complexity*.University of Pittsburgh Press, Pittsburgh, PA, 2007. ProQuest ebrary. Web. 8 June 2016.

Hume, David. *Of the Standard of Taste: Selected Essays*. Oxford University Press, Oxford, 1998.

Kant, Immanuel. *Critique of Pure Reason: The Cambridge Edition of the Works of Immanuel Kant*. Cambridge University Press, Cambridge, UK, 1998.

Latour, Bruno. *Reassembling the Social*.Oxford University Press, Oxford, 2005.

Latour, Bruno, Graham Harman, and Peter Erdélyi. *The Prince and the Wolf: Latour and Harman at the LSE*. John Hunt Publishing, Alresford, 2011.

Malabou, Catherine. "The Future of Continental Philosophy." *Youtube*, uploaded by European Graduate School Video Lectures, 21 January 2015, www.youtube.com/watch?v=XSwdelsSQPU.

———. *Before Tomorrow: Epigenesis and Rationality*. Polity Press, Malden, MA, 2016.
Meillassoux, Quentin. *After Finitude: An Essay on the Necessity of Contingency*. Trans. Ray Brassier. Continuum, London, 2008. Print.
Reid, Alex. "Composing Objects: Prospects for a Digital Rhetoric." *Enculturation*, vol. 14, 2013. Web. 1 April 2013.
Rickert, Thomas. *Ambient Rhetoric: The Attunements of Rhetorical Being*. University of Pittsburgh, Pittsburgh, PA, 2013. Web.
Rivers, Nathaniel. "We Have Never Been Critical." *Iteneration*, http://tundra.csd.sc.edu/itineration/node/52
Sullivan, Patrick. "The UnEssay: Making Room for Creativity in the Composition Classroom." *College Composition and Communication*, vol. 67, no. 1, 2015, p. 6.
Vygotsky, Lev Semenovich. *Mind in Society: The Development of Higher Psychological Processes*. Harvard University Press, Cambridge, MA, 1980.
Žižek, Slavoj. "Afterword: Objects, Objects Everywhere." *Slavoj Žižek and Dialectical Materialism*. Palgrave Macmillan, New York, 2016, pp. 177–192.

3 To Care or Not to Care

The Supposed Indestructability of Wonder

What might the OOO pedagogy of wonder and indirect knowledge look like in practice? Take, for example, Ian Bogost's critique of the show *The Wire*. *The Wire*, Bogorst argues, unfolds as a drama that, as opposed to developing a knowledge of the objects in its universe (ranging from Maryland Transit Authority buses to bottles of Colt 45 malt liquor), instead "ignores" these objects in its "correlational" pursuit of truths about the human condition. In short, *The Wire* is "incapable of giving its viewers any sensation of the constituent parts of its subject (Baltimore), unless those parts are mediated by the actions of its human agents" (115). I imagine, on the other hand, that Bogorst would celebrate the new trend in Norway, where around half the country is tuning in to watch "slow television" productions of, for example, *Knitting Evening*, which traces the production of a sweater for nine hours, or another show that traces the chopping of wood and production of a fire over 12 hours (Russell).

In these shows, as producer Rune Møklebust explains, there is no narrative or story imposed top-down onto the content, but instead the story emerges organically; the "stars" of the shows, often objects and animals, reveal their own stories. In one episode that simply follows a wondering cow, viewers at first watch as it ambles around a river; eventually, however, they want to know why the cow is doing what it's doing, curious as to where it could possibly be going and why (Russell). In other words, objects that are initially in the background slowly reveal different qualities in their interactions with other objects, disclosing something of their hidden depths in a drama that unfolds without the imposition of narration. Bogorst might say that these shows appeal and persuade through an attunement to objects and ambiance. A composition pedagogy informed by OOO might cultivate this kind of rhetorical attunement, this an openness to objects, as a heuristic.

There are other potential uses of OOO for composition pedagogy as well. Laurie Gries, for instance, has developed a rhetorical methodology for tracing the rhetorical circulation of images across new media, describing their adventures into new (and often unintended) configurations of signification. And take for example this recommendation by OOO philosopher, and former college writing teacher, Levi Bryant: Tracing the etymology of the word *ethos*, Bryant suggests that rhetoricians extend their definition in light of OOO theory. He argues that, "Rather than treating *ethos* as the features of credibility an audience attributes to a speaker, we should instead see *ethos* as referring to the *ecology* of ideas or texts within which people *live*." In short, Bryant recommends an "epidemiological approach" to *ethos* that will enable rhetors to take advantage of the geography of ideas—that is, the fact that ideas are more likely to be accepted, understood, and available in some places rather than others. As a result, "the ability of a rhetor to persuade an audience will not simply be a function of whether they're seen as credible by their audience, but rather whether or not their enunciations resonate with the *ecology of ideas* within which the people dwell" ("Rhetoric, Ideology, and the Ecology of Ideas"). Bryant's insight clearly reflects the priorities of OOO, and resonates nicely with ecological theories of rhetoric. It's not difficult to imagine other similar uses of OOO to, if not redefine, at least supplement our work.

After all, recent rhetorical theory similarly demands that we move beyond symbolic accounts of rhetoric and writing as well as the subject. It is doubtlessly for this reason that OOO and SR appears now to many rhetoricians as the "heir apparent" to Heideggarian destruction and Derridian deconstruction. New materialism points to modes of inquiry and understanding beyond reason and symbolic critique; and for writing teachers, this is appealing because it suggests ways to forefront *invention* as opposed to *anti-rhetorical* symbolic mastery. We can understand the significance of Bogorst's wonder in terms of invention. In recommending a pedagogy of wonder, Bogorst follows OOO to suggest that wonder adheres to, or emanates from, ordinary objects, forming a "shell" around them. In this way, Bogorst argues for wonder as a kind of purified "interest," an *attunement* to the world that will enable students to invent and create as opposed to merely replicate discourse. Bogorst's theory of wonder is well represented in our field in Brown and Rivers' multimodal composition pedagogy; wonder, they claim, will allow students "to *invent* new ways of producing meaning through an attunement to the constraints and affordances of new media" (31). Rickert too theorizes invention—beyond the persuasive symbolic performances of humans—in terms of an attunement to our entanglement in environments, bringing into play the persuasiveness of moods and affects as well as things and circulations. In these theorizations, wonder, as the ground level of our affective interface with the world, becomes a *method for rhetorical attunement*, a way to transcend our logocentism and greet objects through their allure.

But what is this "allure" or wonder if not a form of the (co)relationality that Bogort and Harman deny object relations? While I've tried to mark some interesting potentialities for what Laurie Gries calls an object oriented rhetoric in her essay "Agential Matters: Tumbleweed, Women-Pens, Citizens-Hope, and Rhetorical Actancy," for reasons I began to develop in the last chapter, I also believe we should be skeptical of an "object turn" in rhetoric. In addition to Malabou's critique of SR's account of change, and Zizek's critique of OOO around the weirdness of the subject, we can see from the perspective of our own discipline the problem affectivity introduces to thinking subjects as objects (and of thinking objects without subjects). On the one hand, the *pathos* of *things* has long been understood in our discipline. And yet, as Lance Langdon, interviewing Daniel Gross, points this out, the *pathos* of the subject is different: "You write, following Aristotle I think, that '[T]he pathos of stone allows it to become a part of the wall, the pathos of a plant to grow, the pathos of an animal to perceive imminent danger and shriek a warning to others.'" However, Langdon characterizes Gross' argument about how this understanding of *pathos* is complicated in the subject:

> you note that even as we humans share this capacity for movement with inanimate objects, we are unique in our capacity to imagine, our *nous poietikos*, 'the human faculty that allows us to extend into every domain of being and be moved even by things that are not there in body.' So, pathos involves a distinctly human type of orientation.

What's different here is the kind of touch, causation, or suasion that characterizes human desire. Where OOO argues for the importance of understanding the world as indifferent to human designs, neuroscience theorizes a destructive human indifference that is *indifferent even to its own indifference*, offering, as we'll see, a "weirder" and more radical account of causation and the touch. It is also for this reason that the "more basic sense" of our *nous poietikos* "points to our being as a conduit, a vessel, for outside powers" (Langdon). In short, understanding the weirdness of the neuroscientific subject returns us to the question of the relation between radical contingency (otherness), affectivity, and power.

SR and OOO open up important questions about form, consciousness, causation, and change that challenge basic assumptions about knowledge and learning. However, in bracketing the subject, in simply discarding the transcendental, these theories also—in the name of overcoming "correlationalism" and finitude—discard the significance of *desire* and *care* to learning invention and learning in general. As we'll see by further following Malabou's neurophilosophical account of wonder, our understanding of pedagogical care is closely tied to the question of the relation between power and pedagogy. Yet, for OOO, moving beyond correlationalism means precisely no longer caring about the relationality between human subjects and the world. Recall in the last chapter Bogorst's argument (echoed in our own field by Rivers) that our logocentric privileging of forms of reasoned critique and inquiry (including science) works against our student's natural interest in things: "the real obstacle to youthful interest in science arises not from a distaste for mathematics or the natural world but from a latent dissatisfaction with the way science melts the shell of wonder around ordinary objects" (129).

From this perspective, it is because so much pedagogy—compromised by its imbrications in human purpose—disrupts the allure of real objects that Bogorst argues that care in fact works *against* learning. "To wonder," as Bogorst defines it, "is to respect things as things in themselves" (131); that is, to respect things is to not care about their uses and correlations for humans. And for Bogorst, wonder is too often construed by educators in terms of rational intent: "wonder becomes an intentional curiosity, the equivalent of Martin Heidegger's *care* (*Sorge*)" (129). In this way, Bogorst critiques pedagogical care, via Heidegger, as the apogee of Meillassoux's correlationalism; care viewed this way opens the subject to indoctrination to the symbolic order, as opposed to a deep knowledge of things. Care just gets in the way, for the allure of objects secures the purity of wonder; therefore, in wondering, students might *resist having to care*.

However, as I'll argue below, I think Bogorst misreads Heidegger's account of care. But moreover, wonder, viewed outside of relationality and finitude, acquires a stability for Bogorst that pathological neuroscience calls into question. In Bogorst's theorization, through wonder real objects are "suspended" in between their intrigue and their utility; wonder, "like Iris's rainbow" (129), which suspends the goddess Iris as she delivers her message, is both the medium and the sign. That is, where an object's intrigue and usefulness may dissolve, wonder itself remains—like a rainbow—as a *trace*. Wonder traces a supplemental system of difference that enables (through its "suspension") objects to engage each other in their allure. And viewed in terms of a suspension or trace, wonder remains—as I'll argue in relation to Derrida's theory of the trace below—essentially *indestructible*. As the (indirect) interface between real objects—the mark of our "poetic" and metaphorical (i.e., indirect) relation to things—wonder's own quality, lacking finitude, cannot be called into question.

In short, Bogost's distinction between wonder and care itself comes close to the transcendental, as wonder becomes the guarantee of a touch that is both undeconstructed and indestructable. *In OOO as well as in Derrida, there remains a transcendental residue, a trace that can never be accounted for at the level of the material*: and in both, there is a "poetic" or indirect discourse that remains undeconstructed. Neuroscience—as we can see in the plasticity of neuronal traces—complicates this picture, demonstrating at a material level that wonder is in fact relational, finite and, indeed, delicate. And it is the delicacy of wonder that requires that we understand the relationship between writing pedagogy and power.

Malabou's Spinoza: The Affects of Power

In the Introduction and Chapter 1, we began to see the rhetorical relationship between affect and power. For instance, as Langdon, Belli, Abraham, and Gross and Alexander all remind us, the recent focus on positivity has links to contemporary neo-liberalism and divestment in education. In other words, through its focus on positive productivity, under the banner of care, writing instruction repeats the work of power. As Jill Belli argues, the positive education movement "echo[s] the shift towards neoliberal values and austerity measures over the last decade. . . . In a very real way, then, the struggle against positive psychology and positive education is also the struggle against austerity, contingency, and the mandate to do more with less." Furthermore, as I argued in Chapter 1, the focus on positive emotions does not recognize the value of failure to learning, viewing writing education solely in terms of jobs and productivity. Again, the rhetoric of positivity and productivity reflects the situation of power in neo-liberal capitalism, trading on the reduction of plasticity to flexibility.

But through Malabou's neurophilosophical account, we gain a more complicated understanding of the relations between rhetoric, power, and biology—i.e., bio-power. Malabou, as we'll see, describes an essentially *fragile* relationship between affect, the brain, and power under neo-liberalism. In short, it's not just that neo-liberalism requires a flexible productivity that reduces our plasticity, it also requires that we *do not care* about this. And as we'll see, writing pedagogy not only repeats the work of neo-liberal power in requiring flexible productivity, but potentially also in inspiring a careless *indifference* to this situation (and indifference to our own indifference). But to understand the contemporary situation through which affect is related to power, we need to begin with an understanding of Malabou's theory of wonder as a capacity for care, action, and meaning making.

Classically, wonder is the capacity to be surprised or astonished at the unfamiliar, the other, without judgment. It attunes the subject to objects in the world as well as to the interior experience of the self (as an object). In this Cartesian formulation, the subject is "touched" by wonder and other affects, and consciousness (what is touched) is thereby understood to *preexist* affect. For Descartes—whose account of wonder began a conversation inherited, as we'll see, by Spinoza, Heidegger, Derrida, Deleuze, Damazio, and finally Malabou—the main function of wonder is to reveal to us that of which we were previously ignorant by way of a "pure openness" to alterity, to both good and bad things in the world (Johnston & Malabou 17). As the first of Descartes' "passions," wonder is the primary affect to the extent that, characterizing an affective openness world—as opposed to an already joyful or sad relationship to it—it occurs prior to experiences of feelings, consciousness, and reason. It is the affect that opens us to reflect on *difference*, preceding and inspiring meaning making in general. All of this follows from the Aristotelian tradition in which wonder is the *affect of reason*. In other words, as Malabou explains in her lecture "Emotional Life in the Neurobiological Age: On Wonder," wonder is the feeling of surprise at the *reflective*[1] relationship between mind and body, self and world. Therefore, as the originary affect that precedes all others, as the feeling of the reflective relationship between the mind, body, and world, wonder is the *philosophical emotion*. As the origins of humanity's quest for truth and knowledge, it is also *indestructible* precisely because it is the essence of what makes us human, the affective foundation of the transcendental reason separating the human from the animal.

For both Descartes and Spinoza, as Malabou demonstrates, "wonder is what attunes the subject both to the world and to itself" (Johnston & Malabou 9), and the other affects are positive and negative variations on wonder that give texture to the temporal experience of consciousness. Neither positive nor negative, classical wonder is therefore essentially *dispassionate*; it is our reaction to objects before we judge them, the prelude to our judgment or thought about them. Malabou follows Luce Irigaray in emphasizing this pre-predictive aspect of wonder. We wonder before judging: "To wonder is to open oneself up to difference before granting it a value or establishing hierarchies. The anteriority of wonder to judgement. . . . Wonder is the passion of difference" (*Changing Difference* 11). It is our originary openness to otherness, the pure sensation of our existence—the touching of our autobiographical consciousness, the "I," and our affective protoself.

Malabou situates her theory of wonder in relation to Spinoza's, with the insights granted by neuroscience. This requires that she take into account the historical relationships between affect and power. For Spinoza, in interpreting or mapping the overall state of the organism, emotions modulate—increase or decrease—the power to persist, to act. As Spinoza argued through his theory of the *conatus*, when we feel joy, we feel more open—open to action, open to difference—whereas when we are sad, we are more pliable and obedient, lacking the power to act. Joy, in effect, is the increase in the power of self-determination; sadness, on the other hand, results in a lack of agency. In *Ethics* E2P7, Spinoza further argued that this increase or diminishment in the power to act is identical to the ability to think—"the order and connection of things is identical to the order and connection of ideas." As a result, the sad subject is more easily controlled by external forces, objects, and the other in general; indeed, Spinoza recognized that power required the "sad passions" in order to function in his time. In his "Theological-Political Treatise," as Deleuze points out, Spinoza claims that the power of the despot and the power of the priest draw from this same source—in short, that they both require an increase in the *sad passions*. Where power of the priest requires *repentance*, the despot requires *hopelessness*, and both are facilitated where the subject feels less capable of acting. In other words, both forms of power required the suppression of the subject's ability to act, to think, in order to change their own situation.

But does power today still require sad passions? And given what we've seen about contemporary neuroscience, is it still the case that increased sadness enables objects and the other to have increased power over us? Looked at one way, it's as if the situation has reversed itself. After all, the composition theorists cited above are arguing that it's *positivity* that has a relation to power in neo-liberal capitalism. And by theorizing the co-opting of wonder by power, OOO comes to a similar—but different, given to the extent that it brackets the question of care altogether—conclusion. Relatedly, as I argued in Chapter 1, we know that the reduction and control of plasticity today involves fostering an ostensibly positive, productive flexibility. However, as Malabou's theorization of wonder demonstrates, power today requires neither positive nor negative affects, but instead the capture of wonder itself. As Malabou argues, while in the classical account of affect, wonder has *no opposite*—affectability is viewed as essentially indestructible—neuroscience shows that that the opposite of wonder, the breaking point of flexibility, is a totally destructive *disaffection*. Therefore, in the motor scheme of plasticity, power requires not sadness—which can always be converted therapeutically to happiness—but precisely disaffection, the preclusion of the therapeutic conversion of sad affects.

Given this, as we'll see, a rhetorical understanding of *pathos*, of empathy, cannot help in this situation, for this presumes that a symbolic command over emotion can stand in for embodied experience. Nor can we simply teach *writing as process* to instill productive positivity and flexibility. And of course, in the face of disaffection, critique is useless (equally useless is the supposed allure of objects in inspiring wonder). To demonstrate this, I'll follow Malabou's neurological theory of wonder as it relates to power by further developing the complexity of her theory of explosive plasticity; in doing so, I'll continue to argue for the importance of Malabou's account of plasticity to writing pedagogy—that is, for the importance of plasticity as a habit of mind. Ultimately, I'll argue that the neuroscientific account of wonder requires that we theorize not only how we inculcate emotional intelligence and inspire wonder in our students, but also the productive and destructive dimensions of *writing technologies* that mediate the affective experience of wonder and conscious processes of writing and reasoning.

Deleuzian and Derridian Critiques of Classical Wonder

In order to understand Malabou's neurophilosophical contribution to wonder, we need to begin with the Deleuzian and Derridian critiques of the classical account that she builds upon. This returns us to questions opened in Chapter 2 about the nature of "the touch," for, as we know, wonder in the classical account is the affect of the subject's self encounter with difference, with the other. In critiquing classical metaphysics, Deleuze and Derrida (each in their own way, as we'll see) asked in what sense it is that conscious experience "touches" affective embodiment. For Kant, as we know, the subject is divided between transcendental apperception and empirical sensations (what Foucault called the "transcendental-empirical doublet"), such that the "I" does not have access to its transcendental forms. "I" cannot know myself in terms of what gives rise to my thinking, since I can only know myself through that thinking. Heidegger called this "touch" *auto-affection*. In brief, auto-affection describes the experience of inner-speech, the way thought addresses another within. The paradox of the subject as both one and two, both a unity and a division, has caused all sorts of problems for philosophy: auto-affection is naïve Cartesianism *par exemplar*; it's the problem behind the philosophical debates over causation and OOO's theorization of the touch discussed in Chapter 2. The paradox of auto-affection characterizes the classical account of the brain–mind relationship, which doubtlessly has contributed to the disfavor with which neuroscience is still received in the humanities.

While there have been many critiques of auto-affection taking many different forms, as I'll demonstrate following Malabou, neuroscience offers a more powerful critique of auto-affection than OOO, Heideggarian destruction, Derridian deconstruction, and Deleuze. Understanding Malabou's account of auto-affection—which builds on Heidegger, Derrida, and Deleuze—is essential to grasping how neuroscience can allow us to better understand the openness of the subject to learning, the other, and difference in general, as well as the significance of *care* to understanding invention in writing pedagogy. Following poststructuralism, we can begin by asking: is our experience of voice the result of language touching consciousness, or consciousness touching language? Is self care implicit to this experience? Is our inner language simply an auto-affective mirror of conscious thought? We regard to the latter, we know otherwise, of course; after all, poststructuralism has taught us that we don't speak language as much as it *speaks us*. But poststructuralism ends—as Malabou argues—in a problematically disembodied account of writing as arche-writing that fails to understand the explosive potential inherent to the materiality of the auto-affective touch. As we've begun to see, neuroscience offers an embodied account of the touch between language and thought, brain and mind that opens new questions concerning pedagogy, ideology, and power.

While the auto-affective touch is the haptic variant of the mind-body relationship, there are of course other sensory tropes for auto-affection in the philosophical tradition, such as the aural ("hearing our own voice"). In this way, in late works such as "To Speculate—On Freud," auto-affection becomes important for Derrida as a paradigmatic example of the *metaphysics of presence* and *logocentrism* that deconstruction deconstructs. Derrida argued—critiquing auto-affection and the metaphysics of presence it presumes—that there is in fact only *hetero*affection, a radical non-reciprocity of self to self, such that what the self touches or hears is always other than itself. Our experience of self-sameness is simultaneously the experience of the other. The deconstruction of auto-affection led Derrida to revise his core concept, logocentrism; he coined the term "haptocentrism" to reflect how "touching" exceeds even *logos* (speech, vision, and hearing) in establishing metaphysical presence in philosophy.

Descartes is Derrida's ultimate thinker of haptocentrism and the focus of Derrida's deconstruction. Descartes posited a constant touch between the soul and body, but to do this he spatialized the soul *punctually* in the pineal gland, creating a contradiction that persists in our inheritance of a spatially-oriented metaphysics: "if there is a spatiality of the soul, how can it be reduced to a point," Malabou asks (Johnston & Malabou 22). In doing so, Descartes located the soul, paradoxically, *both* across the body and specifically within the pineal gland. In other words, the pineal gland is a metaphorical space in which we discover the "soul's hand" touching the body, "the nonspatial space of the soul's self touching" (22). Malabou follows Derrida in arguing that the Cartesian soul therefore becomes ideal rather than material, evidencing a disembodied mind despite Descartes' attempt to link mind and body. In this metaphorical space, "the difference between activity and passivity is felt as such" (22). While Descartes understood wonder as the conscious mind's basic auto-affective feeling of the world, his formulation here is paradoxically both active and passive; the Cartesian subject is both touching and being touched.

The problem Descartes fell into can be illustrated by touching one's right palm to one's left palm—which one is touching and which being touched? Which is giving, and which is receiving? Resulting from this paradox of auto-affection in the classical accounts of wonder and subjectivity, philosophy has long debated the relationship between self and other, generosity, and the "gift" of consciousness.

Derrida's heteroaffective deconstruction of Cartesian generosity offers one solution to this classical paradox of the touch. As Derrida pointed out, for Descartes, wonder (the foundational affect)—as well as generosity—has to first pass through the penal gland, creating an (always already divided) self-presence, such that the healthy generous subject takes pleasure in "feeling themselves give." For Descartes, generosity is therefore literally *selfish*; affect becomes a gift, something given to us by our relationship with the other. Derrida finally "stresses the possibility of elaborating a new, non-Cartesian meaning of both wonder and generosity, a wonder and generosity that wouldn't know or be aware of their own openness" (Johnston & Malabou 24). However, deconstructing the auto-affective touch (as a metaphysics of presence) required that Derrida theorize a non-metaphysical touch as that which "*structurally loses contact with itself*," characterized by discontinuity and self absence. We are touched, in other words, but don't know who the "I" is that's being touched—the touch of affect appears to us from the outside, as a *gift*, passively received. In short, Derrida's heteroaffection, his theory of the touch, *bypasses materiality*. From the perspective of Malabou's scientific materialism, this is a problem.

Deleuze's critique of auto-affection takes a different tact. In re-reading both Descartes and Spinoza, Deleuze (contra Derrida's reading) demonstrated that this auto-affection is not a simple conscious *reflection* of self to self, but rather a space that opens within self encounter. Auto-affection is not reflexive and immediate, but is translated onto a surface—what Deleuze calls the "plane of immanence"—that is a kind of painting or imaging or mapping of the auto-affective experience (Johnston & Malabou 45). In Descartes, the body and the face becomes such a plane—i.e., the expressive face is the spatialization of the auto-affective experience. We can see here the origins of the "fingerprint" theory of embodied emotions, discussed in Chapter 1, as critiqued by Barrett.

As Malabou explains, for Deleuze, wonder is the "'pure affect' of the face" (Johnston & Malabou 47). Wonder plays a "major role" in constructing the self, as it is "the least expressive of all passions, but it is at the same time the very site of conversion of physical needs into ontological signs" (47). Wonder exists directly between passion and thought, and this is reflected in the inscription of the blank facial expression (one that unifies its different parts) that is its sign. In this way for Deleuze, Descartes, like all philosophers, translates events onto his own privileged surface. This process of inscribing mental events onto the face is, for Deleuze, the definition of the "concept," and he argues that all philosophy projects concepts onto different surfaces, or planes of imminence. For his own part, Deleuze asserts that the brain itself is a "screen" upon which affects play as concepts.

So we have here two different lines of critique of Descartes's wonder. On the one hand, deconstruction demonstrates that the Cartesian account of affect belongs to the "haptocentric" metaphysics of presence. And on the other, Deleuze argues instead that Descartes belongs to a non-metaphysical philosophy that, in its own way, inscribes events onto a plane (the face) as concepts. In addition to these critiques, we have OOO's account of the touch and wonder. Having considered these, we can now explore how neuroscience has built on Spinoza to realize a more radical deconstruction of the subject than any of these theories, reintroducing the material question of care.

Malabou's Spinoza: Plastic Transformations in Deleuze and Derrida

As Damasio argues, for Spinoza, the continuous variation of affective encounter comprises the feeling of existence, the power to act that he called the *conatus*. For Spinoza, wonder is associated with the *conatus* as "the fundamental and most important joyful passion" (Johnston & Malabou 40). When we view an object in its singularity, difficulty (by which Spinoza does not mean complicated but rather rare and unknown), or excellence, we desire it, and judge it to be good. This increases the joyful passions and therefore the power of the *conatus*—that is, the power of the subject to act. As Malabou puts it, wonder "reveals to us the beauty of difficult things and attunes our mind to their scarcity and rarity" (42). Again, wonder is not theorized here, as it is in Descartes, as a *conscious* engagement with the world, but rather as an affective clearing or opening: "the call of being, the tendency to turn the conatus toward the ontological beauty of the necessity of things" (42).

What is gained from this return to Spinoza? Against the classical tradition, Spinoza's account of wonder allows us to understand the ways affect constructs self without abandoning materiality. That is, against Cartesian auto-affection which presumed the stability of subjective consciousness, a voice ("I think") that precedes affects, Spinoza presaged a subject constituted by affective experience. We've already seen how Derrida builds on Spinoza's critique, arguing that in fact auto-affective experience is impossible and that we are in a sense fated to be strangers to ourselves. In claiming

Spinoza as a proto-neuroscientist, Damasio, as I already began to develop in Chapter 1, argues that there is a neurological mapping between ideas and bodily states; that is, the brain represents the homeostatic situation of the body, and therefore the power of mind and body correspond.

In short, neuroscience theorizes auto-affection such that—in opposition to the classical conceptualization where a unified subject is affected by exterior objects or interior feelings—the materiality of affects *precedes subjectivity*, giving rise to consciousness, and auto-affective voice. For neuroscience, the structure of the self has three components: 1. The protoself: the homeostatic neural structure that maps at each moment the body. 2. Core consciousness or "thick consciousness": this is the location of the "feeling of ourselves;" at this level the modification of the protoself occurs as "pure affective awareness with no cognitive function" (Johnson & Malabou 32). 3. Extended consciousness and the autobiographical self: the memories and experiences that form self-consciousness. The protoself, core consciousness, and the autobiographical self each "touch" each other in the protoself's process of homeostatic maintenance. The process Damasio describes begins in the non-symbolic and non-pictorial—that is, material—affectivity of the protoself.

Around the complexity of the touch between the different levels of the self, Malabou follows Damasio to claim that the neuroscientific account of auto-affection is more radical than either deconstruction or Deleuze. To demonstrate her point, I'll begin here by considering how neuroscience demands that we rethink Deleuze's theorization of the concept and the "plane of immanence" (Deleuze *Spinoza*). Recall that for Barrett, the *concept* appears not on the face, nor even in the brain, but is distributed between the protoself and the social through interoception. Barrett, in other words, radically challenges the spatialization of the subject/object relationship in her theorization of the concept. The brain's mapping of the body's affective state marks the coincidence between thought and events in the body in just the same way as the Deleuze's "plane of immanence" inscribes internal affects onto an external (brain) "screen." But it's important to note here that for Barrett, the brain's "signs" appear exactly at the level of materiality. Barrett's deconstruction of the "plane of immanence" points to one way that neuroscience problematizes the transcendental subject at the material level.

Driving this point home, Malabou argues that in theorizing heteroaffection, both Derrida and Deleuze require recourse to a "heterobody . . . a nonorganic body" (Johnston & Malabou 68). For Deleuze, this is of course the plane of imminence. For Derrida, it is a surface between the subject and object, irreducible to biological determination. Derrida's heteroaffectivity requires that the touch occur on an external surface, an immaterial extension of the body. For example, Derrida argues in *On Touching* that "No one should ever be able to say 'my heart,' my own heart, except when he or she might say it to someone else and call him or her this way" (Johnston & Malabou 68). In other words, we are so alien to our body that even our heart cannot be our own; we touch our heart only through an external other. But Malabou asks Derrida, "Why shouldn't we say 'my heart' "? In other words, why do the humanities continue to posit a moral injunction insisting we must move beyond the biological? And further, she asks Deleuze, "When I clasp my hands, is it really two planes that I join?" (68). In other words, why must the body be "at a distance from its own organs" (69)?

In short, both Deleuze and Derrida "look for the outside outside the body" (27), distancing the body from its material, organic reality. It is as if there is a second, symbolic body—one not subject to the same destructive forces as the material body—a kind of "body without organs." This body, not unlike the Cartesian mind, is envisioned as an imaginary and inorganic extension or surface of the body, not actually existing in real space; it is somehow able to "stand in" for the damaged biological body, a stable surface upon which new traces can be written even where the neurological traces of the brain-surface have been disturbed (Malabou "Emotional Life"). In Deleuze, for instance, we can see the continuation of a philosophical tradition that *always presumes* that the sad passions can *always* be converted into happy ones by appealing to this symbolic body; even when we are sad, we are still in a sense capable of wondering at symbolic difference. As he puts it: "We are completely enclosed in this world of affection-ideas and these affective continuous variations of joy and sadness, so sometimes my power of acting increases, okay, sometimes it diminishes; but whether it increases or diminishes I remain within passion because, in both cases, I do not possess it" (Deleuze "Gilles Deleuze, Lecture"). Self care always remains possible because there is nothing outside of it. Even the depressed subject can mobilize their pride and re-*project* a positive identity through a symbolic conversion of negative feelings (Malabou "Emotional Life"). It's this durability that neuroscience challenges (I'll explore this in much further depth below).

And as for Derrida, Malabou accepts his critique of auto-affection, to a point. She agrees that, "Without the capacity to be surprised by objects, the subject wouldn't be able to have a feeling of itself" (Johnston & Malabou 9). In other words, she advances Derrida's idea that there is an essential ambiguity to wonder: "What are the soul, or the mind, struck by: the surprising object or its own capacity to be surprised? What do the soul or the mind wonder at: the other or themselves?" (9). However, Malabou's account of plasticity demands that we see Derrida's ultimate privileging of the symbolic over the material; as Malabou is fond of pointing out, Derrida finally *leaves the symbolic-material binary itself undeconstructed*. Deconstruction retains something of the classical faith in the durability of wonder in its recourse to the externality of the trace, inscribed on a separate, inorganic body. Specifically: "For Derrida, there is no deconstruction of wonder without wonder. Heteroaffection is still an affect. The possibility of losing the very ability for the individual to feel or get affected by something or someone is never envisaged" (Johnston & Malabou 11). In other words, it is impossible to deconstruct without first *wondering about the very thing we intend to deconstruct*; indeed, philosophical thought in general requires wonder. It would seem then that in both the classical system and in Derrida, wonder is a supplement to deconstruction that is itself *undeconstructable*.

Malabou's plasticity, on the other hand, exists fully within the closure of material form. As Malabou argues,

> Plasticity designates the future understood as a future within closure, the possibility of structural formation: a transformation of structure within structure, a mutation 'right at the level of form' . . . the possibility of a closed system to welcome new phenomena, all the while transforming itself, is what appears as plasticity
>
> (Malabou, *Future* 192–193)

And, as we've seen, the potential for hetero-heteroaffection—the possibility of a final, explosive, complete material transformation happening "right at the level of form"—is what is not possible in Derrida, for whom the symbolic is always, in a sense, conserved in the play of the trace, the ongoing chain of signification.

Derrida develops his key concepts of arche-writing—the graph, the trace, the process of erasure and emergent inscription through which new binaries emerge out of old ones as opposed to resolving dialectical advance—to efface the integrity of identity and classical form. Deconstruction, in other words, is an assault on the formalist tradition from within, the presumption of auto-affective self closure that characterizes Descartes *cogito* and Spinoza's *conatus* alike. It is only in relation to the other that the self takes form, Derrida argues, and inner-thought/speech must always be thought in relation to the other/external/writing, to the point that inner-thought cannot be thought without first mastering the conventions of the other. Identity always *passes through* the external, and in this way the individual can never be auto-affective, self-touching, "true" self of classical and enlightenment philosophy. The self, that is, always already bares the trace of the other. Writing, external to speech, characterized historically by its lack of presence is, of course, the general model of this process of supplementarity for Derrida.

Ultimately, what deconstruction deconstructs, as Malabou argues in *Plasticity at the Dusk of Writing*, is form (74). The trace (the graphic element outside of Being) is the trace of the supplemental other within form that always undermines it, and for Levinas, "The trace is inconvertible into forms" (47). Another way of thinking this, as we've seen, is through the problem of the "metaphysics of presence" and auto-affection—for Derrida, form does not touch itself. To demonstrate the *potential* damage that this thinking of the trace does to her plasticity, Malabou follows Derrida's argument about hospitality. For Derrida, the threshold of the home—its boundary from the outside—has always already been compromised by an originary relation of the self to the other. Before the boundary of the home is thought—and at the moment of its origination—we are already bound to the stranger though the necessity of hospitality. The idea of home cannot be thought, then, without the external other, and even then, only through thinking from the place of the other's intrusion—an imagination that substitutes the other for the self within the self—in order to master the thought of the home. To make the ideal home, free of external contamination and intrusion, involves always first mastering the thought of the outside intruder.

In retort, one might think that Malabou would stage her attack on Derrida's privileging of the external symbolic by emphasizing nonlinguistic, pre-conscious forms of meaning, such as, for example, the emotional meanings we make of affect. Indeed, this is Kia Jane Richmond's approach when she argues that "our tendency to value writing above all other kinds of meaning making, is complicated by theories of multiple intelligence posited by Howard Gardner and a theory of emotional intelligence" (72). But this argument does no damage to deconstruction; after all, we can easily understand emotion and other nonlinguistic forms of knowing in terms of the trace; emotion, for example, is "written" from the grammar of our affective experience. In short, Derrida's trace can easily account for the essentially linguistic nature of the nonlinguistic.

Instead, to get beyond the metaphysics of presence, to change the transcendental, Malabou argues that there has to be an explosion into something *altogether new*. And this explosive transformation must occur *from within* the transcendental subject itself—we do not discover the difference within difference that is plasticity in the body (severed from consciousness) or in the external object. The plastic explosion occurs *in between* the material (the brain) and the symbolic (consciousness), in *translation*. To state that the alterity of the trace is inconvertible to form is to fetishize it, to place it outside of the economy of the constancy of material exchange. So while translation will always entail a touch between these different orders, the material and the symbolic, Malabou describes difference *within the touch itself*. Again, the transformation of the transcendental occurs from within itself; and for Malabou, following neuroscience, the touch between *brain and mind* is characterized precisely by *difference itself*.

In other words, what Derrida misses is the convertibility of form from within—the explosive potential of form, the auto-hetero-affection of plasticity and the hetero-heteroaffection of its explosive potential to become other than itself. As Malabou argues, "*One must be in good shape to welcome the trace*." And we can see this at the level of the brain, of course, where the pathological subjects of neuroscience are in no shape to "welcome" the neurological trace. Only the shape of form can be effaced by the trace, and "form cannot be 'undone' without calling on *the support of form*, including the aid of its power of explosion" (46).

Finally, where Derrida reads Heidegger's exceeding of metaphysics not as a metamorphosis, but as another version of the philosophy of presence, for Malabou, the deconstruction that proceeds from the trace, the concept of the other, or writing, is in fact only *describing form* after the fact of the Heideggerian destruction of metaphysics and deconstruction. What the deconstructionists encounter is not the absence of form, but the metamorphized form that deconstructed form—the plastic transformation of the transcendental. While form can never again have its statuary solidity, nor can it be "written" away. Ultimately, Malabou shows that plasticity emerges as another supplement in the deconstructive system, replacing Derrida's writing, because it exceeds the trace inasmuch as it "marks the *difference of the grammatological instance from itself*" (79). The trace cannot be recuperated in the plastic because it cannot describe the mutability of the "chain of substitutions" in which writing finds its place as the privileged supplement. Instead, the brain is the privileged model because "neuronal traces don't proceed as do writing traces: *they do not leave a trace*; they occur as *changes of form*" (79).

Without resorting to a metaphysical account of the symbolic, without positing a non-material, inorganic body, what neuroscience offers is an account of a heteroaffection that nevertheless does not ignore or reduce the symbolic. Clearly, as we've seen, the relationship between the protoself and autobiographical consciousness in Damasio does not ignore the importance of the symbolic. Indeed, it is only out of a (sometimes willful) ignorance that neuroscience is reflexively associated in the humanities with reductive accounts of the brain. In fact, Damasio's redefinition of the subject theorizes auto-affection as a nonconscious structure explicitly irreducible to biology. For Damasio, "The nervous system is . . . a distributed structure, acentered and with shared receptivity" (Johnston & Malabou 27). The plasticity of this system represents the "internal law of mutual compensations" (27) that regulates the fragile structure, a structure that must constantly cooperate in order to maintain its form in relation to both internal affects *and* external sensory data. The automatized computer metaphor of the brain, inherited from the classical prioritization of subjectivity over affect, is no longer applicable—neuroscience understands plasticity in terms of the psychic and social experiences that give form to the individual neural structure. There is nothing reductive in this account.

Rethinking Heidegger's Tool Analysis: Brains That Wonder and Care

Ultimately, what neuroscience teaches us is that, contra Bogorst's theory, wonder is *essentially* linked to care. Where affects map the state of the body, emotions for Damasio (following Spinoza) signify a "concern" with it; where affects create self attachment, emotions in general—and more specifically, wonder—are the mechanism of self care (Johnston & Malabou 51). That is, wonder opens *the possibility of concern or care*, the tendency towards survival in general, and therefore directly underlies "basic value" or the *conatus*: "Feeling in general, and wonder in particular, lay the foundation for care, the care of ourselves, the care for ourselves" (51). Indeed, "wonder is the very expression of these vital impulses" (54). The affects are thus intrinsically related to survival, to self care; "Being itself is survival, or endeavor," and Nature is present within us in this way (53). In other words, wonder is the emotion required to *care*, and care is what is required to act in a way that produces an equilibrium between joy and sorrows, essential to both well-being and survival in general.

As Malabou argues, the neuroscientific account of wonder, "tends both to erase and to underscore the border between auto- and heteroaffection" (63). That is, wonder describes the feeling of the weird experience of auto-affective self-presence that passes through the other. So where in Derrida's vision of heteroaffection, wonder appears as a "gift"—the gift of wonder as the experience of the other within me wondering—Malabou theorizes wonder as somehow closer to a sense of self—that is, in terms of interestedness, desire, and care, something closer to Spinoza's *conatus*. But where Spinoza spoke of the special power in the soul taking pleasure at its own self-presence—pleasure in the operation of the harmonious function of body and mind—Malabou argues that because the soul *qua* protoself is the *other* of consciousness, auto-affection in fact passes first through the experience of the other: wonder is the "affect of the other as such" (10). Indeed, for Malabou, the pleasure (one side of wonder) we feel experiencing the self is actually the feeling of the encounter with the other—consciousness feeling the protoself. But again, at the same time, she stipulates that there is something very genuine about our feeling of auto-affective experience; we have: "a consistent perspective, as if there were indeed an owner and knower for most, though not all, contents. I imagine this perspective to be rooted in a relatively stable, endlessly repeated biological state" (32). In other words, Malabou is willing to go a long way towards saying that there is indeed something like an auto-affective self-presence; but the structure of this voice is distributed, constantly evolving, and—as I've promised to soon show—fragile.

In the neuroscientific account, wonder "coincides with the passage from core consciousness to autobiographical self" (32), marking the experience of the self as it opens to consciousness. Or put another way: *wonder is the emotional experience of the excess in the protoself* that enables its plastic metamorphosis both within itself and into consciousness. Indeed, the "passage" between the (internal and external) other and consciousness is characterized by an *excess* or *overflow* of meaning that precedes it. Wonder in this way describes the emotional experience of our plastic capacity for learning, concept formation, and difference in general. And it is only to the extent that we are invested in the world through wonder, because ready-at-hand objects appear to us meaningfully *as* something in different contexts (e.g., hammer-as-weapon)—indeed, because we *care*—that we are capable of the differences that mark invention and learning.

This neurological account of care allows a stronger reading of Heidegger than we find in Bogorst's and Harman's readings of the tool analysis, adding another wrinkle in OOO's potential to inform composition pedagogy. Contra Bogorst, I don't read Heidegger's account of our primordial concern or care (*Sorge*) in terms of reasoned intentionality. For Heidegger, concern and mood (*stimmung*) form the background of experience, and are the requirement of human intelligence and learning; care is the "thrown-open-ness" of the subject into time—its "being-towards-death." It is a projection of care into the future, a constantly unfolding concern, that wonder anticipates. For instance, as Heidegger intuited of the predictive process model, when I walk into a room, my brain makes predictions about a range of potentialities, including whether there will be a floor that will support my weight or if the people in the room are friendly, to concerns about the lighting or the temperature. Most of these predictions (i.e., there will be a floor) never rise to consciousness. Indeed, predictions tend rise to consciousness only where things break down—for example, if my brain predicts incorrectly that there will be adequate lighting in the room, jostled, I will need to consciously adjust my brain's prediction if there's no light. It is simply and clearly not the case that "I," a singular cogito, process all of these things at the level of consciousness. In Heidegger's terms, it is generally where what is "ready-at-hand" breaks down that we begin to consciously theorize about them as "present-at-hand." But beyond Heidegger, Malabou understands care—and its affect, wonder—as the embodiment of this affective interface, the space between the subject and world. Wonder is in this way the emotional experience of a primordial openness to the world: a surplus of meaning, the plasticity in excess of the affective system that allows intelligence to adapt, metamorphosize, change shape.

So we have here two different readings of Heidegger's tool analysis as it relates to wonder. On the one hand, OOO's own take on Heidegger's tool analysis emphasizes the reality of objects outside of their correlation to human thought. Again, for OOO, we only ever encounter objects partially, and we "touch" objects only from within intent; and furthermore, this situation is not unique to humans because objects have this same experience with each other. On the other hand, in Malabou's materialist account of wonder (and affect more generally)—as the "background" or interface between the subject and objects—wonder lacks the stability we find in OOO. OOO implies the existence of a mystical world of ideal (as opposed to material) forms in which *difference itself* is a stable law guaranteeing a universe of discrete essences, thus reimporting back into ontology the transcendental reality it denies the subject. Neuroscience, on the other hand, discovers in the materiality of consciousness, its plasticity, the law of *difference within difference itself*.

Again, neuroscience accomplishes this deconstruction without recourse to external concepts or to the conscious meaning making of the subject; again, the deconstruction of auto-affection is experienced at the very level of materiality. What neuroscience demonstrates is that mind and body have the same (plastic) essence. Indeed, maintaining the distinction between the two is no longer useful, as it is "the organism as a whole that is capable of wondering, that persists in life" (Johnston & Malabou 55). Auto-affection is the mutual mirroring of mind and body; the underlying protoself is reflected in conscious experience and *vice versa*. And again, it is clear that "something remains nonsubjective in this process" (55). Wonder thereby marks the essential "*strangeness or estrangement*" of subjectivity (33). This is the deep weirdness of the neuroscientific subject: Wonder is equally the self amazed at difference, at the other, at *objects*, and *also* the self amazed at its own self difference. This amazement at the simultaneous withdrawal of the subject from both self and objects is more fundamental, and more complicated—given that it is relational and dynamic, constantly emerging in relation to difference—than the subject's withdrawal from objects alone.

In the auto-affective touch that gives shape to conscious experience, there is something nonconscious, which is precisely the internal heteroaffective mapping—a mapping that is never experienced as a "self touching" because it remains invisible and detached from the experience of the "I"—of the overall affective state. Given the originary nonsubjective character of affectivity, we must, Malabou reminds us, consider the possibility of a total, final detachment of the protoself and the "I." This finally turns us to Malabou's account of the accidental in self formation and the destructive dimension of plasticity, the most radical form of difference within difference.

Explosive Plasticity and Hetero-Heteroaffection: Power and the "New Wounded"

As I began to develop in Chapter 1, plasticity has two dimensions, productive and destructive, reflecting the potential of each brain to take a unique shape in ongoing processes of pliable self creation. Plasticity is the "accurate balance between the ability to change and the resistance to change" (Johnston & Malabou 56). However, in cases like Phineas Gage, as we saw in Chapter 1, destructive plasticity can potentially result in the irrevocable *destruction of self*. In such cases, a new self forms, a new identity is sculpted out of the (damaged) material through plasticity—like other sufferers of neural (and social and psychic) trauma, Gage become unrecognizable to those that knew him. Complicating both rational and rhetorical theorizations, this new self is in no way an "invention." Rather, "The destructive plasticity forms what it destroys. It is not a simple annihilation or suppression to the precise extent that it has a result. This result is the formation of 'someone else,' a new self, a self that is not able to recognize itself" (58). Destruction in this way calls attention to heteroaffection at the very level of materiality; as Malabou states, "Destructive plasticity is a biological deconstruction of subjectivity" (58).

And it is also in this way that Malabou offers most radical critique of Derrida's heteroaffection, recognizing the possibility of a "hetero-heteroaffection": that is, the *explosive* potential of destructive plasticity to radically disrupt and transform subjectivity, a biological/material deconstruction of the subject.

As we know, when the protoself is damaged or destroyed—as in the case of Phineas Gage—the subject presents as indifferent, and furthermore, *indifferent to their own indifference*. What Oliver Sacks' or Damasio's neuropathological cases demonstrate is that the disappearance of affect is in itself an affect, or modification, in which the subject becomes radically *disaffected*. Malabou argues that Damasio's insight challenges the very idea of heteroaffection, given that "the patient is less heteroaffected than *not affected* at all. He has become other, a new person, a nonsubject" (Johnston & Malabou 8). This is what Malabou calls *hetero-heteroaffection*, the possibility that the self-touched-by-the-other becomes *other-in-itself*.

Recall that in the classical formulation wonder has *no opposite*, understood as the basic emotion that underlies all others; in the classical tradition (including Spinoza, despite his prescience) it was always possible for the subject to move from the sad passions to greater forms of perfection. In Spinoza, the auto-affectivity of the subject, the core, primitive self, is preserved—the individual can convert sad passions into joyful ones, the symbolic can always stand in for the biological, as the subject can always mobilize their identity, projecting it in more positive ways. This presumption of *persistence* remains as a trace (quite literally in the case of deconstruction) even in contemporary thinking about auto-affection—from psychology to deconstruction to OOO. But neuroscience reveals that wonder does have an opposite, which is total disaffection, the lack of all care, *indifference to indifference*. That is, neuropathology has demonstrated that the ability to wonder can indeed be destroyed, can become totally other than itself, and that cases of neurological trauma can result in the complete loss of auto-affection. Yet, as we've seen, these disaffected subjects, unable to wonder, are often able to think and reason perfectly fine, despite not feeling. Such subjects, characterized by a profound indifference, or "cold blood," are untouched by wonder;[2] acting without feeling or care, their personality becomes unrecognizable to friends and family. Malabou calls these subjects the "new wounded" of neuroscience. They are those that are profoundly unable to make new meaning of their trauma through a symbolic reintegration; the accident or psychic wound is in effect "meaningless," and meaning cannot be recuperated through any hermeneutic schema or rediscovered in the patient's language or history.

Again, in the tradition inspired by Spinoza's critique, it was always understood that the subject can be recuperated, can re-project their ego—that is, can *reintegrate symbolically*. As we've seen, even as the biological body is damaged, there is still a non-organic, symbolic body that one can (re)project oneself into or through; the symbolic is always able to substitute for the biological where the biological is damaged. We can see this idea continuing into psychotherapy, and in turn, resonating through contemporary rhetoric and writing pedagogy, especially in our accounts of invention and development. Malabou quotes Freud in "Thoughts for the Time on War and Death" making this point quite clearly; for him, the protoself is finally "imperishable": "The primitive mind is in the fullest meaning of the word imperishable. What are called mental diseases inevitably produces an impression in the layman that intellectual and mental life have been destroyed. In reality, the destruction only applies to later acquisitions and developments." Mental disorders, in other words, are regressions to "earlier states of mental life," to a "primitive mind" that is—like the Cartesian soul—itself indestructible (qtd. in "Emotional Life"). We can see here how faithful philosophy remains to wonder as the guarantee of reason and that which distinguishes us as the symbol-using animal.

For these reasons too, as Malabou argues elsewhere, in Freud and Lacan, all traumatic experiences are finally superficial: "For Freud and for Lacan, it seems clear that every external trauma is 'sublated,' internalized. Even the most violent intrusions of the external real owe their traumatic effect to the resonance they find in primary psychic conflicts" (*Post Trauma*). This is because of the difference between the real and the Real in Freud and Lacan, where the Real is the transcendental, "always already" of the unfulfilled desire that—with the character of the signifier, the "lack"—structures the mind. For example, in the case of brain trauma inflicted by war, the external blow cannot have a causative power in the psychic suffering of the patient. Rather, the "real" of the blow merely awakens in the subject the "always already" traumatic nature of the "Real"—that is, of our subconscious which is characterized by the "lack," by unfulfilled desire—which is to say, the psychic reality that is more real than the physical one. For both Freud and Lacan, physical trauma can only ever be a repetition of originary, psychic trauma, and therefore the trauma that it seems to cause is in realty only ever the subject confronting psychic reality—the death drive.

How has rhetoric and writing pedagogy inherited the presumed indestructability of the *conatus*? This is precisely what drives our disciplinary focus on flexibility, productivity, and positivity discussed across this book as they relate to invention and other dimensions of composition. Additionally, we need to consider how automatized pedagogical programs—such as where writing is taught only in relation to high-stakes tests—and the overlearning of mechanized forms (such as the five-paragraph essay) affect wonder. Furthermore, I believe that the current failure to recognize the "new wounded"—and relatedly, the relationship between plasticity, pedagogy, and power—drives an overly-optimistic embrace of new media and writing technologies, outside of the historical cultural relations between writing and care. It is in part through this embrace that writing pedagogy potentially *creates or reproduces the very carelessness and indifference that power capitalizes on today*. And this disaffection is currently advancing—as in the case of our social epistemic pedagogy—under the banner of pedagogical care. I'll address these problems in Chapter 5, but first, I need to further establish the relationship between the new wounded, power, and pedagogy today. Around the relations between wonder, reason, auto-affectivity, and embodiment, we can see that there are interesting pedagogical questions concerning the role of writing technologies, invention, and the disaffection of the subject.

Neo-Liberalism and the Politics of Indifference

Why does it matter that wonder finds its opposite in a destructive disaffection? What's the consequence of having privileged the symbolic over the biological? And what is at stake for writing pedagogy? Here we finally join the biological and social, the scientific and the philosophical, rethinking the transcendental in terms of a neurophilosophy. For Malabou contra Freud, the "new wounded" revealed by neuroscience gain us insight into a contemporary political power that requires a *careless flexibility* (a concept that will be explored in more depth in Chapter 5). As we've seen, for Spinoza, power requires the creation of sad passions that diminish the power to act. Contemporary power, however, is different. For Malabou, the current political situation is characterized not by inspiring sad passions, by diminishing the power to act, but by making the subject indifferent to their diminished power by *destroying wonder* through traumatic blows to the protoself. Malabou explores the question of the relation between the emotions and power, arguing that while Deleuze was right, in his analysis of Spinoza, to argue that historically sovereign power required the "sad" emotions of the subject, today, by demanding our docility and flexibility, power is aimed precisely at our *indifference*. The difference is that, where on the one hand various forms of tyranny require depression and decreased action, the neo-liberal economy requires instead our suppleness, our mobility—that is, it requires that subjects flexibly occupy different nodes within a network. But perhaps even this network metaphor implies too much resistance, as what power really requires is not that we become relatively stable nodes, but something more flexible still. The indifferent "new wounded" subject *ceases to care what node or position he/she occupies*. And we are all—potentially at least—the "new wounded."

Damasio clearly and in many ways describes similarities between political and social trauma and brain trauma. For instance, in *The Feeling of What Happens*, he compares his patients to the emotionally detached characters that populate Samuel Beckett's *Happy Days* (Damasio). And he supplements his case studies—which always, significantly, describe his patients in a social context—with analogies to subjects without neurological lesions, disaffected individuals he encounters in real life. He describes, for example, a disoriented old man boarding a ferry in Stockholm who reminds him, in his presentation, of one of patients. Therefore, as Malabou argues: "how can we not be struck by the general similarity between the behavior of a social outcast and the person with a brain lesion? . . . Traumatized subjects, disconnected from their affects, present symptoms analogous to those that accompany brain disorders, even though they are not related to any lesion." She continues the analogy, describing the catastrophic anonymity of accumulated forms of social and political violence:

> It now appears that the impact of social war is just as forceful as a brain lesion, and no less violent than being struck by a bullet or an iron bar. Even if such blows do not always occur as sudden events, but tend to be more continuous or harassing, their sense, like that of a brain lesion, remains dissimulated between an absence of sense, again, social conflict without dialectic, as anonymous as a natural catastrophe. An absence that reveals the very coolness of the political and the social today.
>
> ("Emotional Life")

It turns out that neurological and social trauma *alike* are characterized by *indifference to indifference*. In trauma brought about by accidents resulting in pathological lesions and neurological disorders ranging from Alzheimer's to Parkinson's to AD/HD, *patients present the same indifference* as those suffering from socio-political trauma, PTSD, rape, and various forms of exile and other events causing post-traumatic stress. That is, the biological fact of plasticity sheds light on the social accident, the chance destructive encounter with otherness. Or to put this differently, *social and political traumas are capable of neurological destruction—the destruction of neural connections—no less than physical traumas*.

In Malabou's words, "Neurobiology shows that every psychic blow, a depression, a personal crisis, a sentimental or professional failure, have consequences on the equilibrium of the emotional brain and acts like a snip of scissors in the frontal lobe neural networks" ("Emotional Life"). The lesson of the accident is that plasticity is the hinge between the physical and the social. Just as we have no recourse to the symbolic over the biological, nor is the biological more fundamental than the symbolic: *both* are inscribed at the level of materiality. Again, from a pedagogical perspective, this fact gives renewed force to psychologist Silvan Tomkins' claim that "the absence of the affective support of interest would jeopardize intellectual development no less than the destruction of brain tissue" (343).

Malabou cites Naomi Klein's *Shock Doctrine* in its astute description of political strategies meant to produce meaningless shocks, apparent accidents that seem both "natural" and senseless, typified by Alan Greenspan's policy of inducing political shocks following disasters in order to realize the neoliberal agenda of opening markets. In short, these political shocks are meant to separate subjects from their feelings, to appear as so meaningless that they inspire only indifference. As Malabou argues, "Political violence currently wears the mask of meaningless accidents, pure nonsymbolic attacks against the symbolic which gradually provoke the disappearance of the capacity to wonder" ("Emotional Life"). Just as the physiological accidents and shocks that destroy the protoself produce a pathological indifference, so to do these social shocks produce and require the indifference of political subjects. Realizing the political agenda of opening markets to enable the uninterrupted flow of capital, recklessly destroying local economic systems, requires that subjects *no longer care enough to resist*. Incapacitated by social shocks, these events—having the character of accidents—are simply meaningless. *In other words, it is precisely this indifference, as opposed to sadness, that power requires today*.

Although perhaps lacking Greenspan's sophistication, we can also view president Donald Trump's political strategy in these terms; the apparent randomness of his policies and his shocking outbursts have a deadening effect, and he explicitly claims that much of this chaos is purposeful. For example, responding to hurricane Maria's devastation of Puerto Rico, Trump obscured the government's lack of hurricane preparation and aid, making its catastrophic effects appear meaningless, going as far as to blame the Puerto Ricans themselves for the failed recovery (and by extension, for the hurricane itself). Violence here is made meaningless, a matter of mere chance; what is political appears as merely accidental. Finally, it's more difficult to resist this senselessness, and many citizens respond only with increasing indifference to events that would have outraged them in the past. Trump's politics seem at war on our capacity to wonder, our ability to make sense of violence, our capacity to remain open to difference.

The Retreat of Intelligence: Writing Technologies, Attention, and Disaffection

It is within a culture characterized by this disaffecting power that we receive increasingly indifferent students in our classrooms; and as I've argued across this book in different ways, it is our job in the humanities to make sense of this increasing senselessness. As writing teachers, this will mean understanding the relationship between writing pedagogy, writing technologies, and wonder. Where we've largely failed to recognize the embodied relationship between wonder and care, affect and reason, Malabou's theory paves the way for an understanding of the emergence of a novel and pervasive disaffection in the classroom—a disturbing disruption of our student's motivation and concentration. As I'll argue in Chapters 4 and 5, the capacity for "deep attention," through which culture has been traditionally transmitted and disputed across generations, is rapidly eroding, giving way to new forms of attention, some of which are manufactured *at the level of affectivity* by technologies with the goal of maximizing profit in an "attention economy." In the attention economy, attention is divided into increasingly smaller units to be bought and sold, desire is replaced by consumption, and care is replaced by indifference. As this happens, our students increasingly withdraw from school, friends, and family, their intrinsic motivation replaced by the disinterestedness power and its technologies require of them.

Therefore, counter Spinoza's formulation, it appears that objects gain power over us where we are increasingly disaffected, where wonder is absent. And here I have specifically in mind the increasing influence that objects and technologies hold over us in today's attention economy. These persuasive technologies, which form and deform attention below consciousness and at the neurological level, replace wonder—and concomitantly, reason—with their own forms, scripts, and imperatives. And power, doing little to reverse this situation, benefits from an increase in indifference. The rest of this work will consider, therefore, the complicity of our own pedagogy in this situation. How do writing technologies work to shape consciousness, and how can we help increase our students' power to act through writing?

While I will explore this situation further in Chapters 4 and 5, for now it's important to understand that, for Malabou, we are faced with a previously unthinkable retreat from being in which there is not even recourse to the necessity of care and self preservation that defines being for Heidegger, or to the possibility of Freudian symbolic reintegration. Today we are threatened by the possibility of a true, non-metaphorical retreat from Being, a retreat marked by meaninglessness, where being cannot even be meaningfully recuperated as retreat. Yet at the same time, it is conceivable that after the destruction and deconstruction of metaphysics, we find ourselves in a new epoch—following an explosive transformation within the transcendental—in which new concepts and new subjects emerge. So we must ask: What is this new subject that, through the dispersion of attention, is no longer within itself, more susceptible to the imperatives of objects and technologies, no longer close to meaning and Being? And as teachers, especially as writing teachers, we have been left to wonder how—is it even possible?—do we inculcate care and intelligence in this new moment of their retreat? Following contemporary neuroscience, Malabou's plasticity characterizes this simultaneously destructive and creative moment in which we find ourselves, a moment where the neurosciences have opened new clearings in which we might reimagine the subject.

Notes

1. Etymologically, wonder connects admiration to astonishment or surprise; the Latin word for surprise, "*mirari*," underscores wonder's connection to reflective, philosophical consciousness. This will become important in Chapter 4, given the relationship between discipline, reflection, and power in writing pedagogy.
2. It's worth pointing out that the opposite can also happen. Damasio describes patients that retain their feelings and emotions but not their first-person consciousness. He describes a particular case in which a patient in a great deal of pain, after a surgery that creates a small lesion in the frontal lobe, claims to still feel the pain, but without any pain sensation. The patient still felt affect—the protoself remained intact—but not *consciously*.

Works Cited

Abraham, Matthew. "Rhetoric and Composition's Conceptual Indeterminacy as Political- Economic Work." *College Composition and Communication*, vol. 68, no. 1, 2016, pp. 68–97.

Barrett, Lisa F. *How Emotions Are Made: The Secret Life of the Brain*. Houghton Mifflin Harcourt, Boston, MA, 2017.

Belli, Jill. "Why Well-Being, Why Now? Tracing an Alternate Genealogy of Emotion in Composition." *Composition Forum*, vol. 34, *Association of Teachers of Advanced Composition*, 2016.

Bogost, Ian. *Alien Phenomenology, or, What It's Like to Be a Thing*. University of Minnesota Press, Minneapolis, MN, 2012.

Brown, James, and Nathaniel Rivers. "Composing the Carpenter's Workshop." *O-Zone: A Journal of Object Oriented Studies*, vol. 1, 2013, pp. 27–36.

Bryant, Levi. "Rhetoric, Ideology, and the Ecology of Ideas." *Larvalsubjects.com*, 10 June 2012, https://larvalsubjects.wordpress.com/2012/06/10/rhetoric-ideology-and-the-ecology-of-ideas-hasana-sharps-spinoza/

Damasio, Antonio R. *The Feeling of what Happens: Body and Emotion in the Making of Consciousness*. Harcourt Brace, New York, 1999.

Davis, D. Diane. *Inessential Solidarity: Rhetoric and Foreigner Relations*. University of Pittsburgh Press, Pittsburgh, PA, 2010.

Deleuze, Gilles. *Gilles Deleuze, Lecture, Transcripts on Spinoza's Concept of Affect*. Les Cours Vincennes, Paris, 1978.

———. *Spinoza: Practical Philosophy*. City Lights Books, San Francisco, CA, 1988.

Derrida, Jacques. *The Post Card: From Socrates to Freud and Beyond*. University of Chicago Press, Chicago, 1987.

Gries, Laurie. "Agential Matters: Tumbleweed, Women-Pens, Citizens-Hope, and Rhetorical Actancy." *Ecology, Writing Theory, and New Media*, 2011, pp. 67–91.

Gross, Daniel M., and Jonathan Alexander. *Frameworks for Failure, or What Happened to the Social Turn in Writing Studies? Pedagogy*, vol. 16, no. 2, 2016, pp. 273–292. Print.

Harman, Graham. "Intentional Objects for Non-Humans." *Pour une Approche Non-Anthropologique de la Subjectivite*. University of Toulouse, France, 17 November 2008.

Heidegger, Martin. *Being and Time*. Suny Press, Albany, NY, 2010.

Johnston, Adrian, and Catherine Malabou. *Self and Emotional Life: Philosophy, Psychoanalysis, and Neuroscience*. Columbia University Press, Columbia, 2013. *eBook Collection (EBSCOhost)*. Web. 19 August 2015.

Klein, Naomi. *The Shock Doctrine*. Metropolitan Books, New York, 2007. Print.

Langdon, Lance. "The Passions of Rhetoric and Composition: An Interview With Daniel M. Gross." *Composition Forum*, vol. 34, *Association of Teachers of Advanced Composition*, 2016.

Malabou, Catherine. *The Future of Hegel: Plasticity, Temporality, and Dialectic*. Routledge, London, 2005.

———. *Plasticity at the Dusk of Writing: Dialectic, Destruction, Deconstruction*. Columbia University Press, Columbia, 2010.

———. "Emotional Life in a Neurobiological Age." *Youtube*, uploaded by Cornell University, 9 August 2013, www.youtube.com/watch?v=H4oFump89W4.

———. *Changing Difference: The Feminine and the Question of Philosophy*. Polity Press, Cambridge, UK, 2016.

Rickert, Thomas. *Ambient Rhetoric: The Attunements of Rhetorical Being*. University of Pittsburgh, Pittsburgh, PA, 2013. Web.

Russell, Helen. "Norway Braces Itself for Nine Hours of Live Knitting." *The Telegraph*, 31 October 2013, www.telegraph.co.uk/news/worldnews/europe/norway/10417764/Norway-braces-itself-for-nine-hours-of-live-knitting.html

Appendix 3.5: Pedagogy Breakout 2

Taking the "Low Road" to Embodied Pedagogy: "Tacit Knowledge" and Wonder in Writing

Recall from Chapter 1 that concepts, like emotions, have no fingerprint. It is therefore the case that, as Lisa Feldman Barrett's laboratory has shown, when individuals are asked to give an example of a bird, what bird they select is highly dependent on context (for instance, around Thanksgiving North American respondents are more likely to answer "Turkey"). As Barrett argues, concepts make predictions based in categorical *similarities*:

> concepts aren't fixed definitions in your brain, and they're not prototypes of the most typical or frequent instances. Instead, your brain has many instances—of cars, of dot patterns, of sadness, or anything else—and it imposes similarities between them, in the moment, according to your *goal* in a given situation.
>
> (How Emotions Are Made 89–90)[1]

While the classical account of concepts views them as stable abstractions, they are in fact convenient and flexible groupings bound together only by their efficacy in *predicting* the meaning of various stimuli.

In critiquing Bitzer's "rhetorical situation," Richard Vatz famously argued that "No situation can have a nature independent of the perception of its interpreter or independent of the rhetoric with which he chooses to characterize it" (154). He was (quite rightly) making the phenomenological point that there are no "situations" independent of the perceiver with objective characteristics. However, from the perspective of neuroscience, even the phenomenological situation is a virtuality. The situation is, in fact, a prediction by the brain that precedes phenomenological cognition. We must therefore revise our thinking on situatedness accordingly; neuroscience gives materiality to Thomas Rickert's theory of rhetorical *attunement*—the suasive background circulation of mood, affect, and energy that precedes agency. But this background needs to be thought always *in relation* to the body's interoceptive system, which works alongside the concepts and the affectability of the nervous system (i.e., the brain) to create predictions.

This casts into doubt, as we saw in Chapter 3, on the value of OOO in theorizing attunement *qua* wonder, metaphor, and indirect discourse, given the necessity of theorizing situations *in relation to* the body (again, a predictive process much weirder than OOO's divinations). Relatedly, when we view writing as a set of predictions made by the brain in managing the body's interoceptive budgeting system, we need to revise our idea of what it means to learn to write in the first place. Extrapolating from neuroscience and neurophilosophy, we must emphasize the importance of embodied dispositions—shaped from hetero and hetero-heteroaffective accumulations—open to difference. That is, we must also inculcate plastic habits of mind, openness to (internal and external) difference.

Therefore, as opposed to teaching a critical or rhetorical approach towards emotions—for example, "critical empathy" (e.g., Leake) or emotional reeducation (e.g., Worsham), as important as these may be—we need above all to inspire or enable wonder.

But how?

In Appendix 1.5, we saw that—against the received idea of conceptual expertise—transference may require emotional attachment to new knowledge (Driscoll & Powell). And more than this, it appears that to the extent that any concepts transfer, they must be linked to embodied, affective experience. For example, Chris Anson's compelling essay "The Pop Warner Chronicles: A Case Study in Contextual Adaptation and the Transference of Writing Ability," on the problem of the transference of writing concepts and skills, describes a situation in which a professional writer highly versed in all of these writing concepts—who turns out to be Anson himself—struggles to produce brief summaries of his son's football team for a local newspaper.

Drawing on his own experience and the research on transference, he concludes that: "we can't expect students to effortlessly and uniformly transfer writing ability just because a foundational course has introduced them to process knowledge or audience analysis or metastrategies for analyzing their context. Adaptation and success require continued situated practice and gradual enculturation. These processes often take place mostly tacitly" (541). In short, he demonstrates that our ability to perform in different situations requires an acquired "tacit knowledge" within discourse communities that are always contingent, temporary, and unstable. And in our reliance on tacit knowledge in writing situations—what Salomon and Perkins term "low road" transfer—we discover the limits of writing expertise and conceptual knowledge of writing in general. Tacit knowledge, at the intersection between embodied affect and conscious thought,[2] describes the "low road" we take to allowing us to perform in different writing situations, knowledge related to our automatic, embodied, and practiced relationships to writing (533). Below, I will consider some ways that we might take the "low road" to wonder and learning.

Embodiment and the Counter-Process Tradition: The Road (Recently) Less Traveled

From the 10,000 miles above view, there are two diametrically opposed traditions concerning how writing is learned, one of which has been mostly ignored following the process movement. Simply put, one tradition holds that learning to write can be taught conceptually, and that these concepts, through practice, potentially transfer to new situations. The other holds that writing cannot be taught at all, at least if one means that there's a knowledge about writing that can transfer to novel situations. Relatedly, Chris Anson's work on transfer—in arguing that *neither* group believes that there's potential for automatic transfer between situations "without significant cognitive effort" and *also* "some degree of learning" and experience within the new situation (539)—labels these traditions "weak negative transfer" theories and "strong negative transfer" theories. The position, calling into question the very idea of writing "expertise," was dominant among language scholars even as freshman writing courses begin to proliferate, and it still has its adherents today in (controversial) theorists such as Stanley Fish. Additionally, certain linguistic theories following Noam Chomsky argue that language is primarily *acquired* as opposed to learned. Nevertheless, the former position clearly dominates today, and it's no wonder. From our contemporary perspective, the latter position remains hopelessly bound to a troubling innatism that, historically, has tied expression to "character" and "native ability," spuriously linked to social categories such as race, gender, and social class. Indeed, it is something of a testimony to the ascendancy of our discipline that style is no longer widely understood as something one possesses by birth—a mark "mental discipline" and superior breading.

However, while we must obviously strongly repudiate this kind of thinking that has no place in the contemporary world, it's worth considering that, in a rush to distance ourselves from these backwards politics (politics that also happen to undermine our strongest claims to disciplinarity), we may have reduced the complexity of the "writing can't be taught" or "strong negative" position. Indeed, as the work of theorists such as Thomas Kent makes clear, there is a certain amount of correspondence between contemporary postprocess theory and the "writing can't be taught" tradition. In short, what neuroscience shows us is the value of *both* traditions. Writing is *both* something learned through embodied acquisition and *also* something that can be taught through appeals to critique and reason.[3] However, as should be clear by this point, we cannot teach to reason alone.

In the "writing can't be taught" tradition, Robert Ochsner's fascinating, flawed, and mostly overlooked *Physical Eloquence and the Biology of Writing* (1990) makes the strong case for taking the "low road" towards an embodied writing pedagogy. For Ochsner writing skills are "acquired" rather than "learned" through the activation of internal mental structures. Drawing on (now dated) biology and neuroscience, he posits an auto-affective subject, whose "inner language" or biogrammar is ideas or propositions, that expresses ideas more or less well according to "harmonies" between language and embodiment. In a culture that privileges oral over written work, Ochsner calls for "kinetic and visual melodies" that wire the brain to effectively produce texts through above all and always through *practice*. For instance, he recommends that writing be the only mode of communication in a class. As well, he calls for "auditory melody," the attunement of sound to language (for example, having students read their texts out loud). He's against in any way teaching writing as a cognitive act—writing to express abstract ideas and internal thought—and instead wants students to practice the physical form of language in various ways in order to break through sedimented, embodied habits learned through schooling. As I read it in the light of neuroscience, his approach is radical: "As teachers we must move away from a pedagogy that fundamentally denatures the student's body; we must therefore largely discount writing as a mental or cognitive endeavor. In brief, we must try to de-emphasize writing as a thinking process" (24). He's not calling for a return to old fashioned grammar instruction. Instead, he calls for a pedagogy of *practice* and (following Richard Lanham) *play* in which writing is learned like a foreign language, activating the unconscious and natural disposition to communicate while also wiring the brain and body in new ways.

By taking the "low road," the goal is finally to create harmonies so that the expression of inner ideas (the "inner voice") in writing has the rhythm and sound of speech. Indeed, for Ochsner, eloquence—a quality he values, from the perspective of embodiment, over reason—is a *physical* embodied attunement to the writing situation. But in addition to concrete *experience*, what this requires, above all, is *motivation*; students have to *desire* to communicate effectively in a given situation in order for acquisition to occur. In other words, our "natural" desire for persuasion is underwritten by a libidinal economy in which the subject develops. Indeed, motivation, he stresses, is always "from within" (49).

While Ochsner problematically views motivation as intrinsic[4]—indeed, as a matter of natural character—his argument nevertheless resonates with my theorization of embodiment, disaffection, and wonder, calling into question the rationalism of social epistemic and process pedagogies. His embodied pedagogy demands that we consider motivation differently than we do where we privilege reasoned engagement. As Ochsner explains, the problem for classical curriculum (and this will be a main theme of Chapter 4) was that it was rooted in "discipline and boredom" (25). But as we've seen, our social epistemic pedagogy suffers from a similar problem. What we can recycle from Ochsner's idea of intrinsic desire is that motivation, tied to desire in general, is an embodied disposition as opposed to a reasoned awareness.

From the perspective of a plastic pedagogy, the question of embodied motivation is fundamentally the question of wonder; to take seriously the primacy of affect is to take seriously motive. We must recognize that the pedagogical privileging of autonomous reason over affect is frequently, as Ochsner argues, *demotivating*. Instead, writing instruction must begin in an authentic recognition of the affective entanglements of desiring subjects; this returns us to the question of wonder, the affective connectedness to the other that opens students to the forms of reasoned inquiry we value in the academy. In response to the question, "what would a writing plastic pedagogy rooted in wonder look like?," it's likely the case that the answer is clearer for what it excludes than for what it includes—e.g., pedagogies based in auto-affective self expression as well as ones based in rational programs. But fortunately, I think there is much in the affective turn to help answer this question.

Prediction Error and Tacit Knowledge: Learning as Embodied Experience

As we've seen, from the perspective of neuroscience, learning is the resolution of a "prediction error"; that is, the brain only takes in new information when a prediction goes bad, disrupting interoceptive equilibrium and the efficiency of the brain's function. For example, in baseball, a batter's brain must make predictions about the ball—what kind of pitch, where it will be—before all of the sensory data has registered. In other words, the batter must take the "low road" to learning and improving their performance hitting a given pitcher. But conceptual knowledge plays a role too, including, for instance, a knowledge of the type of pitches in a pitcher's repertoire. Imagine if a major league pitcher known for his high-velocity fastball (92+ mph) suddenly just soft-tossed in a high-looping "eephus pitch" at about 58mph. While a major league batter would have no problem with that pitch in many contexts, there's a disproportionate chance that he won't make good contact because he's not disposed to predict it in the context of a game (this has been a tactic of savvy veteran pitchers, such as Livan Hernandez). But if the same pitcher attempts the same pitch too frequently, it likely won't be as effective—the batter will have *learned* through his failure by matching categories. That is, the, the brain will have learned to make automatically predictions through experience, aided by concepts.

Likewise, a student writer that gets feedback (in one form or another) on a dangling participle might make a similar conceptual adjustment—although, without an affective response to the feedback, the student probably won't adjust at all. That is, it's less likely—although not impossible, given that reason is rarely divorced from affect in practice—that the student will begin to attend to dangling participles solely because they have been *reasoned* with. And it's especially unlikely, absent a basis in affect, that this knowledge will transfer (Immordino-Yang & Damasio). As we've seen, for learning to occur, the categorization process likely *needs to be linked to affect.*[5] This is all, of course, entirely counter-intuitive and weird, as we like to think of reason, learning, and emotion alike as our *reactions* to things in the world—not as adjustments to predictions that register below conscious awareness. But neuroscience underscores that, beginning at a level beneath conscious awareness, we form new concepts only when old concepts are no longer sufficient to the brain's task of prediction. With these things in mind, we can rethink some of the enduring pedagogical questions of our discipline from an embodied perspective.

What's taking shape here is that learning has the character of an *event*—a disruption of the nervous system's homeostasis—that passes through the social/external. And we can better see the significance of the negative—*failure, destruction, explosion*—to learning. For example, it's unlikely that students will form a stronger concept of "audience" without being put in a situation in which their habituated, automatic predictions (resulting from schooling in the five-paragraph essay) are no longer rewarded. It's unlikely students will change an old writing process (perhaps one rooted in procrastination) without that process leading, one way or another, to an affective agitation. The brain itself will resist discarding the five-paragraph essay so long as it continues to yield rewards, like good grades, in their classes.

On the one hand, it's becoming clearer that we need an embodied theory of learning that emphasizes tacit knowledge within novel situations, creating affective provocations beyond the reward-punishment system of grades, recognizing and rewarding a multiplicity of intelligent contributions to composing in the digital age. Indeed, where grades are the primary motivator, where writing is limited to the student-amateur writing for the teacher-expert, we find a real but very narrow range of affective provocations, making it more unlikely that students will abandon hardwired habits learned through schooling (as opposed to through education). On the other hand, by multiplying the connections between writing to feeling, we multiply the potential for the predictive errors that give shape to learning, as well as for success construed as intelligent contributions irreducible to linear reason. This would suggest the value of, for example, public rhetoric and service learning to concept formation (which I'll explore further in Appendix 5.5). However, as we'll see, it also suggests the value of rhetorical theories of pedagogy, such as Jenny Rice's, which highlights tacit knowledge as a form of preconscious knowing, subject to alteration below the level of critical reflection.

But before further exploring this, we need to be careful here: there is nothing in neuroscience to suggest that learning *qua* explosive disruption must result from traumatic or otherwise dramatic events, or even from events that originate outside the subject. The analysis of causation in Chapters 2 and 3 reminds us that the "cause" of learning may seem totally disproportionate to the effect, like pushing a button that triggers a nuclear explosion. So learning can happen following both external and internal disruption. Following findings from pathological neuroscience, Immordino-Yang and Damasio show that "the very neurobiological systems that support our social interactions and relationships are recruited for the often covert and private decision making that underlies much of our thought" (4). In other words, private reasoning reuses neural circuits identified with sociality, further blurring the line between auto and heteroaffection. Immordino-Yang and Damasio's discovery resonates with other neuroscientific findings, such as the fact that neurons fire both when engaging in and observing a behavior.[6] Similarly, we know from neuroscience that when we remember something, we activate the same neural pathways that formed—linking image and affect—during the original experience (even though, as Proust's famous example of the madeleine demonstrates, memory degrades over time, becoming more about the rememberer than the remembered).

What I really want to emphasize here is that learning can potentially result from manifold experiences—from both within and without—and each speaks to the brain's heteroaffective touch. As Immordino-Yang and Damasio put it:

> Why does a high school student solve a math problem, for example? The reasons range from the intrinsic reward of having found the solution, to getting a good grade, to avoiding punishment, to helping tutor a friend, to getting into a good college, to pleasing his/her parents or the teacher. All of these reasons have a powerful emotional component and relate both to pleasurable sensations and to survival within our culture. (4)

Relatedly, we know that humans seem to have a unique ability to learn directly through language. As Andy Clark argues following the work of Roepstorff and Frith, language enables an ability for top-down "script sharing," such that "one agent's action may originate in the brain of another agent" (286). As opposed to other animals who learn only through bottom-up "training," through language, the human capacity for developing new conceptual models extends outwards into the brains of others.

Clearly, therefore, we need not entirely dismiss "classical" pedagogical techniques; learning may occur in response to a lecture by a trusted teacher (or, potentially, the dreaded and feared one) just as it might in moments of failure. For this reason, it may therefore prove useful to once again, as did the ancient Greeks, theorize the affective relationship between teacher and student to learning (as I will in Chapter 5). In short, in addition to novel exposure to rhetorical situations and genres, neuroscience suggests the significance of embodied, heteroaffective relationality *in general*—between students and teachers, students and other students, students and outside texts, students and their own texts, students and different situations—to learning. But what's novel here is how the neuroscientific theory of learning as prediction error enables us to see the importance of the relations between affective, embodied wonder and the failures and events that result in learning. Thankfully, new rhetorical theories of non-critical reflection and embodied, tacit knowledge help us in understanding this relationality between wonder and the symbolic, moving us toward a pedagogy that cultivates plastic habits of mind.

Tacit Knowledge: Experts and Open Wounds

In contemporary rhetoric, I greatly value Jenny Rice's work "Pathologia," which discovers wonder in the experience of being wounded. Rice argues that "we begin to theorize the wound itself as the beginning of dialogue." Where Micciche speaks of the "pain" involved in resisting cultural codes, Rice argues that the resulting wound of such "lacerations" is in fact the beginning of healthy dialog: "Being an interlocutor is possible only because of the lacerations, because I have undergone an experience with the outside, with my interlocutor" ("Pathologia" 40). Following Hawhee, Rice argues that through a "critical toggling" between epistemic and descriptive rhetoric—that is, describing the wound as opposed to critically or dialogically engaging with it—we open up new potentials for public rhetoric to understand pathological discourse and persuasion in general. In Rice's pedagogy, describing the wound "opens" the student to the sensorium, "connective tissues of publicness itself" ("Pathologia" 37–38), where they are first implored to "spill their guts" as opposed to responding through stock forms of reason. In describing the wound, we remain in a state of wonder before it.

However, of course, wonder is not only a negative response (in fact we seem to associate it more with positivity). Jody Shipka similarly emphasizes the importance of wonder in her call for teachers to more explicitly allow students to discover topics and invent arguments through their own emotional connections to the world. In Shipka's work, *hobbies* become important sources of academic inspiration, as in her multimodal compositions rooted in her passion for antiques, photography, and Maryland history. Subjects emerge through her hobbies where they intersect, leading her into more academic engagements with them. From the perspective of these theories, wonder connects students to their own affective experience (as opposed to, for example, objects). Beginning with embodied experience, students are led to goal-directed writing and rhetoric.

Relatedly, in her essay "Para-Expertise," Rice argues for the value of subjective and "tacit knowledge"—that is, our embodied, affective experience of the world outside of expert knowledge; for example, how to maneuver a key "just so" into a quirky lock on a door ("Para-Expertise" 126)—as essential to the distributed and goal-directed rhetorical work of posing and solving problems. Tacit knowledge "thrives," as Rice argues, "in the spaces where our bodies live, move, and work" ("Para-Knowledge" 127). For Rice, given that we *know more than we can tell*, embodied experience can serve as a basis for problem-forming and invention, leading to "alliances" with experts, underscoring the role of the amateur in public rhetoric. The act of problem-forming, essential to "cultivating rhetorical expertise" ("Para-Knowledge" 135), is therefore distributed—linking embodied experience, environment, and extra-individual collaboration—as opposed to reasoned or dialogical. Importantly here, Rice is undermining the received concept of writing as symbolic *expertise*.

Tacit knowledge is the accumulation, or mapping, of our *felt* experience of the world. What is at stake here is a rhetorical pedagogy that moves composition beyond a reliance on models of expertise, which is to say models that imagine composing as a matter of *personal and symbolic* as opposed to *relational and affective* mastery. By investing "pedagogical emphases toward helping students identify '*pivot points*' in those areas where they have para-expertise" ("Para-Expertise" 134, my emphasis), we can teach students to act into their environments while also valuing the unique significance of their tacit knowledge, their embodied experience. On the one hand, this "pivoting" may be read as a form of flexibility, and any theory of tacit knowledge must also entail resistance. However, we can also understand pivoting as essentially related to wonder, connecting our tacit, embodied experience to the goal-directed work of writing, reason, and rhetoric. Just as reflecting on the wound connects us to the public circulation of affect (the sensorium), so too does reflecting on embodied, tacit knowledge prepare students to represent problems to themselves, thusly providing a point of entry into the work of public rhetoric.

Wonder and the "Ghosts in the Stacks": An Assignment

For my part, I've tried to incorporate wonder into pedagogy in various ways, formal and informal (with more and less success!), and I'm especially interested in thinking about the relationship between heteroaffective wonder and *academic* work. This is both because I believe great scholarship begins in wonder and also because I believe it has the potential to inspire wonder in our students. I teach a course on "pathological rhetoric," focusing on the rhetoric of pathological ideas held by one population or another to be true in some place or period, ranging from scientific racism to contemporary fake news. In one assignment, after having introduced some of the now embarrassing "knowledge" of early (late 19th- and early 20th-century) psychology and sociology (e.g., hysteria, eugenics, the social hygiene movement), I have students visit the library at our school to find books from that period—works that students like them, less than one hundred years ago, would have cited in their own papers as knowledge. The assignment is meant as a heuristic, and is connected to a larger research project, but here is the relevant portion:

Ghosts in the Stacks

You will search deep in the library stacks and find works of scientific racism/sexism/bigotry that are "hidden in plain sight." That is, you will find an old book from the era in which scientific racism was popular—for our purposes we'll say about 1890–1940—in the library.

Having found this book I want you to imagine that you are a student [at our school] in the early 20th century. You've taken a class, and you've been presenting the "knowledge" in the book you've unearthed as *fact*. You don't need to read the entire book, but what I want you to do is explore it, thinking about how students engaged with the book at the time. Then, you have two options. **In either case, I want you to write a paragraph or two detailing your findings:**

1. In this option, you will consider how the work may have affected those students so long ago, considering how a passage worked rhetorically to create powerful affects. Do you see ideas underlined? Do you see pages dog-eared? What's on those pages? Does it tell you anything about what students might have found important at the time? When was it last checked out? In short, describe how the *rhetorical structure* (e.g., *logos, pathos, ethos, kairos*) of those pages or passages likely impacted those students [at our school] so long ago. In other words, the goal is to consider how the book's presentation, tone, word choices, sentence structures, metaphors, and other rhetorical devices may have *affected* those students.
2. If you don't see any markings in the book, you might instead locate a powerful example of a dangerous idea presented in the book. Simply explain what it says, and reflect upon it: I want to know how the author's *rhetorical choices* (e.g., *logos, pathos, ethos, kairos*) makes *you feel*. In other words, try to find *something* in the book that reflects the dangerous ideas of scientific racism, and reflect on (write about) how the book's presentation, tone, word choices, sentence structures, metaphors, and other rhetorical devices affect you.

Of course, not all students have an emotional experience with these texts, or in realizing that they are connected to abominable ideas by a direct line in the very place they live—but some do. And I recognize too that the first option, the idea of reconstructing the feelings (or what rhetoric created those feelings) previous generations of students, involves artifice (indeed, the construction theory of emotions precludes such easy access to emotions across time and space). Nevertheless, I hope that the assignment will allow students to draw on their emotional experience to represent a problem to themselves. That is, I hope that, by dwelling in their embodied response, it will inspire them to wonder about the *otherness* of these knowledges.

Notes

1. In some ways, Barrett offers a similar account of objects as OOO, which also theorizes a situatedness in which we encounter objects in accordance with their use, a caricature of the underlying "real object." However, there is a crucial distinction here. Barrett is arguing that tools and objects and emotions are each simulated or

predicted at a level below conscious awareness, and furthermore claiming that this process occurs always in *correlation* to social goals.

2. Jenny Rice describes the tacit knowledge in, for example, knowing that you need to jiggle a key into a lock that just doesn't quite work right. We don't necessarily think consciously about this work, but understand and address this problem at an embodied level ("Para-Expertise").
3. We can see this very clearly, for instance, in Barrett's neuroscience, in which learning straddles the biological and the symbolic.
4. In viewing motivation as "natural," Ochsner fails to see the significance of resistance to the politics of disaffection in the "attention economy," and the potential for technologies to disrupt (or replace) the libidinal economy that drives development. Further, Ochsner overemphasizes style and form in positing that motivation comes primarily from a drive to self display (Malabou reminds us that desire is more complicated than this).
5. Again, it's obviously true that many received pedagogical practices—giving grades, for instance—can create an affective context and have long served this role.
6. This has led many to postulate, controversially, the existence of "mirror neurons" that have the specific task of mirroring. Others argue that special neurons need not exist to explain this phenomenon—that mirroring is a function of the brain more generally.

Works Cited

Anson, Chris M. "The Pop Warner Chronicles: A Case Study in Contextual Adaptation and the Transfer of Writing Ability." *College Composition and Communication*, vol. 67, no. 4, 2016, p. 518.

Barrett, Lisa F. *How Emotions Are Made: The Secret Life of the Brain.* Houghton Mifflin Harcourt, Boston, MA, 2017.

Clark, Andy. *Surfing Uncertainty: Prediction, Action, and the Embodied Mind.* Oxford University Press, New York, 2016.

Driscoll, Dana Lynn, and Roger Powell. "States, Traits, and Dispositions: The Impact of Emotion on Writing Development and Writing Transfer Across College Courses and Beyond." *Composition Forum*, vol. 34, *Association of Teachers of Advanced Composition*, 2016.

Hawhee, Debra. "Rhetoric's Sensorium." *Quarterly Journal of Speech*, vol. 101, no. 1, 2015, pp. 2–17.

Immordino-Yang, Mary H., and Antonio Damasio. "We Feel, Therefore We Learn: The Relevance of Affective and Social Neuroscience to Education." *Mind, Brain, and Education*, vol. 1, no. 1, 2007, pp. 3–10.

Kent, Thomas. *Post-Process Theory: Beyond the Writing-Process Paradigm.* Southern Illinois University Press, Carbondale, 1947, 1999.

Leake, Eric. "Writing Pedagogies of Empathy: As Rhetoric and Disposition." *Composition Forum*, vol. 34, *Association of Teachers of Advanced Composition*, 2016.

Micciche, Laura. "The Trouble With Affect." *JAC*, vol. 26, no. 1/2, 2006, pp. 264–276. Web. 4 June 2015.

Ochsner, Robert. *Physical Eloquence and the Biology of Writing.* State University of New York Press, Albany, NY, 1990.

Rice, Jenny. "Para-Expertise, Tacit Knowledge, and Writing Problems." *College English*, vol. 78, no. 2, 2015, p. 117.

———. "Pathologia." *Quarterly Journal of Speech*, vol. 101, no. 1, 2015, pp. 34–45.

Rickert, Thomas. *Ambient Rhetoric: The Attunements of Rhetorical Being*. University of Pittsburgh, Pittsburgh, PA, 2013.

Shipka, Jody. *Toward a Composition Made Whole*. University of Pittsburgh Press, Pittsburgh, PA, 2011.

Vatz, Richard E. "The Myth of the Rhetorical Situation." *Philosophy & Rhetoric*, vol. 6, no. 3, 1973, pp. 154–161. *JSTOR*, www.jstor.org/stable/40236848.

Worsham, Lynn. "Going Postal: Pedagogic Violence and the Schooling of Emotion." *Journal of Advanced Composition-JAC*, vol. 18, 1998, pp. 213–245.

4 Writing Pedagogy and the Crises of Attention

From Distraction to Disaffection

In Chapter 3, we saw that where sovereign power required sad passions—that is, a diminishment of the power of reflection leading to reason—contemporary power instead exploits disaffection. In both cases, and especially from the pedagogical perspective, the correspondence between wonder and power is closely related to *attention*. Where reason, and the capacity to act, begins in an affective capacity to remain open to difference through wonder, attention exists somewhere *in-between* embodied affectivity and consciousness. We can see this in Joddy Murray's definition of the "coolness" (an openness that is not yet joy or sadness) of the affects related to attention:

> Finally, another significant "cool" or rational emotion are feelings associated with attention. For example, the reticular activating system may cause a heightened awareness of the number and frequency of blue cars around because I just painted my car blue. The heightened attention can also come from a sense of awe, or a sense of amazement following a seemingly new piece of information or discovery, and this awe or amazement may naturally lead to a sense of concentration associated with focused attention.
>
> (Murray 104)

Simply put, attention entails and requires affective investment.

As I illustrated in the Introduction, the classical account of attentive cognition, in Mike Anderson's words, "is contemplative (or, perhaps better, reflective, mirrorlike) in character; such a mind—withdrawn, narcissistic, engaged only in its own productions—needs inner objects to behold, to alter" (282). And as we've already seen, the relation of power to the active capacity for focused, reflective attention, for phenomenologogical introspection, has a socio-historical character. By inspiring sad passions, sovereign power diminished the capacity for deep reflective attention—that is, for both action and thought. It should be no surprise then that, at the dawn of modern writing instruction, the classical pedagogy's emphasis on mental discipline was widely associated with a regressive *boredom* during what I'm calling the first modern crisis of attention. But where the classical curriculum was understood to have failed because it created boredom and other "sad passions," the modern writing pedagogy emerged around the *biological* problem of attention to combat a perceived spread, and the biological threat, of stupidity.

As we'll see, a biological, transcendental attention became in both discourse and practice the guarantee of reason as reflective intelligence. And in agreement with Spinoza's critique of power, the emergent disciplinary power worked (even more systematically than in the classical curriculum) to produce docility by increasing the "sad passions." However, as I'll later demonstrate, today a *second crisis of attention*—characterized by a disaffecting power and the "new wounded"—entails novel relations between bio-power, technology, and the neurobiological subject.

"Utterly Stupid and Uninteresting Lectures on Rhetoric": Biological Attention and the Dissolution of the Classical Curriculum

Sometime around the middle of the 19th century, seemingly overnight, it occurred to just about everyone that just about no one was paying attention in school. Students were bored out of their wits by pedantic lectures and increasingly skeptical about the value of a language education that stressed memorizing and reciting obscure rules in obscure languages. No longer able to inform or inspire, the old methods of instruction that comprised the "classical curriculum" no longer seemed to work. As one author put it in *The New England Magazine* in 1879, "It has appeared that the classical curriculum, although incomparable as a mode of mental discipline, fails in all cases thoroughly to inform the student, and in the great majority of cases to inspire him" (Baldwin 575). As a result, in the newly student-centered classroom, the care and attention of the student—around an emergent bio-power—would replace the classics as the central subject of language education. But in the long history of higher education, perhaps nothing was less likely than this decline of the classical curriculum.

The first freshman writing classes appeared out of this decline at Harvard through a pervasive anxiety over the biological problem of attention. This anxiety spoke to the entanglement of concerns over the decline of reason, morality, and the species. At the end of the 19th century, the Harvard Committee of Composition and Rhetoric began publishing highly influential reports that revolutionized writing instruction from the university all the way down through the grammar schools, effectively ending the classical curriculum and leaving us a legacy of compulsory freshman composition. While the trace of the aura of the classics reappeared in the newly formed disciplinary studies of English Literature, in the Harvard reports, language was brought down to earth and denuded. The rhetoricians of the classical curriculum were left exposed—off came the gowns—in a modern "student-centered" classroom. There, the writing teacher would serve in a new role as technician of student attention and practitioner of care rather than as cipher of Truth.

By the turn of the century, few academics, artists, and intellectuals could resist commenting on the relation between attention, human development, and education. William James built his brilliant challenge to faculty and empiricist psychology around a systematic study of attention (James 403). British psychologist James Cappie argued that attention "may be said to underlie every other mental faculty" (qtd. in Crary 17). Freud made attention the condition of meaning. At the same time, physicians discovered the startlingly long delay of the "reflex arc"—between stimuli and nervous response—proving that our perceptions are not of the immediate present. Bergson theorized attention as freedom, a capacity for transforming the expected course of events.

Anticipating the emergence of the newly conceptualized attention, artists, especially Cezanne, and philosophers, especially Nietzsche, explored the counter-intuitive fact that sustained focus resulted in dissolution rather than unification (Crary); Walter Benjamin later made this fragmented attention the basis of his esthetics. At a moment in history prepossessed with the effects of industrialism on the individual, the family, the culture, and even the species, attention was directly connected to the period's ideas of progress and "degeneration": "Culture and command over the powers of nature are solely the result of attention: all errors, all superstition, the consequence of defective attention" (Nordeau 56).

And just as William James challenged the earlier faculty psychology through attention, the proponents of a new writing instruction posed a challenge to the classical pedagogy by appealing to new certainties about attention. From the "current-traditional"[1] pedagogy popularized by Harvard's freshman English course to its various alternatives—e.g., writing instruction based in the personal/experiential; literature; non-literary texts; and even in classical rhetoric, with no writing instruction at all (Brereton 14–17)—there appear regular preoccupations with attention and its disciplines. That is, the new intelligibility of attention and the subject cut across the family of writing pedagogy discourses, characterizing the current-traditional pedagogy as well as the more socially directed pedagogy of the progressivists that is today "everywhere in our work" (Emig 12).

The concern over the relevance of the classical curriculum to the lives of students, and its concomitant failure to secure student interest, is visible across the "family" discourses surrounding writing curriculum and pedagogy in the late 19th and early 20th centuries. This concern begins in relation to relatively crude theorization of boredom rooted in a two-dimensional "transactional" concept of attention—attention as simply either present or absent (Comstock). However, in these conversations, reflecting similar developments in modern psychology and art, we can see the emergence of a *new* form of attention, attention as a finite capacity of a *biological subject* that would become a central object of study in progressivist discourse.

This *reflective attention*—that is, attention that, operating like a beam or searchlight, holds ideas before the mind for instrospective examination and expression—served to unify the subject in an auto-affective, fully-present experience in the face of dissolution and fragmentation. In the classroom, constantly threatened from both inside and outside by fragmentation, this attention became the guarantee of reason and subjective unity through its volitional, suspensive powers. That is, by paradoxically harboring the "conditions for its own disintegration" (Crary 47), reflective attention emerges here as both the problem and the solution, setting the table for wholesale reconsiderations of both curriculum and pedagogy.

Early critiques of the classical pedagogy around the problem of boredom culminated in the 1897 *Harvard University Report of the Committee on Composition and Rhetoric*, which resonated throughout the world of education. The report sounded the death knell of the classical curriculum and was the driving force behind the freshman writing courses that would quickly proliferate shortly after, and especially between 1920 and 1940 (Berlin, *Writing Instruction* 65). And we can see both in the report, in the 1,170 student self-reports, and in broader pedagogical conversations by teachers, proto-psychiatrists, education theorists, and other stakeholders, that the decline of the classical curriculum was framed by a broader conversation about *care* and *attention*.

As the 1,170 student self-reports collected by the committee for their 1896 report make clear, students were no longer connecting to the classical pedagogy, that their feelings about it were entirely negative. Simply put, when they were finally asked by the Harvard Committee, they characterized the old curriculum to be too boring, too abstract, and too out of touch with modern needs. Student #42 vehemently argues against "the utterly stupid and uninteresting lectures on Rhetoric" he was subject to in high school, calling the curriculum a "waste of time." Many students make similar comments on the ways the content of their education seemed remote both from their lives and from their individual intellectual development. In all of these ways, we can see that classical pedagogy worked to reproduce the relationship between affect and power described by Spinoza. However, at the same time, this system of power was cumbersome and inefficient. Resistance was common. As Student #7 comments, "we took no interest in it" and often faked attention.

The failure of the classical curriculum to secure attention comprised one side of the push to institutionalize writing instruction; on the other side, there was the question of modern *distraction*. The Harvard Committee specifically argued that writing courses were needed because other institutions had broken down, failing to deliver moral and literate students. And their concerns were shared by far more progressive thinkers as well. In the scholarly discourse there was a pervasive anxiety over outside threats to the purity of language, a language no longer secured against its usage on the streets, even by the elite few trained in usage at the highest levels. The following quote from *English Journal* in 1912 is typical of how the decline of language was linked to social decline in general:

> We are no longer a Bible-reading people; the church and Sunday school are fast losing their hold; family life is less intimate and watchful; respect for law and authority is decreasing, while forces of evil are steadily multiplying in our midst. The moving pictures and the vaudevilles, cheap and commonplace if not immoral, the trashy magazine, the daily newspaper with its scandal and vulgar comic supplement are but a few of the agencies at work which have already helped to bring about a cheapening of ideals, a lowering of standards, and a blunting of fine sensibilities and distinctions.
>
> (Breck 68)

Seemingly everybody agreed—modern technology was a distraction, a threat to an already overburdened attention and proper usage. For example, E. L. Godkin, the author of an incendiary and widely circulated essay entirely devoted to this concern, titled "The Illiteracy of American Boys," lamented the influence of newspapers and "dialect novels" (4). Around the problem of finitude in the face of modern distractions, language was compromised at the very point of its usage.

Therefore, beginning "about the year 1870," as the Harvard Committee points out, *most* classes began to rely on writing as a disciplinary technology: "the classes increased in size nearly fourfold, so as to become wholly unmanageable for oral recitation . . . so that at last the whole college work was practically done in writing." By replacing oral examination, by replacing memorization homework, and by replacing in-class oral recitation with written exercise, writing, in its expanded role, was originally valued for its disciplinary efficacy. And it is as a result of the disciplinary value of writing that *instruction in writing* is in turn justified: "the need of facility in written expression was, of course, correspondingly increased." Indeed, writing during this period was a "mere incident" of discipline in education and "no longer an end" (411).

The ongoing discipline of the subject is justified because attention (and subjectivity) always threatens to dissolve where it is overburdened, where demands are made upon it at a developmentally inappropriate level. And to combat this situation, the "wearisome" experience of writing—the negative affects associated with discipline—was justified. According to the Harvard Committee on Composition and Rhetoric, writing instruction "involves steady, daily drill, and drudgery of a kind most wearisome" (421) as well as "severe, constant, daily discipline and practice" (413). The cultivation of embodied lower level composing skills required disciplinary intervention; "errors" were a clear sign of a lack of both volitional attention and embodied discipline, and writing instruction was institutionalized to intervene and remediate. Even classicists Day and Kingsley at the Yale English Department argued instruction should be "best calculated to the art of fixing the attention, directing the train of thoug" (qtd. in Crowley 278) and recommended "frequent exercise" (Crowley 49). But strangely, this diagnostic vision of writing instruction was in fact most overtly expressed by progressivists like Scott, who viewed errors quite literally in the terms of organic pathology as an "outward sign of an inward lesion" (470). It is not difficult to see why G. Stanley Hall's flinty statement was often repeated by language teachers: "the good teacher is a *pedotrieb*, or boy-driver" (235).

For example, we can see the emergence of these new disciplinary techniques in the panoptic system described in the Harvard Report (Comstock). In this system, students produced writings that were always collected but only occasionally graded. Making the student the *potential* subject of an irregular surveillance forced the student to act *as if* they were constantly visible. Resistance within this system, as a result, became more difficult (Comstock). As Spinoza would predict, the imposition of the disciplinary techniques had the effect (if not exactly the goal) of creating docility and negative feelings, as we can see through student and theoretical accounts from this time. For example, Student #8 in the Harvard Report characterized the new technique of writing of daily themes thusly: "It was a dreary, mechanical drudgery, unlighted by a single gleam of interest." And although many students likely parroted their professor's insistence that they required daily discipline (internalizing the work of power), the reports nevertheless make clear that bodily discipline was imposed with no genuine connection to development or intelligence; typical is Student #21's claim that "These 'Essáys' were returned with a few criticisms, the gist of which was either 'good' or 'bad,' as the case went. Why they were good or bad the criticism never told. I do not think the instructor knew, and I am positive I did not."

While problems related to attention and distraction appear across diverse discourses on language, writing, and pedagogy (Comstock), it might be surprising to some that they culminate in the early decades of the 20th century in the pedagogy of John Dewey, Fred Newton Scott, and other progressivists. Indeed, a cultivated "reflective attention" or introspection is the *very definition* of "educated" for Dewey: "A person who has gained the power of reflective attention, the power to hold problems, questions, before the mind, is in so far, intellectually speaking, educated." It is the psycho-physiological apparatus at the center of his theory of reflective learning, and for this reason, "the proper recognition and use [of attention] is perhaps the most serious problem in instruction upon the intellectual side" (*School and Society* 147). The progressivists differed from the humanists not in the significance their pedagogy attributed to attention, but rather only in the strictly developmental manner in which they believed this suspensive "power" of a reflective attention must be inculcated in the student. So for Dewey too, overtly, the teacher must cultivate introspective attention through discipline: "it is a discipline, or gain in power of control; that is, a *habit*" (149).

Far from disrupting bio-power, the progressivist pedagogy was *more* invested in biological capacity, *more* invested in discipline. Dewey argued that the pedagogy of the humanists, at Harvard and elsewhere, had only focused on "intrinsic" biological attention, while the next (biological) stage of human development—recognizing man's uniquely social nature—is characterized by *reflective attention*. The humanist pedagogy overemphasized one end of the pole—oscillating between the intrinsic power of stimuli and the volitional power of focus—on which attention was understood to exist. This approach left the student "at the mercy of custom and external suggestions" (Dewey 147). For the progressivist, through development, the student must discover the communicative, pragmatic, and above all *social* utility of correctness, linguistic purity, and composing; composition becomes, in Scott's words, a "*social behavior*."

The fact that the progressivist pedagogy was hardly a disavowal of bio-power is perhaps best captured in the complexity of their disciplinary scheme meant to correct inattention at the "lower order":

> The ill-regulated work of the primary school may breed habits of inattention and general intellectual flabbiness, to the frustration of the work in the higher grades. There must be discipline, from the beginning of school life; and the discipline in reading and writing is within a field of activity necessary for the child both in school and in after life. . . . This discipline must be adapted to the capacities of the child.
>
> (79–80)

Scott, like other educators we saw above, relied similarly on discipline to compensate for the finitude of attention, but tied his techniques more explicitly to bio-power through a normalized, quasi-scientific developmental scheme. Early in development, the disciplines worked at the level of the body to make writing automatic—writing is hardwired into the extremities to free up space at the center. Again, the hardwiring of "lower order" skills, such as mechanical correctness, grammar, and spelling, occurs at first mostly through sheer repetition of the body, especially of course the hands. As Scott argued, "There must be frequent repetition. Abstract ideas easily evaporate unless they are made part of the very stuff of the mind" (148).

Similarly, grammar "must be made concrete" in the subject; spelling must be learned through "drill" (153). For example, in teaching spelling through repetition, the student would develop "a clear picture of the word as it looks on the page, and a readiness in transcribing this visual image with the pen." The sound images of the word would thereby be physically written into the body, and "the motor memories whereby the hand automatically writes the word that is in the mind" (154). Ultimately, not only would drilling command the attention of the subject and focus the student in the right direction, but it would also compensate for the divided nature of language itself as it presents to the attention.

But additionally, and quite strikingly, progressivist pedagogy was tied to bio-power around the problem of attention in quasi-eugenic terms. For Scott, we must have a "fitness" of language to ideas, while the countervailing demands on attention threaten to take us back to the "childhood" of our language—to a recapitulated "savagery." It is this pathological, "savage," and "other" attention of the child that threatens both individual development and the species, justifying intervention: "in brief, the life of the savage is very near to the boy of the twentieth century" (Carpenter, Baker & Scott 93). While avoiding many of the rhetorical excesses of the mental hygiene movement, the progressivist conceptualization of social worth is nevertheless similarly read against the backdrop of recapitulation and degeneration.

The atavistic logic that underscored the progressivist politicization of education extended directly out of their insistence that reflective attention is the pinnacle of social and psychological development. On the one side, reflective attention reduced the relation between stimuli (language) and consciousness to passive reception. But on the other side, reflective attention presided over a problematic abstraction of the subject that failed to account for the lived, situational, and affective processes that comprise learning. That is, viewed as a biological capacity, reflective attention ignores the dynamic, context-specific exchanges between world and consciousness, the ways in which the learner is, as Matthew Crawford notices, "pulled further into some phenomenon" such that "our mental energies are not simply reflected back but refracted." The beam of searchlight attention is a constant, autonomous force of a developed conscious unity "unchanged by what it illuminates"; by failing to deconstruct the subject/object binary, reflective attention presumes a transcendental, auto-affective self-presence.

The New Attention Economy: Compositions of Attention

As we can see, around an emergent bio-power, writing pedagogy during the first crisis of attention produced a "reflective attention" as a guarantee of subjective unity in the face of cultural fragmentation. In Foucauldian terms, the student emerges within new disciplinary institutions, through the relation of their writing and attention, as an impossible "transcendental-empirical doublet." But the situation in today's attention economy, following neuroscience, is different; clearly, after process pedagogy, writing instruction is no longer tethered to discipline. We no longer—at least not to the same extent—greet inattentiveness with *drudgery* (the intersection of attentiveness and "sad passions"). At the same time, however, as I began to establish in the Introduction, there are new and significant concerns about student attentiveness, typified by the proliferation of AD/HD. To understand what I'll call the "second crisis of attention," complicating Foucault's concept of bio-power, we require a new account of the biological in the light of neuroscience. After all, Foucault himself was never very clear on what he took for his model of the biological; his definition of the biological never gets far past his ill-defined notion the "somatic." As we'll see, today a neurobiological vision of attention supports the disaffecting work of power, resulting in a proliferation of AD/HD and other "new wounded" subjects. The question becomes, how does our contemporary writing pedagogy contribute or respond to this contemporary bio-power?

A recent Anderson Cooper report on *60 Minutes* titled "What is 'Brain Hacking' " investigated the new crisis of attention and its relation to new media and technologies. As the episode reveals, Silicon Valley has embraced neuroscience for purposes of "brain hacking," purposefully crafting apps and other technologies that work at the synaptic level to replace *care* with new habits of attention: getting "likes," "earning" new emoji, and so on. Others work by holding their (totally useless) rewards back before offering them in a big burst—for instance, "likes" are parceled out in bursts that accord with algorithmic predictions about user affect. Further, they adjust these bursts to individual habits. On average, as the report claims, we check our phone every 15 minutes—not because of phone alert or message (that is, not because we are rationally persuaded), but because we become habituated to doing so. Eventually we create our own "alerts," embodying the apps attentional program. Perhaps even the very mention of cell phones has you itching to check yours right now.

As former Google product manager Tristan Harris claims:

> Well, every time I check my phone, I'm playing the slot machine to see, 'What did I get?' This is one way to hijack people's minds and create a habit, to form a habit. What you do is you make it so when someone pulls a lever, sometimes they get a reward, an exciting reward. And it turns out that this design technique can be embedded inside of all these products.

For example, Snapchat targets its user's attention through a reward system that recognizes usage "streaks"—that is, the number of days in a row one sends messages back and forth to another user. What they've found is that users don't want to lose their streaks, and young people, especially, become stressed when they are away from the app, going so far as to share their passwords with friends while on vacation to maintain their streaks. And as Harris claims: "Inadvertently, whether they want to or not, they are shaping the thoughts and feelings and actions of people. They are programming people." It would be more accurate to say that apps like these explicitly intend to shape our thoughts *through* our feelings, to program us to embody their imperatives as affective and attentional dispositions. Indeed, by targeting how people *feel*, the background or mood, Silicon Valley is in a "race to the bottom of the brain stem." What neuroscientists have discovered is that through "gameification," these technologies keep us in a continual state of anxiety, so we keep checking in.

The attentional capture of the new cybernetic technologies was recently driven home for me by a particular game that seems to compel children like few I've seen before, *Clash of Clans*. I've heard parents use the word "monstrous" to describe the reaction their children (usually young boys) have to this cell phone game being taken away from them. Lacking the emotional intelligence and disposition to recompose themselves, some children seem to lose all sense of self, throwing temper tantrums violent enough to disturb their parents. Googling "Clash of Clans" and "addiction" yields interesting results, including multiple articles about how a "crippling addiction" to the game almost "sank" the Kansas City Royals' season before manager Ned Yost intervened (Petchesky). Meanwhile, adults remain glued to their phones at a level beyond what most find healthy or socially acceptable. And as I write this, new toy robots have appeared on the market that replicate human emotions; the effect is so powerful, that children are concerned about leaving their "new friends" alone when they leave the house (I imagine we'll be hearing a lot more about these toys and their derivations in the near future, as we move beyond SIRI and towards more emotionally intelligent machines). These examples speak, if only anecdotally, to the novel power of attentional hold of these new cybernetic technologies, their ability to anticipate our predictions and the habituating force of their reward systems. It also speaks to the vision Silicon Valley has of the subject: neurological, finite, *flexible*. In light of this, it's clear that what we require above all are strategies of disruption, ways to reclaim the plasticity of our attention to resist its capture and shaping.

This is a point philosopher and media theorist Bernard Stiegler (like Malabou, a Derrida protégé) makes at length, arguing that programming industries increasingly "have worked together to capture children's attention through psychotechnologies" (*Taking Care of Youth* 58). The attention economy that has formed around the new psychotechnologies competes, through the hypersolicitation of attention, for attention as a scare resource. Indeed, in a highly-organized way, plasticity itself has been grammatized by organizations looking to profit on an understanding of its plastic capacities and limits. While it's certainly not the case that all new writing technologies are *essentially* destructive, we must nevertheless confront that many of them have the explicit goal of grammatizing or otherwise capturing (deforming) attention (through its hypersolicitation) at the neurological level in order to realize their own commercial goals.

Examples of this phenomena are rapidly proliferating, and the disturbing results and psychic consequences of this hypersolicitation are becoming clearer (Hayles; "Attention Spans"). For example, a Microsoft study titled "Attention Spans" using EEG scans demonstrates that the brains of adults and children alike have been reformed, and the "deep attention" that Hayles described as the condition of reason—the ability to attend to what Stiegler terms the "long circuits of knowledge" that comprise culture—has been increasingly replaced by an animalistic vigilance, or "hyper attention." The deformation of attention is the deformation of wonder, of the plasticity of intelligence, of primordial care, of our affective openness to the world. Where attention is deformed, our capacity for critical deliberation is diminished, or worse, colonized, outside of relationships of cross-generational care by external drivers of attention. It is in these ways that Malabou's "new wounded" appear, presenting symptoms that parallel cases of neuropathology.

To be as clear as possible, there is nothing *inherently* bad about these new cybernetic technologies, as attention *always* passes through its supplements; furthermore, we saw above how institutional imperatives also work to control and manage attention. And writing too is, of course, a technology that shapes consciousness (a fact that will become important in this chapter). Neither inherently good or bad, technology has the character of the *pharmakon*—it is both cure and poison—an ambiguity that similarly characterizes destructive plasticity.

Nevertheless, we must recognize the rapidly changing relationship between writers and writing technologies. Above all, we must consider to what extent the interests behind these new technologies, interests that are not our own, work to transform consciousness, to destroy care and reason or to replace them with their own imperatives—that is, what is the relationship between writing, technology, and the new wounded. After all, the new cybernetic technologies are, explicitly, mostly not meant to improve our lives; as a society, we mostly don't feel good about them. They have emerged from a global neo-liberalism, a movement defined by the privileging of the economic over the political, an entirely different milieu than the television or telephones of modernity. And their aim is not, as with previous technologies, to capture our attention in order to sell us things. Rather, their aim is precisely to *sell us*—that is, sell our attention. Facebook is not selling Coke or Hondas to us, they are selling our attentional habits to Coke and Honda. Directed at a synaptic level "below" reflective attention, these new technologies are more rhetorically savvy—more *persuasive*.

Andy Clark describes the situation, rather conservatively, in relation to synaptogenesis and the predictive process theory of the brain:

> Increasingly, our best tools and technologies are in the business of predicting our own needs, requests, and patterns of use. Google anticipates search requests according to past patterns of information about present location, and offers advice and options even before we ask for them. Amazon uses powerful collaborative filtering techniques to make suggestions based on past purchases. Such innovations extend the realm of mutual prediction to include webs of humans and machines, each of which are now busily anticipating the other. Unless checked or controlled this could lead . . . to increasingly restricted explorations of the space of opportunities.
>
> (75)

This "restricted . . . space of opportunities" euphemistically speaks to the hijacking of the plasticity of our brain's predictive processes by machines. Unchecked, it is our intelligent capacity for learning itself that is restricted.

Rhetorical, Posthuman, and Neurorhetorical Accounts of Attention

How has composition and rhetoric responded to bio-power in the new attention economy? And to what extend are we, like the moderns, complicit in the work of power?

Given our discipline's investment in pedagogical care, it's surprising to find that for the most part we've been more interested in embracing new writing technologies than questioning their relation to biology and embodiment. I think here especially of the increasingly vocal calls in our discipline, reviewed in the Introduction, to "bring the funk." Works celebrating new writing technologies and multi-modality—many of which have been explored over the course of this book—are important in that they greet the immense complexity of composing in the 21st century with ideas and proposals worthy of that complexity. *Of course* we need to work towards new understandings of the relations between new media, forms of composition, and persuasion. And *of course* we need to deconstruct the reduction of intelligence to reason and reflective attention. It does not follow, however, that we should simply jettison the tradition that relates reason and discursive writing.

One may well retort, even though all the intellectual momentum in our field seems to be on the side of non-discursive forms, that few overtly argue that composition courses should abandon reason or epistemic writing. Yet, it's worth recalling, that, as Meillesoux argues, "Everything and every world *is* without reason" (53), and that composition scholarship rooted in OOO indeed wishes to abandon the transcendental without negotiation. Furthermore, beyond some dated thinking about "critical thinking" that most postprocess pedagogy is calling into question, intelligence and reason—remarkably enough—have barely been considered in posthuman terms. In the rush to "bring the funk" to composition, we've failed to theorize any enduring value of reasoned discourse in contemporary or posthuman terms. As I've been arguing, what we require is a negotiation with or rethinking of reason, not its simple abandonment.

Richard Lanham's theorization of the attention economy is exemplary in this regard. Where other compositionists have embraced the retreat of the *logos*, Lanham looks forward to dancing on its grave, celebrating rhetorical (and technological) diversity. For Lanham, the new attention economy is all good sport because it is always tied to audience and choice—to the scarcity of attention—which, through a kind of natural selection or invisible hand, enables—rather, necessitates—the survival of the fittest rhetoric. Those who control the rhetorical codes control the power. Reality begins in the formal, stylistic *programing* of the material—nearly everything, after all, from chairs to baseball stadiums, now begins as a computer-generated template. In Lanham's words, "The 'real' world becomes a printout, a printout created increasingly by computer graphics, by digital design" (5). Today, "the important people sit at computer screens and make designs" (5), and power means having *access* to or *understanding* of rhetorical codes. Lanham has little interest in our embodied relation to these codes, focusing instead solely on their flexible deployment and efficacy in commanding attention. The code is merely possessed or not; those that lack possession require only enlightenment.

Yet here, once again, the privileging of reason, consciousness, and the symbolic, metaphysics sneaks in through the back door of rhetorical theory: despite his sophisticated understanding of the relations between technology, attention, and persuasion at a level beneath cognition, Lanham nevertheless views these relations as essentially indestructible, such that a rhetorical metacognition can recuperate the status of the subject in the attention economy. For Lanham, the attention economy is "fun" because, potentially at least, everyone can participate by manipulating its (symbolic) codes. Meanwhile power is reduced to ownership and expertise (simply possessed or not). On the one hand, Lanham means his theory to serve as a bulwark against the rising tide of information that endangers attention (remember that for Lanham, it is the over-abundance of information that is the problem, making attention a scarce recourse). However, his therapy is an epistemic self-consciousness or metacognition of "attention-rhetoric" that can act as "the first line of defense of a child swimming in the information flood" (143). This rhetorical self-consciousness is in fact a flexible oscillation that involves looking both *at* as well as *through* surfaces in order to better persuade and attend. That is, it is in some sense a conscious act rooted in reason, governing the movement between attentional modes.

Ultimately, in Lanham, technology and new media are justified teleologically, through a kind of neo-Darwinism of ideas (more, Dewian), and rationalized[2] outside of relationships of care. In failing to recognize the dialectical sublimation of *technics*—that is, the ways technologies work on us below the surface, for better and worse (which will be the topic of Chapter 5)—the design, the program, the code, becomes everything for Lanham; as a result, his project is indistinguishable from the neo-liberal and corporate imperatives of 24–7 capitalism, his endorsement of flexible rhetorical circulation and productivity reinforcing the work of power in the new attention economy.

Furthermore, at this point, it should be no surprise that object oriented rhetoric offers no quarter in the attention economy. Bracketing the subject, these theories view breakdowns at the intersection of consciousness and technology on equal terms. Again, the subject has no ontological priority in the world of objects. For example, Alex Reid's call for a "glitchy" composition argues that our experience with technologies is characterized by failures and breakdowns: "Cameras, GPS satellites, facial recognition software: we adopt such technologies as an extension of our sensorium. But . . . in doing so we do not create a seamless expansion of our perception of a natural world but rather progressively build out another glitchy realm." The glitch, Reid argues, should be seen as "a key ontological condition," as "features, not bugs." This leads Reid to ask, "What if glitches were the source of agency and thought rather than their limits? If so, then we might also recognize the objections in composing as integral to the process." In short, he argues that the "objections" of technologies might serve as a new heuristic as opposed to something to surpass in realizing some truer, fuller human agency.

My problem here is not with Reid's insistence that we move beyond our reduction of compositions to the terms of discursivity and subjectivity. And it should be clear by now that failure and accidents are important to a pedagogy rooted in plasticity. However, as we've seen, in simply discarding the transcendental, Reid's recommendation that students follow trails of glitches totally ignores the destructive dimension—the disaffecting power—of technological "blowback." The "objections" of both humans and objects are on the same level. Once again we can see that object oriented rhetoric leaves the question of pedagogical care to the side. "Agency is the pinnacle of being human, but as such it is also the human quality that is most easily threatened, by technology, by government, by materiality, or perhaps even twinkies, as the apocryphal legal defense goes," Reid finally allows, somewhat softening OOO's position. But, from the neurological perspective, it is not just agency that is threatened.

Relatedly, Nathanial Rivers, in "Paying Attention with Cache," theorizes attention as a "thing" that is constantly formed and reformed, not a finite resource of the intentionality of an agent. Following OOO and Latour in bracketing the psychological and neurological accounts of attention, Rivers posits that: "The example of geocaching works *not* to demonstrate how students can, despite worries to the contrary, be taught to pay better attention, but how attention itself is contingently refigured by material relations, in particular those mediated by digital technologies such as locative media." However, because Rivers isn't interested in attention at the level of the subject, he brackets the question of finitude, and therefore also the ways that these technologies not only compose, but also *erode* attention. Therefore, his rhetorical theory of attention turns on a now familiar valorization of flexibility—that is, a reduced account of plasticity that can be exploited by power.

Rivers uses the example of geocaching—a "hide and seek" game involving GPS—explaining that its rewards are in fact temporary assemblages of attention, such as interesting views of a landscape that emerge within the game. The game becomes an example of how attention works in general—that is, as a composition. Theorizing attention thusly, Rivers argues that the formation of the social is in this way "risky" because different actor-objects in the network can cause other actors to act in unexpected ways. The geocache not only "grabs" the attention of the participant, but composes it, always in relation to its ambiance. This suggests for Rivers that, in opposition to correlational accounts of attention's finitude at the level of the subject, we need to understand how different objects in our environment compose our attention. He has in mind the pedagogical value of the "allure" of objects composing attention: "The payoff for unpacking attention is the inventional potential, as another area of rhetoric wherein kairos, contingency, embodiment, and mediation are all at play." In other words, not unlike Bogorst's account of wonder, Rivers challenges us to consider how we might exploit the object networks students find themselves as a heuristic. As opposed to being a possession or a "beam" directed at things, it is something that is assembled alongside and through other things that have their own agency. In this view of attention, "Attention is a finite, cognitive resource that must be employed by intentional, autonomous and sovereign actors." For Rivers, on the other hand, attention itself becomes another "thing" as opposed to a finite resource or power of the intentional agent.

Ultimately, Rivers (rightly) challenges the argument made in *The Shallows* by Nicholas Carr, which is essentially a version of "technology is making us stupid." In bracketing the kinds of questions raised in Carr's work concerning psychological finitude, Rivers seeks to imagine more "productive" roles for technology and multi-modality in composition: "Smart phones, iPods, digital cameras, and Garmins aren't simply challenges to attention; they are part of what progressively composes attentions." His point is attention isn't *just* a thing that can be controlled or captured by technology; rather, attention is also formed in relation to external things as a temporary assemblage.

Once again, without resorting to the mechanistic and innatist account of attention we see in Carr (or Flower and Hayes), neuroscience complicates these theorizations. Whether technology extends and changes our humanity through its enhancements or through its glitches, these theories continue to discover the affordances of the cyborg without seeing that nature itself—its plasticity—offers a better model of composition, learning, and difference than does technology. It's not just that objects and technologies *compose* attention—which they most certainly do—but that these temporary assemblages are engrammed through habituation in neural traces, altering the brain's predictive processes below the level of consciousness and concept formation, giving shape to more enduring dispositions. On the other hand, Rivers' endlessly *flexible* theory of attention is—as he seems to recognize to some extent in calling his theory "dangerous"—*entirely formless*. Indeed, it simply brackets (much like the OOO theorists) the question of the relation between finitude, form, and attention.

By returning to the neurological account established in earlier chapters, we can see that the new materialist revision of the stability of modernist "reflective attention" is insufficient. Attention is *neither* the power of volitional reflection on sensory input *nor* a "bottom-up" assemblage. Instead, attention is a function of the brain's prediction process, an assessment of the probability of prediction error: "It is the ability flexibly to extract signal from noise by forming and deploying focused and fine-grained estimates of our own perceptual uncertainty" (Clark 56). For example, when driving along a familiar road in fog, we should generally privilege our top-down knowledge of the road. Attention in this case would emphasize prediction errors that occur where something deviates from our knowledge of the road (for instance, if an unexpected curve in the road were to appear, we'd be highly attuned to it). The prediction errors relative to sensory input on a foggy road, on the other hand, are de-emphasized, given that these errors are likely to be less precise. Similarly, driving fast on an unfamiliar road requires privileging sensory input. The brain works in both situations to continuously "estimate and re-estimate its own sensory uncertainty" (57). As we saw with the "outfielder problem" in Chapter 1, attention works in such situations to create a *balance* between top-down and bottom-up influences, working to increase the value the brain gives to a prediction error (in either direction).

As Andy Clark puts it, attention "is the ability flexibly to extract signal noise by forming and deploying focuses and fine-grained estimates of our own perceptual uncertainty. That ability . . . plays a major role in accounting for both normal and abnormal forms of contact within the world" (57). In other words, attention is at the center of the brain's predictions, an *ad hoc* system through which the brain discovers form in the world as virtualities (as opposed to OOO's essences), increasing the gain at different levels of prediction by forming an estimation of where those errors will be most important in a given situation. The neurological predictive processing model of attention's finitude cannot be reduced in the way Rivers claims. Rather, neurobiology demonstrates that there is no single, stable, internal model that conforms to sensory input, positing that models work to discover the sensory experience they construct, actively carving out sensations from the world that conform to its parameters, until the moment (because

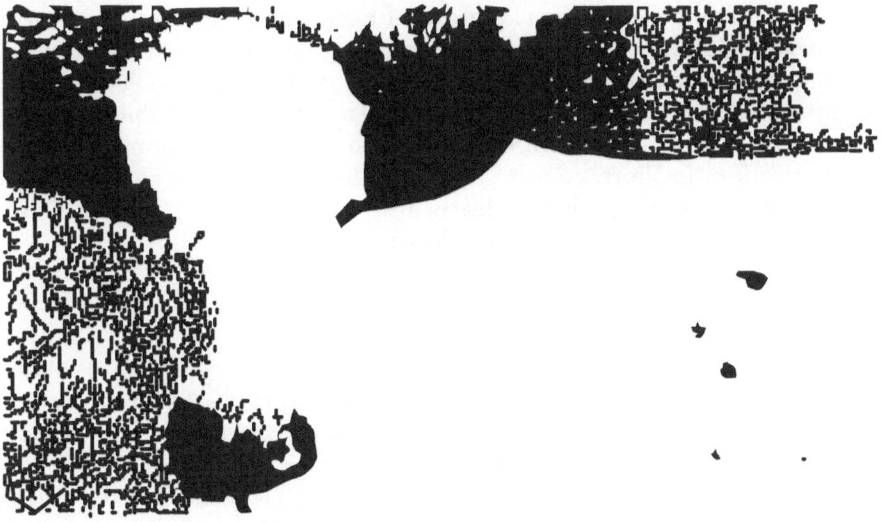

Figure 4.1 What do you see in this noisy image?

"Hidden Cow" by John McCrone, CC-BY-SA-3.0. http://creativecommons.org/licenses/by-sa/3.0, via Wikimedia Commons.

of prediction error) the model can no longer sustain itself. Internal models, in other words, are plastic. But this truly weird idea is made all the weirder for the fact that attention "drives learning" in attuning the agent to a particular level of prediction error, the one itself predicted to have the most significance.

Take for example the image above. As you look at it, the brain will attempt to make sense of the image through rapid-fire predictions against the backdrop of sensory "noise." But once you see it—it's a cow with a large head (the head is on the left, facing you)—it's difficult to un-see it. The next time you view the image, you'll likely see the cow immediately. Just as your brain will focus attention on prediction errors at the level of your *knowledge* of a road on a foggy day, so too will your brain automatically emphasize your knowledge of the cow image over sensory data in anticipating potential prediction errors. Or again, your brain will have calculated that the most useful errors for making a correct prediction will occur at the level of knowledge; visual input will have been estimated to be too noisy to be reliable. On the other hand, where our top-down models fail to detect a predicted pattern, "the scene is sampled in a wandering fashion and no clear stable percept is produced." In this scenario, failure leads to learning, driving "increased plasticity allowing a new model to be acquired and applied" (Clark 71).

As Heidegger argued, intelligence is always already meaningfully engaged with the world—it is because of the temporal nature of cognition, our "being-toward-death," that we always project being into the future as *care*—and cannot be reduced to after-the-fact applications of reason. Understanding this is essential to understanding learning, which, as we can see in the example of the cow image above—and as opposed to consisting in rational and symbolic meaning making out of experience—begins in a primordial meaningfulness that *precedes* consciousness and the symbolic. Human learning from the perspective of plasticity is not a transactional, Cartesian input-output, but entails transformations—a formal modifiability within our largely preconscious (neurological) processes of prediction, care, and categorization. In short, contra OOO, it is *because we care* and meaningfully attend to the world that we learn, and without this primary affectivity, learning is degraded to the computational.

The Contemporary Crisis of Attention: Care, School, and the New Disordered Subject

As Malabou explains, "The philosophical turn from the twentieth to the twenty-first century is . . . notable for the in-depth search for the origin of thinking outside of consciousness and will" (*Before Tomorrow*). In different ways, the most important contemporary thinking has worked to transgress the transcendental by calling into question the "spontaneity" through which the *a priori* supposedly enables both an objective and open correspondence between thought and the world. Indeed, despite the variability of these theories, "all result in the decision to drown spontaneity in a more ancient past than subjectivity." And we can see that deconstructive and posthuman critiques of the transcendental entail the discovery of a non-human "background" that precedes both reason and life; as Malabou schematizes, "For Heidegger, it is an ontological past with no beginning; for the neuroscientists, it is the night of a biological and evolutionary past; meanwhile, Meillassoux evokes ancestrality without human ancestors." Each of these accounts attempt to go beyond the critique of reason to understand the origins of thought, asserting "from which non-conscious, not necessarily human and not programmed, formative instances thinking derives." And yet, as Malabou has shown us, these attempts have hit a dead end. Where Heideggarian destruction and Derridian deconstruction have become "bogged down in the infinite poetization of a dreary messianic temporality," we saw also that SR is fundamentally unable to give content to its speculations on contingency. In short, we cannot simply bracket or abandon the question of reason, but must instead rethink it in terms of plasticity.

I submit that pedagogy requires a new response to contemporary disaffecting power, as critical thinking, metacognition, and reflective attention—that is, the "modernist" pedagogical strategies meant to ensure the advance of reason—can no longer guarantee the coherency of the subject, gaining the subject purchase over technology. Above, I examined the rise of the college writing course in relation to what I termed the "first attention crisis" of modernity. We saw that leaders and educators believed that writing classes could remediate poor writing skills by inculcating a "reflective attention" that could transcend, through critique, technological and cultural threats to both subject and species. Instead, as we saw, it tended to reproduce power through discipline and the concomitant production of bad feelings. The current crisis of attention, on the other hand, happening at the neurological level, is connected to the widespread destruction of both reason and intelligence by a new "attention economy" (Beller; Goldhaber; Lanham) formed around the "hypersolicitation of attention" (Stiegler). In short, the current attention economy differs from the former in that it works "beneath" consciousness and reason; the problem is no longer that students aren't paying attention to truth—or that the power of attention is divided by technologies—but that attentional capacities have become deformed to the point that students can't pay attention in the first place. Discipline alone is not enough to respond to this disaffecting power.

The "new wounded" student with disordered attention is rapidly proliferating in Northern America and now in many other Westernized countries (e.g., Conrad; DeGrandpre; Hallowell & Ratey; Rafalovich; Rose; Schrag & Divoky), and we have responded with new knowledges and new technologies, especially of the psycho-pharmaceutical variety. In the face of the erosion of wonder, Adderall appears as the new "wonder drug" in our schools. And even many non-AD/HD students now come to us with some version of what Harvard psychiatrist John Ratey calls an "acquired attention deficit disorder," rooted in their constant exposure to new media and technologies. "Accustomed to a constant stream of digital stimulation," Ratey demonstrates, these students "feel bored by the absence of it" (Richtel). Given the explosive appearance of these new technologies on the psychic landscape, it should hardly be surprising that there have been explosive psychic consequences among children. But the thing is, we are *all* threatened by the erosion of attention—adults and children alike; a Microsoft study using EEG scans demonstrates that the average attention span has declined from 12 seconds in 2000 to 8 seconds today (Microsoft Report). In 2007, Katherine Hayles wrote that we would not realize the full effects of the reformation of cognition around attention until students that were then 12 reached college. As those students become upper classmen, it's clear to many that Hayles was right.

The situation in the classroom is exacerbated by the fact that most teachers were raised with at least one foot in the modernist dispensation. In that tradition, there was a great value placed on singular focus, on sitting still in a single room, concentrating on just one thing—in short, dwelling within oneself in a way that places one close to meaning and Being through care. "Deep attention"—"the cognitive style traditionally associated with the humanities"—has been replaced by "hyper attention"—"characterized by switching focus rapidly among different tasks, preferring multiple information streams, seeking a high level of stimulation, and having a low tolerance for boredom" (187). And while Hayles reminds us that hyper attention is a functional attentive form given the demands of contemporary society, nevertheless, lacking a capacity for deep attention, students increasingly struggle in college, left to "squirm in the procrustean beds outfitted for them by their elders" (188). As students begin to occupy new forms of attention, the received curriculum begins to *feel* outmoded, and both student and public bodies become increasingly cynical. We can clearly see this in recent enrollment declines in the humanities, where student disengagement from the disciplines is now so advanced that students reflexively and vocally question their very value. Relatedly, perhaps, the failure to include embodiment in our pedagogies has led to a fetishizing of sports and partying on college campuses.

As writing teachers, this new retreat from *logos* has a special relevance, as we have long defined ourselves, or been defined, as practitioners of *care*. We cannot be complicit with the work of power and the attention economy in producing disaffection. As I'll argue in Chapter 5, reasoned, discursive writing (and speaking), in relations of pedagogical care, is the historical form through which students have matured in Western culture. Therefore, the increasing importance of new writing technologies and various non-discursive forms—or "funk" (Banks) and "glitches" (Reid)—within our discipline warrants vigilance and careful analysis with regard to affectivity, attention, and intelligence. And yet, contemporary composition theory has had little of substance to say on the matter. As Kia Jane Richmond points out, the received social epistemic pedagogy has a "lack of interest in the personal" (69). And most recent composition and rhetorical theory—despite an increased focus on, for example, positivity and empathy—has bracketed pedagogical questions of care. Indeed, overall, recent composition theory has been guided by a suspicion regarding universal claims about the caring, personal connection between teacher and student. Reflecting a post-structural (and distinctly rhetorical) skepticism towards the foundational subject, reason, and all philosophical rationalizations and universals, ethical questions of personal reflection, self-stylization, and "spiritual" improvement are frequently viewed as frivolous or secondary concerns.

This reflects larger trends in academic thinking. Where ethics historically required practices of reflective and meditative self care directed at both self and others, modern ethics is often reduced to epistemic reflection on the social and biological conditions of knowledge. As Richmond argues, "Our affinity for the rational and the scientific has left little room for anything that cannot be observed, counted, or measured" (71). It is for this reason too that recent neurorhetoric, which tellingly has had little to say about writing pedagogy *per se*, focuses only on the significance of the brain's affective structure to theorizing *persuasion*. However, because there is an ethical dimension to plasticity, a plastic composition pedagogy must articulate the *embodied* relation between affect, composing, and care.

Additionally, some composition pedagogy simply presumes that our students care reflexively—about their lives, their bodies, their society, their politics, their selves. As we saw in Chapter 4, this reflective care is the guarantee of disciplinary subjectivity. Yet, inattention appears in the classroom precisely as a lack of self-presence, as a lack of seriousness, as disenchantment and *indifference* (Malabou *What Should We Do*). How are we to respond? Hayles summarizes our options: "As students move deeper into the mode of hyper attention, educators face a choice: change the students to fit the educational environment or change that environment to fit the students" (195). And as their devices call out the seductive songs of hundreds of daily tweets, it's increasingly clear that our students will not permit that we lash them to the masts of older forms of composing so that they might, like Ulysses, return "home."

Above I attempted to untangle the relation between writing pedagogy, disciplinary power, affect, and reflective attention in order to understand the history of plasticity's reduction within our own discipline. This may be read as a critique of schooling in general, as well as the disciplinary power through which the student subject takes shape historically within educational institutions. Indeed, usually the Foucauldian interpretation of subjectification lends itself to skepticism concerning the relationship between schools and bodies—the historical ontology is frequently an overt critique of institutions. But we can't understand the contemporary situation in terms of disciplinary power alone; as we've already begun to see in analyzing Malabou's "new wounded," power is now closely related to disaffection.

Therefore, I wish here to push past skepticism towards institutions (more germane to the last century, given the contemporary neo-liberal divestment in public institutions) that ends in their repudiation (as well as the repudiation of the work writing teachers do). To do so, I will turn to the work of philosopher and media theorist, Bernard Stiegler. Across his work, Stiegler, in both critiquing and building on Foucault, has argued that Foucault ignored the value of educational institutions in connecting youth to cultural norms and shared forms of attention and meaning, a requirement of public rhetoric. In Stiegler's words, "Only a being that is educated can develop . . . the shared attentional forms of knowledge of how to live, to do things, as well as cognitive and theoretical knowledge" (2). By following Stiegler, I hope to clarify the developing relations between writing, care, rhetoric, and reason during what we might call the "second crisis of attention," where neo-liberal interests have increasingly replaced the forms of care traditionally fostered by educational institutions. To do so, I will need to address the capture and reduction of intelligence by new technologies that operate at such a pace that they exceed neural functioning, and whose goal it is to reshape consciousness through the inculcation of a form of attention—"hyper attention"—best suited to the manufactured desires of 24/7 capitalism.

An analysis of these relations will finally return us to the theorization of an embodied, plastic writing pedagogy, one that understands writing *as a technology of synaptogenesis*. As we've seen, the brain, its relational and emergent *ad hoc* inscription, cannot be conceived in terms of the durable trace, an indestructible symbolic system, or through rationalized pedagogical programs. Destruction itself, as Malabou's embodied theory shows, occurs *outside of reason*. We only appear endlessly *flexible*—without form, able to constantly "adapt" to situations—from the vantage of a perspective that assumes a certain rigid, essential continuity, model, or identity. I will argue, following Malabou, that a plastic intelligence must foremost work to disrupt this rigidification of reason, to inculcate an openness to the world that resists the automation and habituation of intelligence. To do so, we need to move beyond the privileging of reason over affect, while at the same time realizing the *affective, embodied, value of reason* to intelligence. That is, beyond the question of the affective value of multimodal and non-discursive writing, we must also consider the embodied and affective relationship of reason to discursive writing. I argue that the sustained, embodied forms of attention involved in reasoning must themselves serve as groundings for the dialectical advances of learning, disrupting forms of automation and attentional control, breaking through the blockages of neurologically engrained bad writing and thinking habits.

Notes

1. Alfred Kitzhaber's original label that John Brereton famously described as "about on par with 'Dark Ages' as a satisfactory investigative or taxonomic tool" (xiii) because of its inability to account for the diversity of classroom practices during this period.

2. The sign of rationalization is that it appears that "*there is no alternative*" (*States of Shock* 44). In Lanham, this is the prevailing sentiment: that we are being swept forward by progress in a way only a Luddite would question. Of course, this is also the prevailing sentiment of the era of the Anthropocene—the geological era where the behaviors of man effect and ultimately destroy the environment, the "code" of the Earth—in which it seems to many that we have little choice but to perish.

Works Cited

Anderson, Michael L. "Neural Reuse in the Organization and Development of the Brain." *Developmental Medicine & Child Neurology*, vol. 58, 2016, pp. 3–6. Web.

Baldwin, F. Spencer. "Ideals of College Education." *New England Magazine*, September 1897, pp. 570–580. Print.

Benjamin, Walter. *Illuminations: Essays and Reflections*. Ed. Hannah Arendt. Trans. Harry Zohn. Schocken Books, New York, 1968. Print.

Berlin, James A. *Writing Instruction in Nineteenth-Century American Colleges*. Southern Illinois UP, Carbondale, 1984. Print.

———. *Rhetorics, Poetics, and Cultures: Refiguring College English Studies*. National Council of Teachers of English, Urbana, IL, 1996. Print.

Breck, Emma J. "A New Task for the English Teacher." *The English Journal*, vol. 1, no. 2, 1912, pp. 65–71.

Brereton, John C., ed. *The Origins of Composition Studies in the American College, 1875–1925: A Documentary History*. University of Pittsburgh Press, Pittsburgh, PA, 1995. Print.

Carpenter, George R., Franklin T. Baker, and Fred N. Scott. "The Teaching of English in the Elementary and the Secondary Schools." *Google Books*, 1903. Web.

Carr, Nicholas G. *The Shallows: What the Internet Is Doing to Our Brains*. W.W. Norton, New York, 2010.

Clark, Andy. *Surfing Uncertainty: Prediction, Action, and the Embodied Mind*. Oxford University Press, New York, 2016.

Comstock, Edward. "Toward a Genealogy of Composition: Student Discipline and Development at Harvard in the Late Nineteenth Century." *Writing Stories: Composition and Rhetoric in High Schools and Normal Schools, 1839–1969*. University of Pittsburgh Press, Pittsburgh, PA, 2015, pp. 185–205. Print.

Crary, Jonathan. *Suspensions of Perception: Attention, Spectacle, and Modern Culture*. MIT Press, Cambridge, MA, 2001. Print.

Crawford, Matthew B. "How We Lost Our Attention." *The Hedgehog Review*, vol. 16, no. 2, 2014, n.p. Web.

Crowley, Sharon. *Composition in the University: Historical and Polemical Essays*. University of Pittsburgh Press, Pittsburgh, PA, 1998. Print.

Dewey, John. *The School and Society and the Child and the Curriculum*. University of Chicago Press, Chicago, 2013. Print.

Dobrin, Sid. *Postcomposition*. Southern Illinois University Press, Carbondale, IL, 2011. Print.

Emig, Janet. "The Tacit Tradition: The Inevitability of a Multi-Disciplinary Approach to Writing Research." *The Web of Meaning*. Eds. Dixie Goswami and Maureen Butler. Boynton/Cook, Upper Montclair, NJ, 1977, 1983, pp. 145–156.

Foucault, Michel. *The Order of Things: An Archaeology of the Human Sciences*. Random House, New York, 1970. Print.

Freud, Sigmund. *The Freud Reader*. Ed. Peter Gay. W.W. Norton, New York, 1989. Print.

Godkin, E. L. "The Illiteracy of American Boys." *Educational Review*, vol. 13, 1897, pp. 1–9. *Archive.org*. Web.

Hall, G. Stanley. *Youth: Its Education, Regimen, and Hygiene*. The Echo Library, Middlesex, MA, 2006. Print.

"Harvard University Report of the Committee on Composition and Rhetoric to the Board of Overseers of Harvard College [1892–1897]." *HathiTrust*, 1897. *JSTOR*. Web.

Kitzhaber, Albert R. "Rhetoric in American Colleges, 1850–1900." Diss., University of Washington, 1953. Print.

Malabou, Catherine. *Before Tomorrow: Epigenesis and Rationality*. Polity Press, Malden, MA, 2016.

McCrone, John. "Hidden Cow." *Wikipedia Commons*, http://creativecommons.org/licenses/by-sa/3.0.

Murray, Joddy. *Non-Discursive Rhetoric: Image and Affect in Multimodal Composition*. Suny Press, Albany, NY, 2009.

Petchesky, Barry. "A *Clash of Clans* Addiction Nearly Sank the Royals' Season." *Deadspin*, 21 October 2014, https://deadspin.com/a-clash-of-clans-addiction-nearly-sank-the-royals-seaso-1648848299

Rivers, Nathaniel. "Paying Attention With Cache." *Enculturation*, 2016. http://enculturation.net/paying-attention

Scott, Fred Newton. "English Composition as a Mode of Behavior." *English Journal*, vol. 11, 1922, pp. 463–473. *JSTOR*. Web.

Stiegler, Bernard. "Relational Ecology and the Digital Pharmakon." *Culture Machine*, vol. 13, no. 1, 2012, pp. 1–19. Web.

5 Technology, Intelligence, and the Plasticity of Writing in the New Attention Economy

Stupidity is on the rise. Even if you cannot quite agree with that, likely you'll agree that talk of stupidity is increasing. And you may also agree that intelligence is increasingly hard to recognize in this age where so much information is so easily accessible on our smartphones—no wonder the humanities has long focused on deconstructing it, resisting its reduction to a singular, positive account. In Malabou's three-part lecture on intelligence at UC Irving in 2015, she makes the compelling case that, after Kant, stupidity has in fact been treated better than intelligence by the humanities. In the first lecture, "Intelligence Versus the Intellect," she argues that philosophy is skeptical of or otherwise unable to bring forward the question of intelligence, characterizing it in the inhuman terms of reduction and automation. As Malabou argues, for philosophy, "Intelligence, being blind to its own source, being incapable to render the reason of its own origin, cannot be the origin of reason. Reason starts where intelligence stops being a question. Reason starts where intelligence erases its own traces." In other words, philosophy can only recognize intelligence—that is, give it form—at best *after the fact*, and cannot deduce its origins. We can see this in Kant's definition of genius, which "deletes itself in order to appear paradoxically as what it is." The transcendental is *a priori*; it has no genesis; it is itself without origin such that there is no more to say about it.

In the philosophical tradition that remains at odds with science, intelligence does not touch its (biological) source, but *deletes* it. In this way, intelligence lacks philosophical intelligibility, a positive account of its manifestations. And as a result of this deletion in the philosophical tradition, knowledge of intelligence has been left to the discourses of biological determinism. At the turn of the 20th century, "I.Q." was at the center of the innatist eugenics movement, a tradition that continues into contemporary genetic accounts, such as the human genome project's (failed) attempt to locate a genetic sequence underlying intelligence. The humanities have reacted to the formlessness of the innatist understanding of intelligence with an untenable "paranoia," as Malabou argues, realized as "a reaction against any reduction of the intellect to both the cerebral and the cybernetic; that is, in both cases, to the structure of the brain." This is yet another manifestation of the untenable binary between the biological and the philosophical that Malabou argues neuroscience erases—a "blind spot" that, in light of "profound" changes to social and educational structures, "constitutes major theoretical and ethical challenges of our time." The challenge, precisely, is to combat disaffection by positively thinking intelligence through the lens of plasticity, and in doing so, think the humanities through the biological (and *vice versa*). The ongoing *critique* of the biological reduction of intelligence, as Malabou argues, is useless and misguided given neuroscientific deconstruction and the motor scheme of plasticity.

But in an epoch where a plutocrat preaches populism, where the byzantine and formless programs of neo-liberal real estate markets produced an economic collapse under the weight of their own folly, where it's more important that capital flow through investment sites without blockage than for socially beneficial projects to come to realization, it's not enough to just talk about stupidity and deconstruct intelligence. A generation of social epistemic pedagogy has ended in the ascend of Donald Trump, leaving many compositionists scratching their heads. Of course, Trump (intuitively, at least) understood something that rhetoricians should have grasped immediately (in retrospect!): intelligent ideas and reasoned deliberation were always already vulnerable to the potency of his emotional appeals. Trump won in part by making stupidity itself smart. And we are left to wonder, what is the value of reason without intelligence?

As we've already seen, neuroscience offers a stronger materialist account than competing posthuman theories of our relation to the transcendental, and therefore also of learning, intelligence, and consciousness in general. As opposed to simply bracketing or abandoning reason, biological plasticity, the "external outside" of the humanities, must be viewed as an "internal inside" that will allow us to negotiate or create a rupture *from within* the transcendental.[1] Plasticity, that is, introduces into the transcendental rupture, discontinuity, and modification. Or again, the transcendental, by welcoming its other—the biological sciences—transforms itself from within. Through plasticity, we can introduce a new moment into the history of reason, allowing us to rethink reason and intelligence without resorting 1. to the biological determinism that philosophy has so long critiqued, nor 2. to a disembodied transcendental intelligence, attention, or reason. At the same time, just as we are able to rethink the humanities through the scientific, we can rethink the reduced biological concept of intelligence in its historical specificity.

After all, we cannot simply concede to the forces of biological determinism, reducing intelligence to a quasi-Darwinistic program. Nor can we be satisfied with mechanistic accounts of writing ability—such as we find in the Flower-Hayes model—that view intelligence through computational metaphors, reducing reason to the programmatic. Above all, we must reject the reductionist stance that equates a singular determinate intelligence with writing ability. In the light of plasticity, we cannot imagine learning and intelligence—in either the quality of a student's writing or the student's development as a writer—as merely quantitative. To make intelligence quantitative, and to view learning as a process of addition, is to view it as always and everywhere the same, as a measurable singularity. Intelligence remains the same thing it was yesterday. In this chapter, I'll begin to think through the relations between writing and intelligence in the terms of plasticity. In doing so, I hope to rethink the value of reason in posthuman terms, arguing that there is an essential *embodied* relation between reason (especially reasoned writing), synaptogenesis, and the plasticity of intelligence.

Plasticity as Habit of Mind: Writing, Power, and Synaptogenesis

As I've already begun to develop in Chapter 1, in addition to the political dimension of plasticity that demands our "responsibility in the double movement of the receiving and the giving of form," there is also an *ethical dimension* to plasticity that emphasizes "solicitude, treatment, help, repair, rescue" (Malabou *What Should We Do* 30). In other words, the ethical work of a plastic writing pedagogy requires *care* for the embodied and heteroaffective relations between writing and synaptogenesis, connecting teachers and students in a shared desire for the universals of culture and knowledge[2]. There is a relation between, for example, the "repair" and "rescue" of students, the brain, the formation of attention, and shared desire made manifest through writing. Or as Bernard Stiegler argues, in post-Enlightenment Western culture, "deep attention" is the product of "a socially configured system of care" in our schools, and our "capacity for rational attention" is configured across the school by the "same psychotechnique: writing" (*Taking Care of Youth* 58).

In Western culture, writing has been the supplemental technology enabling the plastic, dialectical process through which individuals particularize the universal (of culture)[3] and form dispositions as the "insistent accidents" we recognize as individuation. As Malabou similarly emphasizes, humans are first *listeners* that "in turn are led to construct and form what they hear and read" (*The Future of Hegel* 10). "Deep attention" to the (always elusive, deconstructed) "universals" of culture and knowledge is the shared, dispositional requirement of the dialectical process of individuation through which we actively stylize or particularize—through writing—what we had merely passively received through listening to the other.

Through the use of writing technologies, new habits and dispositions are, in Stiegler's words, "inscribed, and in some sense *written*, into the brain as synaptic connections . . . engrammed into the individual brain's cortical and subcortical zones" (Stiegler, *Taking Care of Youth* 66) aided by the student's ability to mobilize different writing resources. Dewey similarly theorized the relationship between habits and the materials and "equipment" of technology: "A habit also marks an intellectual disposition. Where there is a habit, there is acquaintance with the materials and equipment to which action is applied" (*Democracy and Education* 46). However, because Dewey—like so many others before and since—viewed equipment as *essentially* secondary and supplemental, he failed to account for writing (and other technologies) in his theorization of plasticity.

On the other hand, neuroscience allows us to rethink this relationship between writing, technologies, and habit to the formation of Dewey's intellectual dispositions. Eventually, as Stiegler argues:

> the student begins to produce these circuits himself or herself by interiorizing and remaking them through classroom assignments. Through this process, the nervous system learns a wide variety of attentional attitudes, raising the level of concentration (attention span) born of synaptogenesis. Brain-imaging technology allows us today actually to watch this process in action.
>
> (*Taking Care of Youth* 66)

Again, as neuroscience shows us, these dispositions, or "attentional attitudes," are foremost embodied dispositions. And our dispositions towards culture and knowledge are born first, not from our reasoned understanding, but *from the accumulation of our embodied affective relations towards them.* Where shared, deep attention to the "universals" of culture and knowledge are absent, we discover only a destructive, careless indifference.

The point again is that writing technologies play essential but variable roles in forming attentional attitudes and dispositions. Writing, like all technologies that form habits and dispositions—as Plato recognized, possessing the nature of the *pharmakon*—has the capacity to both cure and poison, *form* and *deform*, consciousness. And where writing technologies require us to be merely *flexible*, to passively adapt ourselves to their codes and forms, the result may be a deforming erosion of consciousness, care, and attention. Where writing technologies decompose attention in order to synchronize consciousness with their own codes—codes meant to reproduce behaviors of consumption—wonder erodes into disaffection. That is, outside of systems of care, desire is replaced by the destructive indifference of the "new wounded." Recognizing the ethical dimension of plasticity therefore means equipping students with the habits and tools required to resist the reduction of plasticity to flexibility in realizing maturity.

Malabou's mature, "plastic individual" emerges in a dialectical relation to knowledge, the universal, and culture; unlike individual animals that are merely accidental instances of the genus, accidents of human behavior *change the genus* through the will to persist in individuated habits. "Consequently," Malabou argues, "plasticity appears as a process where the universal and the particular mutually inform one another" (*The Future of Hegel* 11). Or again, plasticity "characterizes the relation between substance and accidents," where the accidental is what follows from the event (12). It is in this way that humans, through the will to persist in habits born of accidents, through individuation as *self stylization*, also, in turn, alter the code of the genus through their active "particularization" of it. Malabou clarifies, "if an external change is repeated, it turns into a tendency internal to the subject. The change itself is transformed into a disposition, and receptivity, formerly passive, becomes activity" (70–71). Therefore, "what is exemplary about man is . . . his status as an *insistent accident*" (73). As we've seen, the experience of our "auto-affectivity"—our sense of a unified self—is in fact an "insistence" on a particularization of what comes to us from the outside, from the accident, from the Other.

We thusly form "dispositions" dialectically as idiosyncratic *interpretations* of life through the insistent particularization of the universal, such that "consciousness and will, under the influence of repeated practice, win their force through a kind of self-abnegating" (75). But where the formation of habits demands only the reception of the code or program, individuals will fail to develop dispositions that particularize the universal through this dialectical process of affective encounter with otherness. For this reason, where power automatizes and mechanizes dispositions towards flexible ends—for instance, through commercial, management, and marketing programs that compete for command of psychic space by grammatizing attention—education will work against the formation of individuated dispositions. It is in this sense that a plastic writing pedagogy is inherently also ethical and political, making both teachers and students responsible for what we do with our brains when we write.

Indeed, Pierre Bourdieu, who was (somewhat surprisingly) prescient in his theorization of neurological plasticity, reminds us that we cannot think the virtualities that manifest through constructed dispositions outside of ideology and power: "To deny the existence of acquired dispositions, in the case of living beings, is to deny the existence of learning in the sense of a selective, durable transformation of the body through the re-enforcement or weakening of synaptic connections" (136). And as Bourdieu recognized, just as reflective intelligence informs the plastic disposition, it simultaneously reduces intelligence by excluding its other practical and even magical (i.e., analogic) forms:

> In order to free our thinking of the implicit, it is not sufficient to perform a return of thought onto itself that is commonly associated with the idea of reflexivity; and only the illusion of the omnipotence of thought could lead one to believe that the most radical doubt is capable of suspending the presuppositions, linked to our various affiliations, memberships, implications, that we engage in our thoughts.
>
> (9)

For Bourdieu, habitus, as the "illusions" formed by our presuppositions (our immediate and spontaneous "attunements" to the world), operates much in the same way as Barrett's interoceptive system, preceding consciousness and reason. While our habits and dispositions, like our emotions, come to us *as if* automatically or "naturally," they are originally social constructions. And the reflective attention that is the basis of the "scholastic disposition"—which we've identified with Dewey and the modern tradition in composition, itself an illusion that manifests in the academic "game"—is inherently limited to the extent that it remains divorced, through its esthetic disinterestedness, from practical purpose. Through it, the plasticity of our intelligence is captured and reduced by the social structure that privileges the scholarly habitus over others, the valorization of the "game" of scholarly reflection coming at the cost of both practical purpose and social equality. Finally, reflective metacognition gives us no purchase over our habitus, but is rather (as we've seen) very much a manifestation of a particular socio-historical situation, and a vision of intelligence limited to scholastic as opposed to practical purpose.

However, to combat the ideology of the scholarly disposition, of reflective reason, we nevertheless require precisely reflective reason; Bourdieu argues that we can only "reconstruct" practical logic by "including in the theory the distance between practical logic and theoretical logic" (52). He continues, "to do this requires a constant effort of reflexivity, the only means, *and itself scholastic*, of fighting against scholastic inclinations" (52). To engage the fight otherwise is impossible; indeed, "each agent, in order to win, can and must use the best weapons produced for and by the previous state of the struggle" (120–121). The long chains of reason embodied in and through discursive writing are in fact required for transgressing the reduction of intelligence to neo-liberal flexibility *as well as* the social codes that inform the scholarly habitus. Or again, discursive writing is a foundation of the dialectical and plastic openness of intelligence; reason remains, paradoxically, the requirement of its own transformation and transgression. In addition to suggesting problems with any overly-enthusiastic embrace of "funky" modes of composition at the cost of traditional discursive forms, all of this casts doubt on OOO's claim that "indirect discourse" can get us around the (transcendental) problem of correlationalism. We simply cannot transgress the transcendental from its outside.

Further, to rethink scholastic reason and reflective attention in this way is to reimagine reason in the terms of practical and social purpose. This has obvious consequences for theories of public rhetoric, and requires, again, that we transgress the transcendental center of reason as rational agency precisely *through the tools of the transcendental*. As I will argue below, contra OOO and SR, such a transgression must begin in the inculcation of reflective reason as grounds for the dialectical advance of learning. And as I argued in earlier chapters, a *consiousness of the brain's plasticity* appears to us at this moment as the form of this transgressive reason. Additionally, it will require that we think of reason—and the forms it takes in writing, such as epistemic discourse—in practical terms, both as a neurologically "durable" and embodied form of attention and also in the terms of *care* and *practicality* denied to it where reflective attention is programatized and reduced to scholastic indifference. Reorganizing the relation between reason and practicality in this way will allow us to theorize intelligence positively as a plastic disposition that resists habitual deformations of attention and reductions of intelligence. In other words, adding to Bourdieu's theorization of intelligence as a conditionability to a habitus, we should add the plastic capacity to *un-condition* ourselves. This is where Bernard Stiegler's pedagogical theorization of the synaptogenic relationship between writing and care—and the erosion of attention, intelligence, and plasticity by new media—becomes especially useful. Stiegler gives new urgency to Bourdieu's call to theorize attention, intelligence, and reason beyond their scholastic reductions, emphasizing the *practical* and transformative (magical) work of writing and public rhetoric.

Down and Out in the Attention Economy: Writing Technics and Plato's Pedagogy

Bernard Stiegler's account of organology and synaptogenesis compliments and clarifies the ethical dimension of Malabou's plasticity. Like Richard Lanham, Stiegler is another media theorist similarly interested in cultural therapeutics; however, as opposed to Lanham, Stiegler confronts the complex value of reason and care to a plastic writing pedagogy in the contemporary attention economy. In doing so, across his works, Stiegler explores the consequences of the second crisis of attention as it relates to the erosion of reason and intelligence. As John Tinnell argues in recommending Stiegler to writing studies, Stiegler's early works are considered among the most important by media theorists. At this point, I would like to linger some on Stiegler's often difficult thinking about technology, both as a way to separate it from more facile accounts of the deleterious effects of technology (such as Nicholas Carr's *The Shallows*), as well as to begin to substantiate and extrapolate from the extensive conceptual vocabulary he offers us for theorizing writing pedagogy today.

Above all, Stiegler's work tackles the contemporary erosion of intelligence, examining how new media destroys social and psychic ecologies by replacing the traditions of writing and shared attentional forms. For Stielger, the dialectical relation between human and technological evolution has been replaced by a permanent technical innovation that evolves on its own terms and at its own pace; while inorganic technologies used to adhere to organic, human time, they are today fundamentally characterized by a speed that exceeds and overwhelms human consciousness, imposing their own temporality and spatiality, their own organology. Humans no longer master tools through use—tools also use us. It is in this way that plasticity is reduced to flexibility, as the human is subordinated to the mechanistic, and the public work of rhetoric to power: "[new media] short-circuits that public life and public debate founded on the republican school, and does so by capturing and destroying attention, superimposing audiovisual programme schedules on scholastic programs, and competing against the latter by use of the colossal means at their disposal" (Stiegler *States of Shock* 23–24). This situation has some obvious ramifications for composition and public rhetoric, demanding, for instance, that we rethink the relation between writing (as technic), social goals, and the evolution of human attention and intelligence.

Stiegler schematizes the embodied relation of attention and memory to technology in terms of primary (stimuli), secondary (remembered), and tertiary (external, technological) *retentions*. Following Foucault, Stiegler demonstrates that these technological "tertiary retention systems" (e.g., stone tablets, books, the internet) are necessarily and "organologically" linked to human nature—that is, external technologies reconfigure human being at the level of the somatic (as when they rewire the brain). Varying across cultures and history, these external technologies work as organic, archival supplements, connecting humans in relations of care to the long-term forms of dialogical cultural memory. Without tertiary retention systems, we would simply cease to be recognizably human. Each cultural moment or milieu is characterized by the textured and neurobiological relations the culture has to its specific tertiary retention systems, as different technologies give rise to different human and cultural "protentions" (that is, latent human potentialities). Or again, humans realize their biological potentiality differently based on their cultural relations to different technologies.

And for much of the history of Western culture, *writing* has been the privileged tertiary retention system. For example, as Stiegler points out, Kant theorized learning, maturity, and individuation within culture precisely as *reasoned writing before a literate public*. This is because discursive writing is precisely the form of a transindividuated attention structure—"addressed to *all*" (*Taking Care of Youth* 26). Individuation, as the addressing of the self before the shared attention of the transindividuated literate world is, per Kant, the basis of a mature Western culture. And dialogic writing is the technology that developed, with the ancient Greeks, to connect us to the storehouse of transindividuated culture by shaping this common attentional form: "Alphabetical vocalic writing, which appeared between the 8th and 7th Century B.C., allowed the constitution of a singular attentional process which is the very basis of ancient Greek civilization. They called it the *logos*" ("Relational Ecology" 4). Through writing, the "West will be formed—and ceaselessly reformed, deformed and transformed as the process of psychic and collective individuation based on writing as the technique of the formation of attention ("Relational Ecology" 4–5). As a result, "the mnemo-techniques that is writing is the condition of possibility of reason (of *logos* and its logic) as theorematic faculty" (*States of Shock* 7). And writing, the historically privileged form of reason, connecting us—through the reasoned disputations that result in individuation—to the disciplines and therefore the *logos*, is optimally fostered within relations of care in educational institutions.

Without the curated disputation of transindividuated reason that begins in the "deep attention" cultivated by the disciplines, our students will be left to "adapt to educational neglect and carelessness, to fend for themselves" (Stiegler *States of Shock* 23) in a situation where the authority of knowledge has *regressed*. We must see, as Kant did, the role of writing in "the formation of maturity as a kind of attention called rational consciousness . . . as *also* and *still* and *always* being a *knowledge* of writing, in turn opening a political space as the *critical* space of writing before the entire literate world" (*Taking Care* 130). For a literate public that shares the required deep attention, "writing is already an 'auto-capturing' of attention" (*Taking Care* 24) that is the basis of mature dialog—in other words, writing is the technological condition of the critical spaces of both public rhetoric and Western culture in general. However, as we'll see, for Stiegler—as opposed to the modernist and Dewian take on Kant—"rational consciousness" is not a transcendental possession of the subject but something that emerges within the shared desires and affective exchanges between teachers and students. Quite surprisingly, to demonstrate this, Stiegler turns to the classical thinker ostensibly *least* interested in writing as a practical and transformative therapeutic technology, and *most* associated with teleological reason: Plato. What Stiegler finds demands that we rethink the relations between rhetoric, philosophy, pedagogy, and writing.

The Primacy of Pedagogical Care: Rethinking Plato's Critique of Writing and Rhetoric

While writing remains the basis of "rational consciousness" and maturity in Western culture, the situation is changing rapidly as new tertiary retention systems become increasingly important. As Stiegler argues, at rates faster than the speed of nerves, destructive digital technologies replace individuation with their own prefabricated, depersonalized imperatives, working as systematic impediments to thinking, creating autotomized synchronies of psychic and cultural participation with the goal of the profit of a nihilistic oligarchy. This process through which attention is short-circuited, the process of *dis*individuation, is not philosophical or abstract, but material and concrete. However, a therapeutic response will first require new concepts and theorization of this present moment. It might make sense to turn, like Lanham, to rhetoric to discover a pedagogical response to the persuasive form and capacities of new technologies. However, Stiegler, quite surprisingly, instead re-reads Plato's *critique* of rhetoric, uncovering within the philosophical tradition *the primacy of a Platonic pedagogy*, even over reason.

By turning to the philosophical tradition and the original theorization of *anamnesis* and *logos*, we can see that the "first question" of philosophy is neither ontological nor epistemological, but *pedagogical*. As Stiegler demonstrates, we discover in Plato the "battle" waged by pedagogy for intelligence: "teaching is not simply the first question asked by philosophy; it is philosophy's *practice*, at least in the Academy, where Plato is following Socrates' teaching strategy, contrary to the methods of the Sophists . . . it really is a *battle* for intelligence" (*Taking Care* 107). From the perspective of a now familiar rhetorical critique of reason ranging from Derrida to Lanham to most of contemporary rhetorical theory, Plato famously condemned writing as an external aid to memory. But Steigler argues that, as opposed to merely condemning writing in his attack on the Sophists, Plato was in fact primarily concerned with the Sophist's erosion of *anamnesis* and the care for the self: "As *hypomnesis*, [writing] tends to atrophy what Plato considered to be the only worthwhile attentional form: *anamnesis* that is, thinking within oneself" ("Relational Ecology" 6). In other words, Plato did not so much condemn writing as assert the primacy of an ethics of pedagogical relations (relations that Foucault called the *care for the self and other*). Plato, of course, found *many* uses for writing:

> He himself writes ceaselessly, and if he never stops noting that Socrates does not write, it is evident that Socrates was very well read. The reference to the alphabetized textuality and the consideration of discrete elements of language are constants in the *Dialogues*, and the entire dialectic that Socrates engages in across each of these dialogues is based on the Greek cultural heritage which itself is founded through writing. (7)

Far from wishing to expel writing wholesale, Plato was pointing out that writing was a *pharmakon*—both poison and cure. His concern was that technologies, having the character of the *pharmakon*, could work to promote forgetfulness, "as recollection, contrary to the Sophists, requires a kind of attention the learner *forms itself as a knowledge* by inscribing it on long circuits of transindividuation" (*Taking Care* 172). Rather than condemning writing and rhetoric wholesale, Plato was in fact opposing the poisonous use of the technology of writing by the Sophists that did not—through pedagogical care—attend to the *logos* (that is, did not inculcate a healthy attentional form), and therefore, worked *against individuation*.

Individuation occurs for Plato through pedagogy—that is, in dialogic relation to "a collective individuation of which Socratic dialogue was the anchor" ("Relational Ecology" 6). There is, therefore, an important dialogical, reasoned dimension to the process of individuation—inscribed along long circuits of thought that are, as Stiegler argues, plastic synaptic connections—which requires symbolic intergenerational exchanges between teachers and students. Through writing, neural circuits and the cultural "circuits of transindividuation" overlap. In this way, affectability is linked to the fundamentally technical and therefore socio-historical character of writing and reason. Following Winnicott, Simondon, Freud, and others, Stiegler argues that maturity (development into the majority from the minority of childhood) begins in a command of cultural disciplines ("circuits of transindividuation") that comprise the knowledge repository of a culture ("collective individuation"), enabling a rational, reasoned sovereignty. The process is dialectical, as collective individuation only stabilizes in as much as it circulates through transindividuated culture, and *vice versa*:

> For if it is true that there can be no psychic individuation if it is not projected into a collective individuation where it weaves itself into circuits of transindividuation, the converse is also true: there is no collective individuation which holds together (which maintains its metastability, that is, its unity) without going through these psychic individuals, without being individuated and transindividuated by them.
>
> ("Relational Ecology" 6–7)

However, the entitlement of the sovereignty of transindividuated culture—and the status of truth—is never simply stable or fixed, such that the individual need only master the disciplinary rules of a paternal symbolic system, of the other. For Stiegler, maturity comes only through the ability to *question* the code, to rethink the rules—that is, the dialectical process of individuation also requires *reasoned critique*. In other words, as Bourdieu recognized, this questioning of transcendental reason in fact *requires* transcendental reason. This recognition does not, of course, commit Stiegler to a belief in a metaphysical "pure reason," but rather speaks to the inescapability of our logocentrism, as well as, as we'll see, the mutual desire, the libidinal economy, that informs pedagogical relations.

Again, for Stiegler, it is precisely through questioning the code that the dialectic he posits advances. As he argues, individual and collective individuation alike proceed through natural, intergenerational conflict, which is a necessary condition of the formation of deep attention, appearing "only on the condition of being formed via passage through the logical disputations lying at the origin of those disciplines called rational" (*States of Shock* 27). In the absence of reasoned disputations, students fail to individuate because "parental authority becomes unsustainable to this adult-in-becoming, who can develop—become adult, that is, mature—only by learning to break with this parental authority, that is, to critique it" (*States of Shock* 26). And similarly, without individuation, culture itself erodes. Where there is not reasoned critique of *logos*, there is in turn no collective individuation, but only authoritative codes and forms. Here writing and reason find a practical purpose outside of disinterested, scholastic reflection. Just as individuation requires that the individual projects the self into transindividuated circuits, so too does transindividuated culture require the constant reformations that occur precisely through the idiosyncrasies of individual experience in relation to reason. Or again, culture requires individuated, reasoned critique that, paradoxically, provides for its stability (precisely because collective individuation *is* the process of reasoned, individuated critique). Against the neo-Sophist's overly-simplistic rhetoricizing of reason, and following the logic of Plato's *pharmakon*, Stiegler demonstrates that there are "metastable" cultural objects and knowledges the reflect synchronizations of attention upon them, such that knowledge forms within libidinal economies in which individuals always "pass through circuits of transindividuation that weave and metastabilize collective individuation" ("Relational Ecology" 9–10). Culture metastabalizes when different individuals desire or value it in the same (or a similar) way.

Understanding therefore requires not a knowledge of *things*, as in OOO, but a "love of wisdom." It requires a *mutual desire* for the *cultural object* of knowledge—born originally, Stiegler demonstrates, from cults—that presents a mystery that can, the philosopher realizes, never be fully grasped (the transcendental is always deferred). Teaching therefore involves a primary affective relationship emerging through common desire, refuting the sophistry of "simple technique, a cynicism-without-object (without desire), and finally a poison that [not only does not *affect*, but] *disaffects*" (*Taking Care* 110). Here again we discover the significance of Malabou's theorization of wonder. As we've seen, wonder is an affective opening to otherness, and where the teacher fails to inspire wonder (through an originary affective relationality), where writing pedagogy is reduced to "simple technique"—for instance, the current-traditional pedagogy, the study of rhetorical forms, or the critical thinking of the social epistemic—writing threatens to become a numbing, disaffecting poison. At the same time, absent pedagogical care, scholastic failure—experiences of difference that confound predictions—threatens to erode rather than produce wonder, resulting in disaffection.

Disputation, Care, and Wonder: Writing Pedagogy as Mutual Desire for the *Logos*

But recall that wonder is not just positive inspiration. The art of teaching first involves the primary affective relationship in which intergenerational knowledge—understanding—is conveyed *and disputed*. Indeed, wonder describes the affective experience of the structural incompletion of desire and understanding; it opens us to truths and objects incompletely, and this incompletion is always already the grounds for disputation. Writing is the technology that allows us to finally gain understanding of things we desire—indeed, for Stiegler, writing and desire are the *requirement of understanding*—but understanding itself is necessarily incomplete. While "Understanding . . . appeared only with the advent of writing, which constructed its object as a *knowable* object, stripped of mystery," understanding nevertheless is always marked by an "inadequacy or incompleteness. . . . Inscribed at the very heart of the individuation process that is based on the conception of understanding *as desiring* its object." In addition to a certain practicality, mystery and *mythos* are therefore "inscribed" at the center of pedagogy as the systematic excess of desire that comprises (as we've seen) our plasticity and the "magically" transformative potential of pedagogy. I explained this excess in earlier chapters in relation to the *feeling* of being human—that is, to wonder, care, and the human capacity for transformative learning "transcending . . . understanding as such" (*Taking Care* 110).

This is one conclusion educationist Megan Watkins reaches, viewing learning as originating in an affective opening—a mutual desire—between students and teachers. For Watkins, the pedagogical relationship entails an affective, inter-subjective, and reciprocal search for recognition between teacher and student. Affects themselves are fleeting, she notices; what is most important in identification are the processes through which affects "accumulate in the form of what could be considered dispositions that predispose one to act and react in particular ways" (278). That is, affects "accumulate" in such a way that a "*bodily* memory" forms with the purpose of "both aiding cognition and inducing behavior" (279). We can also perhaps recognize here something of Sarah Ahmed's account of "emotional stickiness." What we're seeing is that Damasio's somatic markers—as aids to cognition—accumulate into embodied dispositions, and that outside of affective relations of care between teachers and students, there is the potential for a destructive or corrosive disaffection.

As Watkins argues: "While individuals are innately predisposed to affective response, much of what we respond to, and how we respond, is a consequence of learning: the repeated experience of similar affects accumulating in a dispositional tendency" (283). To support her argument, Watkins observes teachers who, reluctantly, confess that they most enjoy forms of "whole class instruction" (as opposed to group or student directed learning) where their own "animation" seems to become contagious. Such "personality" based teaching, of course, has few adherents in our process-oriented field.

Watkins, however, argues that through the mutual recognition of teachers and students, a "contagious" affective excitement circulates through the classroom. And this pharmacological, contagious circulation doesn't happen unless both student and teacher are bound in a process of mutual recognition, engaged together in disciplinary pursuits that, despite having no end in some "final knowledge," are nevertheless driven by a libidinal economy in which desire keeps student and teacher alike enthralled by knowledge's potential (for good and bad). As Bruno Latour argues, composition "takes up the task of searching for universality but without believing that this universality is already there, waiting to be unveiled and discovered" (474). Reason is therefore driven by the inter-subjective relationality of desire and affectivity, as opposed to its own intrinsic values. In short, within the libidinal economy of the classroom, wonder is contagious and accumulative. So too, however—following the logic of the *pharmakon*—is disaffection.

We can hear echoes of Dianne Davis's affective relationality in Watkins' formulation. And although he was concerned specifically with the emotional (as opposed to affective) difficulties of negotiating teacher–student and student–student relationships in classes employing a highly interactive process pedagogy, Lad Tobin's *Writing Relationships: What Really Happens in the Composition Class* similarly paints a convincing picture of the inevitability that learning to write is essentially "interpersonal."

In short, as opposed to (complete) understanding itself, what teaching imparts is a *common form of attention* to the *logos*, one that, throughout the history of Western culture, is characterized by its relationship with the book—that is, with writing—as the common (but always structurally incomplete) object of desire and attention. On the other hand, as Stiegler argues, Sophism, in its failure to offer a critique of technics, "has lost its object without knowing, still believing more than ever that it *does* know" (111), and for Plato it poisons the youth of Athens by replacing desire (for understanding) with technics. Where technics are received uncritically, imposing their specific temporality and organology from outside of the libidinal economy of pedagogical care, a closure is imposed upon the structural incompletion of desire, and the excess in the system of intergenerational reasoning, the plasticity of intelligence, is eroded.

And in contemporary culture, the hypersolicitation of attention by new technologies threatens to destroy this libidinal economy by replacing wonder and deep attention with an animalistic vigilance, a "cynicism-without-object" (*Taking Care* 110). Collective individuation—culture—is in this way too threatened by the deformation of attention. Again, because knowledge and reason are themselves structurally incomplete, and only form through a dialectical interplay informed by the idiosyncrasies of individual experience, the replacement of the libidinal economy of pedagogy with mere technics, or flexible conformity to cultural codes, blocks or destroys the plasticity of learning and intelligence. Indeed, the contemporary situation has resulted in the reduction of the plasticity of intelligence to a *careless* and *flexible* technical ability. Here pedagogy must intervene as that which "presents a new form of attention and care" (*Taking Care* 111) whose requirement is a transindividuated knowledge (anamnesis) that—although Plato failed to *fully* see this in conceptualizing learning as remembering—requires above all the technology of discursive writing.

Allow me to further linger on the importance of instruction in reasoned and discursive writing to the formation of attention and finally to individuation. For Stielger, writing is essential to the elaboration of attentional forms:

> It is only possible to have this apprenticeship *on one's own* that we call *experience* on condition of *knowing how to pay attention*: individual experience, which is in effect the conquest of autonomy, supposes that one has received as heritage, through education, the *lessons of collective experience out of which the attentional forms are elaborated.*
>
> ("Relational Ecology" 2)

Again, attentional forms are also the *requirement* of the cultural disciplines that produce them: "These attentional forms generate the circuits of transindividuation that thread and weave together the process of collective individuation" ("Relational Ecology" 6). As a result, absent the attentional circuits that are the product and the condition of transindividuated, cultural and disciplinary knowledge—a form of attention that, to this point, dialogic writing has best allowed for—the "long circuits of transindividuation" fail to form just as the learner fails to form attention "*as a knowledge*" (*Taking Care* 172). And when this happens, transindividuated culture itself is threatened.

In summary, given this dialectical interplay between individuation and transindividuation, in desiring cultural objects of attention, there are two potential ways the subject connects to transindividuated circuits—always already via an embodied, organological relationship with technologies—reflecting the duality of the *pharmakon*. The first way, which requires the care of the teacher, happens when "the convergence towards the attractor is achieved by the intensification of each person's individuation" ("Relational Ecology" 9). In a process through which the cultural form is idealized in the synchronization of desire, individualization is intensified because, in the common inter-subjective idealization of the cultural form, individual differences are brought into relief through experience. And in turn, the idealization of the cultural form is made all the more complete because it "tends toward universality in maintaining the diversity that it spans" ("Relational Ecology" 10). The other way works like fascism; when desire is coopted through shocks, psychic wounds, coercion, dependency, etc., this is *dis*individuating. Such an object of attention demands precisely a common, synchronic, *dis*individuated response to maintain it—it is a code we do not critique. In the world of fashion, for example, this distinction is the difference between a cultural style that is sustained precisely through the admission of individuated responses to it, and a military or school "dress code" that enforces a singular, *dis*individuating style.

Importantly, it is this second attentional form that Plato responds to: "This second way, poisonous, engendered by a misuse of the *pharmakon* of the literal attentional technique, is what Plato denounces in the Sophistic practices" ("Relational Ecology" 10). Much is at stake in this distinction. We can see that Plato's critique of Sophism is in fact a critique of a certain kind of rhetoricizing that forestalls or disallows reasoned, dialogical disputation. In this way Stiegler shows that Plato's was not a wholesale repudiation of writing, so much as a recognition of its pharmacological nature. "In opposing what, in writing, could lead to a psychic disindividuation (that is, to false knowledge, or what Winnicott would call a *false self*)," Plato opposes the Sophists for whom, "The literal attentional technique became . . . a *detouring of attention*, and a *deformation* of it, through which collective individuation itself was threatened" ("Relational Ecology" 10). Outside of relations of care, Sophism threatens to deform reflective attention. This is because some forms and codes, absent a critical discourse based in reason, are poisonous; the Sophist is incapable of seeing this.

Knowledge outside of care turns only on the *authority* of the discipline, the symbolic system, the father. And as should be clear by this point, the privileging of reason in this way is immediately and often rightly subject to the skepticism of youth. Learning therefore begins in the common recognition of disciplinary significance: "Otherwise it appears to them as mere 'argument from authority.' And isn't this precisely the case with pedagogy, teaching that seems removed, unnecessary, inessential?" (*States of Shock* 26). Minors can only pass into adulthood through the process of teaching and learning, which creates pathways to the disciplines, and "on the condition of being formed via passage through the logical disputations lying at the origin of those disciplines called rational" (*States of Shock* 27). Pedagogy, that is, gives students access to the disciplines: "Teaching recreates the pathways to these disciplines within those who are taught" (*States of Shock* 27).

Again, learning is not for Stiegler a simple synchronization of the psychic apparatus and the codes of knowledge, but entails also its disputation. Similarly, Diane Davis follows Freud in demonstrating that that the condition of individuation is an emotional relationality that precedes and is the condition of reason. For Davis, we become individuals through a ceaseless, intergenerational, affective response to the law of the Other:

> Identification in Freud is simultaneously loving and rivalrous, a devouring affection. It's not only that identification involves inclusion by virtue of exclusion, congregation by virtue of segregation; it is also that identification by definition involves seizing the other's place, ousting the other from the position that "I," having devoured the other, now presume to occupy. According to Freud, wherever there is identification, there is already and intrinsically war.
>
> (170)

Finally, it is in this intergenerational war that precedes individual experience that we *grammatize* knowledge at the level of the body. So what, exactly, is this grammatization? Stiegler's account of grammatization allows us to further understand the relationship between neural plasticity, writing pedagogy, and individuation.

Grammatization and the Neural Circuits of Attention: Writing as *Pharmakon*

Stiegler's grammatization is, extending Derrida's grammatology, the thinking of "that which made Derrida's thought possible in the first place, namely, technics as the surface on which memory is inscribed, and as such exteriorization, and therefore disindividuation as well as individuation" (*States of Shock* 103). In other words, grammatization is the analysis of the technical appearance of Derrida's arche-writing—which describes the dialectical movement of the world in terms of erasure and inscription, the ways new binaries emerge out of old ones as opposed to resolving dialectical advance—but in the terms of the *pharmakon*. Or again, grammatization examines the external imposition of (especially temporal) structure within a given regime of technology that defines the horizon of human potential. But it is also more generically the process of critically articulating any system through a metalanguage—from writing to baseball—according to the gramme, that is, according to the isolable elements of the system, in a way that in turn alters or disrupts the system. When Plato critiqued writing, he was critiquing the grammatization that brought transcendental knowledge down to earth, as it were—in this grammatization he recognized not only a positive tool for cultural retention (the encoding of abstract knowledge in writing) but also a dangerous and deforming supplement (the potential for forgetfulness where pedagogy no longer need rely on memorization and recitation).

And it is only first through a command of cultural codes—and through a transindividuated but disputed logocentrism—that students can in turn grammatize the *logos* and fashion a critique of its rules and systems through the idiosyncrasies of the experiences they enable:

> Critical processes of transindividuation always put their rules of transindividuation to work while *putting into question* the rules themselves, inasmuch as they constitute a *synchronic unity*. In other words, they put their rules to work in submitting them to a questioning of the experience they make possible. They put them to the test by making them work in a manner that is formal and explicit.
>
> ("Relational Ecology" 11)

It is finally in this process of grammatiztion that we can recognize healthy and unhealthy cultural codes, codes that allow for critique and ones that don't: "It is from the transformation of the conditions of individuation by grammatization, inasmuch as it produces metalanguages, that one can and indeed must distinguish *critical* processes of transindividuation from *acritical* ones" ("Relational Ecology" 11). Importantly, reasoned, dialogic, and discursive writing are essential to the grammatization process. In summary, they enable the subject to *disrupt various forms of automation and determinism.*

Historically, discursive writing has been the privileged form through which the work of grammatization happens. In Stiegler's words:

> Making public use of reason means addressing oneself to precisely that literate public as a power, a will, and a critical knowledge through the nootechnics that, as the formation of a specific kind of attention (now called 'public opinion'), opens up an associated psychotechnical space. A *psycho*technical milieu can become *noo*technical insofar as it also becomes associatively symbolic, a symbolic milieu is 'associated' when those receiving its symbols are able and apt to individualize them through what Husserl calls the communitization of knowledge, without which it is neither knowledge nor intelligence.
>
> (*Taking Care* 25)

In other words, it is through public participation in a dialogic and "associatively symbolic" processes of discursive reading and writing that the individual matures, but this only happens where individuals are "able and apt" to rethink public discourse. The problem, from the perspective of the *pharmakon*, is that writing technologies can also write us, synchronizing consciousness and technological imperative, and thereby "suspend the reader in immaturity" (*Taking Care* 24).

Reason is the mature and productive capacity of thought, the disruptive possibility of "distinguishing between *knowledge*, *opinion*, and *dogma*" (*States of Shock* 21) within public knowledge and the disciplines. But this potential fails to form where dialectical intergenerational work ends. As Stiegler argues, "Over the course of the last few decades . . . the technological becoming of knowledge has disrupted the conditions" of the process of rational, public disputation (*States of Shock* 21). Through the proliferation of attention-capturing digital technologies that have taken the place of discursive writing, individuation and transindividuation are alike short-circuited:

> This normal, necessary scene, however, in which the familial relationship becomes tense and then confrontational so that minors will be able to achieve their majority, has been short-circuited by the capture and diversion of individuation, familial and collective attention towards the objects and subjects of the mass media and, through them, towards objects of consumption.
>
> (*States of Shock* 27)

This short-circuiting happens, as I've already demonstrated, through the replacement of writing by technologies coded to grammatize behavior for the production of capital: "it is indeed the goal of this capture of attention to channel the desire of individuals towards commodities. This destroys the very thing that could found the desire of the social group as the circulation of desire between members of this group" (*States of Shock* 26–27). In other words, the work of grammatization based in writing and individual experience becomes replaced with a technological attention capture that instead grammatizes *individual input as metadata for economic gain*. This happens, for example, with apps or social media that are platforms for user-input that is then auto-grammatized, organized and codified as metadata for commercial and further attention-capturing purposes. This process is poisonous because it replaces the circuits of transindividuated reason with new traces, altering the very physiology of our attention.

As Stiegler argues, this situation requires the "biological model of a human central nervous system technologically produced by technologies of control." The open, plastic system of the brain allows for the formation or deformation of attention in accordance with the technological *pharmakon: "the human brain's plasticity is the necessary ground for both the mind's and society's process of individuation, itself structurally unfinished, and the dual nature of this unfinishedness converges in both the psychic and social aspects of the object of attention*" (*Taking Care* 99). And much in contemporary cognitive and neuroscience confirms this poisonous potential of technology. It has been well established that attention is distributed widely in the cortical areas of the brain associated with visual processing. And as one leading neuroscientist of attention, Earl Miller, discovered, because attention is widely distributed across the brain, it can emanate from discontinuous, discreet processes. Miller posits this happens through a system of "brain waves" that select competing neural representations. This ensures the representation of different systems within the brain. But as Miller states, this discontinuity "comes at a cost" (Miller & Buschman 220). Myriad stimuli compete for our limited conscious capacity. Or in other words, we're "not wired to multitask well. . . . When people think they're multitasking, they're actually just switching from one task to another very rapidly. And every time they do, there's a cognitive cost in doing so" (qtd. in Levitin).

Antonio Damasio comes to similar conclusions. As we saw in Chapter 1, the brain forms images that are coded with emotional "somatic markers," the product of a neural map of the organism's overall homeostatic condition. For this reason, based on the different variables of situation, emotion, and stimuli, there is a potentially endless number of possible outcomes available to the attention: "a diverse repertoire of images, generated to the tune of the situation you are facing, entering and exiting your consciousness in a show too rich for you to encompass fully" (170). This is in part because these images are not projected on a unified screen, as if sensory input were a movie viewed by a little man in the brain (the infamous homunculus), but are rather distributed throughout the interrelated regions of the brain and united by the broader tendency towards homeostasis and persistence (84). Our thought-images rise to consciousness as recommended by their emotional character or "mark," such that most of what *could* appear to our conscious attention never does.

But attention, alongside working memory, is crucial to this process: "since the brain holds and retrieves knowledge in spatially segregated rather than integrated manner, they also require attention and working memory so that the component of knowledge that is retrieved as a display of images can be manipulated in time" (84). Attention, then, is the motor of what we *experience as* auto-affective self-presence. But as we saw in Chapter 4, attention appears as the force of an *ad hoc* conscious integration that is only ever temporary and contingent. Where attention is deformed, the subject is marked by a dis-integrating indifference, overwhelmed with emotional thought-images that they are unable "manipulate"—such subjects, as we've seen in cases like Eliot, can no longer make productive choices. This is the condition of the brain in the contemporary crisis of attention where we find, as Stiegler argues, a "disindividuated mass whose brains have been stripped of consciousness, of their capacity to form long circuits of individuation, incapable of critique extant circuits, a nervous system forever enclosed within strict neurological limits" (*Taking Care* 98).

Beyond States of Stupidity: Some Conclusions

I've attempted to demonstrate in this chapter that historically, discursive and dialogic writing has been the technology through which humans have formed the "long circuits of individuation" necessary for grammatizing discursive knowledge. And while writing was the technology that guaranteed a sovereignty based in reason, it has been replaced by modern and postmodern, analog and then digital, forms:

> the mnemo-techniques that is writing is the condition of possibility of reason (of *logos* and its logic) as theorematic faculty. Analog and digital mnemotechnologies, however, represent a new stage of the process of grammatization, a process through which alphabetic writing led to the foundation of the *polis*.
>
> (*States of Shock* 7)

The question becomes, what is the status of reason, the individual, and the state, when writing is replaced by these new technologies?

Stiegler's response is unambiguous: writing gets replaced by global stupidity:

> founded on a systematic extension of stupidity, which is also to say one of submission, infantalization and regression to minority—it also seems that the legacy of twentieth-century thought is simply to leave the human beings of the twenty-first century totally defenseless and unarmed in the face of a situation that appears hopeless.
>
> (*States of Shock* 3–4)

That is, we are compelled to hopelessly, stupidly, recapitulate technological codes. In short, where we lack a grammatizing, critical discourse on the reasons for cultural codes and templates, we are left only with stupidity—i.e., the dissolution of care, attention, and responsibility.

Following Stiegler's argument, we can see that the danger in Richard Lanham's rhetoricizing is that, in its valorization of the social code, it fails to adequately theorize sublimation in the dialectic it sets in motion. Where Lanham celebrates the competition of various attention structures for the scarce material of human attention, Stiegler links the organology of technologies to the political imperatives that drive them. Lanham views hyper attention as democratic because it doesn't become fixated on an official, hegemonic reasoning. But Stiegler reminds us that where forms command our attention constantly around the margins in the service of capital, we are in danger of failing to contemplate, to grammatize, this experience.

Like some other rhetoricians, while Lanham celebrates the proliferation of technology and digital codes, he remains agnostic about the relationship between the code and consciousness except to the extent that these technologies work as attention capture devices, blind to the poisonous potential of codes that operate at increasing speeds, speeds beyond the pace of consciousness and desire, forestalling critical engagement. Furthermore, short-circuiting the caring engagements with knowledge that would enable the critique of their reasons, this same process erodes attention. Without access to critical reason rooted in deep attention, the codes (and their reasons) remain closed, and consciousness—and the brain—becomes synchronized with them; as a result we all become more the same, disindividuated, and subject to the capital-generating imperatives of the new technologies.

As I argued at the beginning of this chapter, the plastic turn in the transcendental requires a new theory of intelligence and reason. Stiegler's nuanced valorization of the logocentric, as I hope has become clear, does not suggest a simple return to automated or deterministic pedagogical programs. Nor does it settle on a transcendental, scholastic "reflective intelligence" indifferent to practical social purposes or the "magic" of transformation. Finally, a new writing intelligence must rethink reason and intelligence without recourse to any singular program, in the complexity with which plasticity of intelligence joins rhetorical situations. Intelligence cannot be understood in the singularity of the reasoning subject, the "I," or the cogito; rather, intelligence emerges from a primordial care or thrown-open-ness to the world, a goal-directed sense of concern and wonder. Intelligence is not the patterning or organization of sensory input, but is instead that which emerges from plasticity—our spontaneous, *ad hoc*, and meaningful openness to the world. And this primordial concern, as we've seen, is distributed and precedes conscious thought, as opposed to emerging form a singular understanding or process.

At the same time, however, we cannot simply dispense with so-called transcendental reason. As we've seen, reason is in fact the condition and tool of its own disputation and resistance; we cannot, therefore, simply abandon the transcendental, but must continue to negotiate its transformation. Neuroscience, as I've argued, allows us to do exactly this by demonstrating, among other things, the importance of writing and habits of reasoning in forming the deep attentional disposition that is also the embodied requirement of those habits. Plasticity allows us to introduce a transformation from within the transcendental; deconstructing the distinction between the symbolic and the biological, it allows us to rethink intelligence and critique in relation to affective embodiment. This points to the significance of developing an emotional intelligence about writing, an awareness of our productive and destructive affective experiences with writing and other technologies. Relatedly, as I've argued, reasoning as an embodied activity rooted in deep and reflective attention entails resistance where it disrupts automation and the disaffecting powers of technologies.

A plastic writing intelligence is the opposite of the stupidity of all programs and determinisms, and the sustained attention built through reasoning allows us to create intelligent dispositions that short circuit the imposition of other codes or programs, to disrupt the automation of intelligence and external attentional control. In other words, through the sustained focus of reason, we create durable attentional forms, inscribed onto neural networks, giving resistant, plastic form to subjectivity. This "writing" of the self is in this sense fundamental to the care of the self and other and to resisting neo-liberal flexibility.

Notes

1. Indeed, although I will not elaborate further here, the central argument of *Before Tomorrow* is that Kant provided the means for rethinking or changing the transcendental in his own theorization of the transcendental.
2. Of course, by "universals" I don't mean metaphysical certainty. These universals don't exist in any stable way, but our desire for them—our desire for truth—nevertheless characterizes our relation to culture and knowledge.
3. For Stiegler, knowledge forms within libidinal economies in which individuals "pass through circuits of transindividuation that weave and metastabilize collective individuation" ("Relational Ecology" 9–10). Cultural objects (knowledges) metastabilize, forming culture in the same process through which subjects individuate in relation to culture. Through shared attention on desired culture objects (i.e., knowledge), those same objects metastabilize even as they are formed and reformed by individuals. The "circuits of transindividuation," the forms of desire, are shared as attentional structures.

Works Cited

Ahmed, Sara. *The Cultural Politics of Emotion*. Routledge, New York, 2014.

Banks, Adam. "2015 CCCC Chair's Address: Ain't No Walls Behind the Sky, Baby! Funk, Flight, Freedom." *College Composition and Communication*, vol. 67, no. 2, 2015, pp. 267.

Beller, Jonathan. *The Cinematic Mode of Production: Attention Economy and the Society of the Spectacle*. Dartmouth College Press, Lebanon, NH, 2015. Print.

Bourdieu, Pierre. *Pascalian Meditations*. Stanford University Press, Stanford, CA, 2000.

Carr, Nicholas G. *The Shallows: What the Internet Is Doing to Our Brains*. W.W. Norton, New York, 2010.

Clark, Andy. *Surfing Uncertainty: Prediction, Action, and the Embodied Mind*. Oxford University Press, New York, 2016.

Conrad, Peter. *Identifying Hyperactive Children: The Medicalization of Deviant Behavior*. Lexington Books, Lexington, MA, 1976.

Cooper, Anderson. "What Is Brain Hacking." *60 Minutes*, CBS, 9 April 2017.

Davis, D. Diane. *Inessential Solidarity: Rhetoric and Foreigner Relations*. University of Pittsburgh Press, Pittsburgh, PA, 2010.

DeGrandpre, Richard. *Ritalin Nation*. Norton, New York, 1999.

Dewey, John. *Democracy and Education*. Dover Publications, New York, 2004.

Goldhaber, Michael. "The Attention Economy and the Net." *First Monday*, vol. 2, no. 4, 1997. *Firstmonday.org*. Web. 18 February 2012.

Hallowell, Edward, and John Ratey. *Driven to Distraction: Recognizing and Coping With Attention Deficit Disorder From Childhood Through Adulthood*. Simon and Schuster, New York, 1995. Print.

Hayles, Katherine. "Hyper and Deep Attention: The Generational Divide in Cognitive Modes." *Profession*, vol. 13, 2007, pp. 187–199. *JSTOR*. Web. 19 February 2015.

Lanham, Richard. *The Economics of Attention: Style and Substance in the Age of Information*. University of Chicago Press, Chicago, IL, 2006. Print.

Latour, Bruno. "An Attempt at a 'Compositionist Manifesto'" *New Literary History*, vol. 41, no. 3, 2010, pp. 471–490.

Levitin, Daniel J. "Why the Modern World Is Bad for Your Brain." *The Guardian*. Guardian News and Media, 18 January 2015. Web. 21 June 2015.

Malabou, Catherine. *The Future of Hegel: Plasticity, Temporality, and Dialectic*. Routledge, London, 2005.

———. *What Should We Do With Our Brain?* Trans. Sebastian Rand. Fordham University Press, New York, 2008. Print.

Microsoft Report. "Attention Spans." 2014, n. pag. 2015 Consumer Insights, Microsoft Canada. Web. 2016.

Miller, Earl K., and Timothy J. Buschman. "Cortical Circuits for the Control of Attention." *Current Opinion in Neurobiology*, vol. 23, no. 2, 2013, pp. 216–222.

Rafalovich, Adam. *Framing Adhd Children: A Critical Examination of the History, Discourse, and Everyday Experience of Attention Deficit/Hyperactivity Disorder*. Rowman and Littlefield-Lexington Books, Latham, MD, 2014. Print.

Richmond, Kia J. "Repositioning Emotions in Composition Studies." *Composition Studies*, vol. 30, no. 1, 2002, pp. 67–82. Web.

Richtel, Matt. "It Don't Mean a Thing If You Ain't Got That Ping." *The New York Times*. The New York Times, 21 April 2007. Web. 21 June 2016.

Rose, Nikolas. "Disorders Without Borders? The Expanding Scope of Psychiatric Practice." *BioSocieties*, vol. 1, 2006, pp. 465–484. Web. 12 Dec 2011.

Schrag, P., and D. Divoky. *The Myth of the Hyperactive Child and Other Means of Child Control*. Pantheon, New York, 1975.

Stiegler, Bernard. *Taking Care of Youth and the Generations*. Stanford University Press, Stanford, CA, 2010. Print.

———. "Relational Ecology." *Culture Machine*, vol. 13, 2012. Web. 11 November 2014.

———. *States of Shock: Stupidity and Knowledge in the 21st Century*. Polity Press, Malden, MA, 2015. Print.

Tinnell, John. "Grammatization: Bernard Stiegler's Theory of Writing and Technology." *Computers and Composition*, vol. 37, 2015, pp. 132–146. Web. 12 May 2016.

Tobin, Lad. *Writing Relationships: What Really Happens in the Composition Class*. Boynton/Cook Heinemann, Portsmouth, NH, 1993.

Watkins, Megan. "Desiring Recognition, Accumulating Affect." *Affect Theory Reader*. Eds. Melissa Gregg and Gregory Seigworth. Duke University Press, Durham, NC, 2010, pp. 269–289.

Appendix 5.5: Pedagogy Breakout 3

Neurophilosophy, Argument Theory, and the Future of Reason: Towards an Embodied Public Rhetoric

As we've seen, recognizing the plasticity of intelligence requires that we oppose writing pedagogy to the stupidity of all automatized programs and determinisms. Intelligence in this way can never be thought in advance, in accordance with a universal test or assignment that is its measure—I include here our rubrics and writing assignments, at least those that articulate the criteria for performance in advance. Such assignments demand a flexible relationship to ossified codes. We must instead think intelligence in the multiplicity of its forms and in terms of a plasticity whose genius can only be deduced after the fact. As teachers, we must consider how we can recognize and reward different types of intelligent contributions to the social and public work of composition and rhetoric, outside of predetermined "learning outcomes." And beyond rewarding "critical thinking," we must realize the value of different practical and seemingly "mystical" dimensions of reason.

"Argument theory" as it has emerged out of contemporary cognitive and neurosciences allows us to think through this *transformation in the intelligibility of reason* that is also a *transformation in intelligence*. Mercier and Sperber's groundbreaking meta-analysis "Why do Humans Reason?" demonstrates that everyday personal reasoning occurs automatically and realizes its end in socially directed purpose. These discoveries lend themselves towards theorizing a writing pedagogy rooted in public rhetoric, where students work together (always with their teachers, as Stiegler reminds us) towards practical goals through reason and disputation. What they've found is that reason does not work reliably at the level of individual decision making or in epistemic gain; however, research is clear that reason functions perfectly well when *groups* work together, pursuing their own emotionally "biased" solutions while compensating for that bias through "epistemic vigilance"—that is, critical thinking. In this regard, the "confirmation bias" is socially functional.

The authors describe a radically decentered, dialectical conceptualization of reason. In opposition to the classical Cartesian view that holds that the main function of reason is the accrual of epistemic benefits, the authors begin with the fact that the high-order reasoning we do when we reflect on a belief—accepting or discarding a conclusion based on a reasoned consideration of the premises, the work of reflective attention—does not alone *reliably* bring subjects any closer to correct answers or better decisions. And remarkably, nor does reason bring subjects closer to their own stated moral norms:

> Reasoning does not lead to more accurate beliefs about an object, to better estimates of the correctness of one's answer, or to superior moral judgments. Instead, by looking only for supporting arguments, reasoning strengthens people's opinions, distorts their estimates, and allows them to get away with violations of their own moral intuitions.
>
> (68)

Decisions are based in the first instance on *intuitions*—the premises that reason works to justify. In short, "Not only are most decisions made intuitively, but when conscious decision-making strategies are used, they often result in poor outcomes" (69). This discovery has obvious resonances with contemporary rhetorical theorizations of invention and the critique of the social epistemic privileging of the symbolic. For example, across her work Laurie Gries argues for the importance of *inference* as a rhetorical attunement to change and difference; and Jenny Rice, as we've seen, similarly theorizes the significance of tacit knowledge.

Indeed, Mercier and Sperber show that instead of leading to accurate beliefs, reason works to support an "intuitive inferential mechanism"—that is, the beliefs one always already, automatically, has formed about a topic. And individual reasoning works to reinforce rather than correct these conclusions: "when reasoning is applied to the conclusions of intuitive inference, it tends to rationalize them rather than to correct them" (59). In neurological terms, we can say that reason works to confirm our brain's predictions, to support the images recommended by the protoself—the affective biases implied by somatic markers. In short, Mercier and Sperber have expanded the somatic marker hypothesis to apply also to the *representation of arguments*—that is, premises and conclusions, like other images, come marked and are "spelled out" in the new representations afforded by reason (58).

The fact that reason is fallible is well established in the psychological literature, but in an attempt to maintain the Cartesian distinction between reason and emotion, mind and body, cognitivists have traditionally chalked up "error"[1] to human finitude—especially cognitive overload. Mercier and Sperber painstakingly work through the research that demonstrates different dimensions of the "unsound uses of reasoning," the very preponderance of which poses a challenge to the traditional Cartisian view of reason that attributes its fallibility to misuse and finitude. Counter this untenable perspective, the authors extrapolate from their findings to show that reason, in its everyday use, is used not to arrive at better decisions, but rather to anticipate the need to defend or argue for one's decisions (69). In our own field, for example, we often attribute errors in reasoning to our students being overwhelmed by learning to write academic (or any new form of) prose. Of course, individual reflective reasoning sometimes does allow the subject to make better decisions, but these occasional benefits fail to justify its biological efficacy or describe its characteristic features (60). Therefore, the authors turn elsewhere in order to understand reason's persistence in human behavior. If reasoning doesn't help us get beyond our inherent premises, biases, and intuitions, why do we have it at all? The authors theorize that reason must "work" at some other level.

Here is what they found: while reasoning doesn't work well with regard to truth or epistemic benefit, it turns out that it *does* work when applied to the premises and conclusions of *arguments* within social (rather than laboratory) dialogical contexts. Again, reason has a social function: "In particular, it allows people to anticipate the need to justify their decisions to others" (71). The confirmation bias is in this way cognitively *efficient*: "When a group has to solve a problem, it is much more efficient if each individual looks mostly for arguments supporting a given solution" (65). While reasoning does not help individuals make *better* decisions, it does enable us to make decisions we are better able to justify (without regard to truth or usefulness). And where there are more justifiable arguments, groups have a better chance at arriving at truth through reason. So while the confirmation bias is optimal because it best distributes the work of reasoning, this is only the case up to the point that the group dialogically exchanges their arguments. At that point, evaluation of arguments works more objectively: "people tend to be more objective in evaluation than in production" (66). In short, reason works well to *support* and *evaluate* arguments: "Reasoning contributes to the effectiveness and reliability of communication by enabling communicators to argue. It thus increases in quantity and epistemic quality the information humans are able to share" (60).

Again, where individual reasoning is unrealiable, "epistemic vigilance"—the process of the evaluation of *others*' arguments, or even one's own *in social context*—is in fact quite reliable.

For example, in a study, "an average of 40% of participants fail to draw the simple *modus tollens* conclusion that was used as an example (if p then q, not q, therefore not p)." However, when asked to perform the same task in dialogic context, "participants can easily understand a *modus tollens* argument when it is of use not simply to pass some test but to evaluate communicated information; the production of valid *modus tollens* arguments in argumentative contexts is also 'surprisingly common'" (61). That is, epistemic vigilance comes naturally *in social context*.

In short, it is only through social interaction that reason "increases both in quantity and in epistemic quality the information humans are able to share" (60). In describing the findings of experiments on the operation of reason in dialogic context—that is, in situations where groups work together to solve a problem, the authors summarize: "The dominant scheme is truth wins, meaning that, as soon as one participant has understood the problem, she will be able to convince the whole group that her solution is correct. This can lead to big improvements in performance" (62). This is because while reasoning is generally used to support our biases, in group situations our *evaluations* tend to be *more objective*. Extrapolating, we can therefore say that the real value of reflective attention to learning is not in disembodied, individual reasoning, *but its efficacy in relation to social purpose*. Reason is in this way decentered and distributed, and intelligence cannot be thought solely in terms of intentionality. Instead, we must recognize intelligence in varied forms of social and situational contribution, invention and assessment—that is, in its plasticity. A plastic writing pedagogy might furthermore recognize the intelligence behind different contributions to arguments, including affective and social contributions not easily identified with intentional agency. From a different angle, is this not also what rhetoricians like Jenny Rice are arguing for?

Relatedly, while in experimental settings subjects fail to adequately think critically by anticipating counterarguments, Mercier and Sperber argue that this is predictable given that, outside of argumentative context, individuals will naturally focus on reasons to support their conclusion. "Looking for counterarguments against one's own claims may be part of a more sophisticated and effortful argumentative strategy geared to anticipating the interlocutor's response, but, in the experimental setting, there was no back-and-forth to encourage such an extra effort" (62). Within socially directed arguments, however, we naturally use argumentative skills that we may not be able to identify. In short, a habitus rooted in "critical thinking" or "metacognitive" skills turns out to not be helpful in overcoming the limitations implicit to our tendency towards confirmation bias (Ritchhart & Perkins 2005; Willingham 2008); however, such knowledge may help us become better arguers in the same (limited) way learning grammar might help us to be better writers. In the end, it is only where argumentation is highly situated and social—where individuals work together in problem solving, drawing on local knowledge and evaluation as opposed to learned, abstract reasoning skills—that reflective intelligence will be efficacious.

In summary, Mercier and Sperber characterize the asymmetry between argument production, "which involves an intrinsic bias in favor of the opinions or decisions of the arguer whether they are sound or not, and the evaluation of arguments," and epistemic vigilance, "which aims at distinguishing good arguments from bad ones and hence genuine information from misinformation" (72). As we've seen, on their own, individuals don't perform well when evaluating their own argument, working in the role as both "judge and advocate." This leads them to ask if it is not possible that individuals might acquire a Sherlock Holmes-like skill—indeed, a powerful metacognition or reflective attention—that would allow them to represent the different positions of the group in order to evaluate arguments on their own: "Wouldn't it be possible, in principle, for an individual to decide to generate a variety of hypotheses in answer to some question and then evaluate them one by one?" Of course, as the example of Sherlock Holmes proves, this is possible. But it is a "pretranatural" skill that few possess naturally.

Overall, Merceier and Sperber's discoveries about reason resonates with Damasio's, who argues that even the higher-order thinking involved in creativity "is a means to survive and flourish in a social and cultural context," ultimately serving the emotional homeostasis and increasing the power to act of the organism. In this way, all high-order abilities—such as creativity, argumentation, and writing—do not work reliably to advance knowledge at an individual level, but instead *serve social and emotional ends* (Immordino & Damasio 124). Argumentation and writing better allow individuals to respond to situations, and thereby to increase the power to act and realize interoceptive homeostasis.

Indeed, argument theory compliments the neurorhetorical arguments that I've entertained across this book—as we know, the predictive process theory of the brain allows us to understand that, as opposed to merely processing sensory information, mental models work to confirm their own predictions, carving out one of many possible worlds in maintaining homeostasis, creating simulations of the world tensed against the incoming sensory information that it actively seeks. As Clark argues, "Active agents are . . . driven to sample the world so as to (attempt to) confirm their own perceptual hypotheses," actively and selectively (through attention) confirming predictions. For example, a misguided mental model generating a believe that a friend is angry with us will "lead us to harvest sensory information" confirming this belief, treating important incoming information as mere noise while amplifying other information (Clark 71). In this case our deployment of the model "discovers visual evidence for the—false and ungrounded—hypothesis" (73). Similarly, as Merckelbach and van de Ven demonstrated, instructing listeners to listen for the song "White Christmas" in a sound file comprised of nothing but noise results in some listeners (falsely) detecting the song. In summary, predictive processing theorizes that the brain works to

> determine a (frequently self-fulfilling) process of exploratory, epistemically mandated, sensing and acting: a process in which a winning hypothesis (a winning 'take on the world') causes us to sample the scene in ways that reflect both the hypothesis itself and our own context-varying states of sensory uncertainty.
>
> (71)

What argument theory adds to neurobiological theory is a fuller account of the *social value of reason* to cognition, underscoring the potential of writing pedagogies rooted in public rhetoric.

A More Plastic Fish: Persuasion and "Doing What Comes Naturally"

What we can see taking shape in argument theory and neuroscience is in fact a new, embodied way of thinking about invention. To demonstrate this, I'll argue here that our new neurobiological understanding of embodied rhetoric demands a re-reading of the rhetorical pedagogy recommended by an unlikely and undoubtedly controversial figure in our field: Stanley Fish. This may be somewhat unexpected, given that Patricial Bizzell once critiqued Fish as a "brain in a jar" (183). But taken together, Fish's work challenges us to consider *form* as plastic—in his rhetorical grammar, but also in his theorizing of discursive forms that, with no claim to universality, reflect a rhetorical circulation and plastic mutability that precedes truth and reason. And despite its limitations from the perspective of a public rhetoric pedagogy—Fish clearly supports academic disinterestedness over and against practical applications of rhetoric. Fish's theory strongly suggests the embodied value of (deconstructed, heteroaffective) reason. As Fish realizes, "the achievements of argument are always wonderful (in the root sense of provoking wonder)" (*Winning Arguments* 44).

I wish to suggest that Fish's position on invention is remarkably contemporary—it's just that where contemporary rhetoric defines space in the ecological and networked terms of extension and emergence, in articulating a writing pedagogy, Fish argues that in the "bounded space" of the classroom we're better off limiting ourselves to teaching some rough-and-ready forms that will be useful to students. This "bounding" is ostensibly at odds with contemporary rhetoric, which theorizes a networked permeability that connects the classroom to more public spaces, making rhetoric a public act. Some have gone as far to say that Fish's rhetoric does not allow for persuasion at all (Danisch). But I believe Fish is somewhat misunderstood here. Much like many contemporary rhetoricians influenced by poshumanism, Fish's main concern—for which he has become notorious in our field—is against the predetermined political program of the social epistemic pedagogy. So even though I'll have to read him against himself at points, I don't view his theory as ultimately doing damage to pedagogies of public rhetoric—it's just that he wants to limit the "public" to the most immediate, embodied situations students find themselves in (i.e., the classroom). Therefore, as opposed to being "against" the social work of rhetoric and in favor of a naïve current-traditionalism, Fish instead views the classroom itself as a highly situated environment where local problems emerge that demand embodied, rhetorical responses. It also happens to be the environment students find themselves in. In these ways and others, Fish's account of rhetorical invention comes closer to contemporary rhetoricians like Jenny Rice than is generally understood. In calling writing "expertise" (or metacognition) into question, both Fish and Rice assert the value of the local and the embodied to invention.

As Fish makes clear in his most recent work, *Winning Arguments*, "Argument, in short, is embodied; it doesn't take place in just the head but involves almost everything that comes before our eyes" (191). And if we are to understand "head" here as connoting consciousness, given that the brain "comes before our eyes," we're not as far as one might think from a materialist theory.

For Fish there is no path to metaphysical certainty—even the anti-foundational certainty that everything is unstable or uncertain—that would give one purchase over situations in practice. *Any* appeal to transcendental principles, after all, would have to be made from within a situatedness that cannot be escaped. Indeed, we cannot help but act from within our belief that the values and knowledges we project onto the world are right and true; rather, Fish has merely argued that any attempt to *account for* how one value or idea becomes accepted as true over another will always and necessarily reveal contingency, given the inability of humans to dissolve disagreement by gathering together in some hypothetical space of absolute knowledge. Or as Fish puts it, "While truth claims are always universal, the justification of truth claims is always local" (Olson & Worsham 274).

Here's the consequence of this: Rhetorical awareness doesn't position one at some higher reflective level, establishing principles applicable to other situations. As we've seen, metacognitive awareness of the writing process, writing "expertise," does not guarantee transfer or success in new situations. Even the "discourse community," Fish's most famous concept, cannot be a foundation, such that knowledge of the fact that there are discourse communities guarantees success—we will always already require the local knowledge, forms of reason, and embodied practices of those communities. As Chris Anson recognizes, the concept of discourse communities in our field has presumed their relative stability (536); it turns out, however, that they are more "fluid" than we've previously supposed. Instead, agreement has the structure of a battle, and victory is always contingent and temporary. For Fish, we are finite organisms, fated to perceive reality, darkly, through the symbols and rhetorical structures that simultaneously mark the (correlational) difference between thought and reality, thereby making rhetoric, rather than reason, as he puts it, "the medium we swim in" (*Winning Arguments* 2).

There is no dry land or Archemedian point above rhetoric from which we could gaze into rhetorical depths, and any attempt to imagine such a space for invention—a space where reason sets forth its generalizable program—is doomed to fail precisely because that dry land can only be imagined from our watery perspective. And yet, without reflective reason, even though it always comes in the service of rhetoric to justify beliefs, we sink. For Fish, at least where we're situated, the disciplinary modes of production—the writing we do and the language we use—*are the things themselves*. That is, writing and rhetoric are not epiphenomena of some other purer mode of academic engagement; rhetoric (or reasons in service of arguments) is all we have, and therefore, the bounded context of classroom performance will do just as well, pedagogically speaking, as any other space. This is what Derrida meant by logocentrism: despite their slipperiness, we always already can't help but make meaning through the discourse communities we dwell within; even a metaknowledge of their "anti-foundational" instability, or a knowledge of the fact that we occupy different positions simultaneously at the intersection of these communities, does not allow us to simply step outside of them. To participate in disciplines and other discourses requires students to be versed in their rhetorical superstructure, not an ability to critique their foundation or base.

Related to his arguments about theory and logocentrism, Fish has written extensively about how little control we have over our beliefs, how we don't so much have beliefs as they have us. That is, beliefs precede reason, and reason and knowledge are offered to *justify* belief, reversing the rational empiricist formula "seeing is believing" to argue that "believing is seeing." In other words, Fish argues that our "belief systems," our *world views*—which are just the same thing as conscious experience—give us the rhetorical tools through which we recruit facts and knowledge to justify our beliefs.

At this point, the typical response to Fish's "belief" thesis is to question it on the grounds that it doesn't allow us to understand how beliefs *change*; after all, if theory and knowledge can't transcend situations, nor can they give us an intelligibility of how persuasion works with those situations. Just as the strategies for rhetorical performance have no recourse to principles or knowedges that exist outside of them, so too does belief respond only to its own internal structure or web. This caused Robert Danisch to exclaim, Fish "cleaves off rhetoric from persuasion" (418). However, Fish's account of persuasion, in subtending reason to beliefs, has the *structure of the event* (which some have interpreted as Fish arguing that persuasion can't be taught): in his words, "Any authority, no matter how longstanding its hold on your imagination, can be dislodged in an instant, although that instant cannot be willed, cannot be planned for, and need not ever occur" (*The Trouble* 283). Deconstructing classical accounts, Fish's theory of persuasion is in fact radically local and embodied, echoing Malabou's destructive plasticity and theorization of wonder.

Fish argues that any change in belief is at once heteroaffective, having the character of the event or accident (as in Saint Paul's famous revelation), yet at the same time the change can only result from something internal to one's system of beliefs. In other words, suggesting an overlooked materialism in Fish, change and transformation occur within form itself. His strongest example of this is the Nazi that renounces Nazism because it conflicted with a belief he held about his daughter. Importantly, as Fish points out, nothing could have predicted that the neo-Nazi would have shifted his belief (he could have potentially renounced his daughter given the depth of his commitment to Nazism), and each change in belief is so contingent that there is no possibility for a system that could predict or make such shifts intelligible except descriptively, *after the fact*. In other words, changes in belief are explosive events, ignited by an excess already present within the belief system. And while Fish is not optimistic about our potential to persuade anybody of anything through reason alone, through its fundamental connection to affect, reason retains its local, embodied value.

In short, Fish (at least sometimes) recognizes the heteroaffective, plastic capacity of thought to completely and suddenly reorganize itself, to become unrecognizably other than itself, but always, again, in a way consistent with its own internal structure. In his words,

> There is . . . one route by which the fluidity of argument can be arrested: conversion. Conversion—from the Latin *convertio*, to turn or reverse direction—differs from ordinary, everyday persuasion in that what one is persuaded to is not a point, but a vision. Argument (especially in law) proceeds step by step; if *x* then *y*; given these facts, this judgement. Conversion occurs at once, in a woosh . . . and its effects are not limited to a single issue or question.

Conversion, in other words, describes the explosive metamorphosis of our beliefs or worldview, our, in his words, "deeper-than-deep commitments."

And furthermore, what is Fish describing here in the "woosh" of the shifting worldview if not the power and primacy of *affective* experience?

Fish similarly characterizes arguments by their potential for sudden and total transformation. They are, as he says, "protean—ever changing, variable, mutable, kaleidoscopic, voracious—and almost anything can be its vehicle" (*Winning Arguments* 8). As Fish claims, "On those occasions when a political argument is won it is often because an *event* enters the argumentative area sideways and produces an unexpected resolution to a dispute that promised to go on forever." Fish cites as an example the "immediate" shift in American-Cuban relations, which produced a "new normal," literally "within twenty minutes." Domestic disputes have the same "woosh"; they "[do] not so much unfold as erupt," having no formal beginning—"*and by the time you know you're in one, it's too late*" (103). It is the nature of arguments that they are able to mutate, shift forms, and become other than themselves; as Fish demonstrates, the form of political arguments is plastic:

> Arguments can migrate from one political party to another depending on where a rhetorical advantage is spied; everything is always on the wing, capable of metamorphosing into its opposite; reversal and transformation, not resolution and stability, are the order of the argumentative day; nothing stays fixed; everything is ultimately up for grabs. (82)

This account squares with the predictive process theory of the brain. For example, Clark argues that this theory may seem to suggest that we are "doomed (until new experiences are constructed or intervene) to stay, broadly speaking, within the limits of our achieved world view." But this is not the case. Rather, "we are capable of a kind of deliberate, imaginative exploration of our own mental space" (273). Even in the absence of relevant sensory data, we are engaged in a continuous, imaginative "exploration around the edges" of the generative models we form about the world. Given that this work happens at the edges of our generative models, this is not the same thing as metacognition—there is no position outside of the model. Yet, these "wanderings" may, in fact, be the primary source of new ideas and behaviors. We might conceive of our imaginative ability to mentally wander around models as, in fact, a neurological requirement, "mandated" (272) by our brain's acquired prediction of a reality that is never completely stable. That is, the brain itself may *predict the instability of generative models*, resulting in imaginative explorations and invention.

Fish's anti-foundational account of form theorizes Derrida's arche-writing as the system of differences that precedes all content and thought: as he formulates, "when we think through pictures . . . what we picture will have assumed its shape as a consequence of the linguistic differences that mark out and *bring into being* a 'this' which is different from a 'that.' The difference doesn't precede its notation in language: language's system of differences creates it" (*Winning Arguments* 16). What neuroscience adds to this formulation is an essential relation between *emotions* and ideas; that is, the "pictures" that comprise thought don't just appear as symbols, as Fish postulates, but symbols "marked," to use Damasio's terms, with emotion. Furthermore, emotion is the formal condition of thought and difference, as it is emotion that "recommends" ideas to us consistent with the homeostatic functioning of the protoself, which is to say, the organism's internal "mapping" of its affective state. And while as far as I'm aware Fish himself never makes this kind of biological argument, as we've seen, his theorization of persuasion nevertheless *implies and requires* a theory of affectivity.

Finally, through Fish we might realize a rhetoric and heuristic rooted in wonder. It is in remaining open and attuned to the "edges" of mental space, at the intersection of the internal-other and the protean exterior, that beliefs change and take new shapes. Fish's pedagogy suggests one way to exploit this. Ultimately, Fish's theorization reflects the embodied and highly situated value of reason to exploring the edges of our predictive model, both within the classroom and beyond. This implies, once again, the enduring value of a deep, reflective attention—the neurological condition and phenomenological consequence of which is a plastic capacity for invention. And ultimately, Fish's core pedagogical position that form—including grammatical form—generates content offers a potentially useful way to think about invention in the terms of a plastic pedagogy. A more plastic Fish might further develop the idea—already latent in Fish, as I've argued—that these forms are not reducible to argumentation and the symbolic; in short, in making use of Fish's formal heuristics in light of neuroscience and Mercier and Sperber's findings, we must also accept the value of affectivity in shaping intelligence and in realizing intelligent, practical social ends. How might we accomplish this in the writing classroom? I've got some ideas I hope to pilot. One idea I'll mention briefly, recognizing that it needs refinement: I'd like to record peer review and group work sessions, coding the recordings in order to share with students the strengths, and limits, of their contributions. In doing so, in addition to rewarding content mastery, I hope to point out moments of blockage, as well as moments of emotional generosity, profundity, and plasticity. I hope to identify moments of wonder as an opening into difference. Finally, I hope to encourage, develop, and diversify the experiences of emotional intelligence evident in these situations.

Note

1. Indeed, Steven Pinker's new writing guide for students, *The Sense of Style*, makes this case at length.

Works Cited

Anson, Chris M. "The Pop Warner Chronicles: A Case Study in Contextual Adaptation and the Transfer of Writing Ability." *College Composition and Communication*, vol. 67, no. 4, 2016, p. 518.

Bizzell, Patricia. "Composition Studies Saves the World." *College English*, vol. 72, no. 2, 2009, pp. 174–187.

Clark, Andy. *Surfing Uncertainty: Prediction, Action, and the Embodied Mind.* Oxford University Press, New York, 2016.

Danisch, Robert. "Stanley Fish Is Not a Sophist: The Difference Between Skeptical and Prudential Versions of Rhetorical Pragmatism." *Rhetoric Society Quarterly*, vol. 42, no. 5, 2012, pp. 405–423.

Fish, Stanley E. *Doing What Comes Naturally: Change, Rhetoric, and the Practice of Theory in Literary and Legal Studies.* Duke University Press, Durham, NC, 1989.

———. *The Trouble With Principle.* Harvard University Press, Cambridge, MA, 1999.

———. *Winning Arguments: What Works and Doesn't Work in Politics, the Bedroom, the Courtroom, and the Classroom.* Harper, New York, 2016.

Immordino-Yang, Mary H., and Antonio Damasio. "We Feel, Therefore We Learn: The Relevance of Affective and Social Neuroscience to Education." *Mind, Brain, and Education*, vol. 1, no. 1, 2007, pp. 3–10.

Mercier, Hugo, and Dan Sperber. "Why Do Humans Reason? Arguments for an Argumentative Theory." *Behavioral and Brain Sciences*, vol. 34, no. 2, 2011, pp. 57–74.

Merckelbach, Harald, and Vincent van de Ven. "Another White Christmas: Fantasy Proneness and Reports of 'Hallucinatory Experiences' in Undergraduate Students." *Journal of Behavior Therapy and Experimental Psychiatry*, vol. 32, no. 3, 2001, pp. 137–144.

Olson, Gary A., and Lynn Worsham. *Postmodern Sophistry: Stanley Fish and the Critical Enterprise.* State University of New York Press, Albany, NY, 1953, 1954, 2004.

Rice, Jenny. "Para-Expertise, Tacit Knowledge, and Writing Problems." *College English*, vol. 78, no. 2, 2015, p. 117.

Ritchhart, Ron, and David N. Perkins. "Learning to Think: The Challenges of Teaching Thinking." *Cambridge Handbook of Thinking and Reasoning*. Eds. Keith Holyoak and Robert G. Morrison. Cambridge University Press, Cambridge, 2005.

Stiegler, Bernard. *Taking Care of Youth and the Generations.* Stanford University Press, Stanford, CA, 2010. Print.

Willingham, Daniel T. "Critical Thinking: Why Is It So Hard to Teach?" *Arts Education Policy Review*, vol. 109, no. 4, 2008, pp. 21–32.

Index